Land and Livelihoods in Papua New Guinea

Dr Tim Anderson is a Senior Lecturer in Political Economy at the University of Sydney. He researches and writes on development, human rights and self-determination in the Asia-Pacific, Latin America and the Middle East. He is a published author on topics of agriculture and food security, health systems, regional integration and international cooperation.

Land and Livelihoods in Papua New Guinea

by Tim Anderson

AUSTRALIAN SCHOLARLY

© Tim Anderson 2015

First published 2015 by Australian Scholarly Publishing Pty Ltd
7 Lt Lothian St Nth, North Melbourne, Vic 3051
tel: 03 9329 6963   fax: 03 9329 5452
email: aspic@ozemail.com.au   web: scholarly.info

Tim Anderson
Land and Livelihoods in Papua New Guinea
ISBN: 978-1-925333-00-8

Design: Art Rowlands
Cover image: The Author

Set in Adobe Caslon Pro 10.5pt

Table of Contents

Acknowledgements

The early research in this book was supported by some small grants from the University of Sydney, and travel assistance at different times from Aid/Watch, the Australian Conservation Foundation, the Bismarck Ramu Group and the Centre for Environmental Law and Community Rights (CELCOR). Later on, additional research and final organisation of the book were supported by the Interchurch Organisation for Development Co–operation (ICCO & Kerk in Actie). I am grateful for all that assistance but, as the standard author's disclaimer goes, I take full responsibility for my own words.

Some parts of the chapters here were previously published. In particular, some elements of chapters two, three and four draw on my 2006 article in the *Pacific Economic Bulletin*. Chapter Five draws on my 2008 *Pacific Economic Bulletin* article and my 2011 paper in the *Journal of Australian Political Economy*. Chapter Six draws heavily on my 2006 report to CELCOR, Chapter Eight uses some material from my 2005 *Pacific Economic Bulletin* article and Chapter Nine adapts material from my chapter in Professor B.N. Ghosh's 2011 book, *Global Food Crisis*. The publication details are cited below.

Finally I must express my gratitude to all my Papua New Guinean friends, who taught me so much about their culture and people. I am particularly grateful to my good friends Yat Paol and Howard Sindana, without whose guidance I would not have met so many others nor gained whatever insight I have into their beautiful country.

Thanks to *the University of Sydney* and to *ICCO Kerk in Actie*
for supporting the research of this book.

Sources

2005 'Challenging 'integrated conservation and development' in Papua New Guinea: the Bismarck Ramu Group', *Pacific Economic Bulletin*, vol.20 1, pp. 56–66.

2006 'On the economic value of customary land in Papua New Guinea', *Pacific Economic Bulletin*, vol.21:1, pp. 138–52

2006 'Oil palm and small farmers in Papua New Guinea', Report for the Centre for Environmental Law and Community Rights, Port Moresby

2008 'Women roadside sellers in Madang', *Pacific Economic Bulletin*, Vol 23, No 1

2010 'Land Registration, Land Markets and Livelihoods in Papua New Guinea', in Tim Anderson and Gary Lee (Eds) (2010) *In Defence of Melanesian Customary Land*, Aid/Watch, Sydney

2011 'Melanesian Land: the Impact of Markets and Modernisation', *Journal of Australian Political Economy*, No 68, December 2011, pp.86–107

2011 'Agricultural liberalisation and its 'high risks' for food security' in BN Ghosh (Ed) (2011) *Global Food Crisis: Contemporary Issues and Policy Options*, Wisdom House, Leeds

Land and Livelihoods in
Papua New Guinea

Land and livelihoods in Papua New Guinea

ℰℐ

A slow motion drama is in play in Melanesia, above all in Papua New Guinea, where the 'omissions' of the colonial era are being addressed by neo-colonial forces. The economic interest of the big powers has its focus on land – always a key resource but increasingly valuable in times of multiple food, financial, energy and ecological crises. At stake are the livelihoods of most of the country's seven million inhabitants, 85% of them rural livelihoods. This book argues that notions of the country's 'economy' and its 'development' have no real meaning without an inclusive focus on both these livelihoods and the role of customary land.

Papua New Guinea, almost alone in the world, did not have its indigenous land tenure system dismantled by the colonial powers.

About 97% of the nation's land mass is legally recognised as still in the hands of families and clans. Further, there is virtually no feudal legacy, and therefore no large landowning families. This means that, at times of uncertainty or crisis, almost all people have access to basic food and shelter, as well as to social identity and social support. That is the good news. Highly productive gardens and crops ensure that rural Papua New Guineans are insulated from the impact of a global food price volatility which has shaken many other countries. Further, domestic produce markets support a thriving (but often unrecognised) cash economy, at least where there are good roads. In sum, the country has probably the most equal distribution of land on earth, and to some extent this substitutes for the great lack of state services.

On the other hand, these same families and communities have very little access to health services and schools, and most have poor roads. In addition, many communities are isolated and even the existing main roads are not well maintained. Income generating activities often centre on meeting the demands of secondary school fees yet, despite tremendous efforts by parents, costs are often prohibitive. Most children cannot complete school, nor can they access adequate health care. Health services are expensive in the cities and virtually absent in rural areas. In many cases, communities create their own elementary schools and health clinics.

With billions of dollars in gas and mineral revenues in recent years, the PNG Government does not lack resources. Rather, it is an inherited elite culture – including inherited liberal notions of 'user pays' – that has left communities to their own devices. So most people are not hungry, and virtually none are homeless; yet education and health indicators are very poor.

As part of a long-term neoliberal strategy to commercialise customary land, PNG's problems of underdevelopment are sometimes blamed on land–owning families. If families only 'mobilised' their land, gave it over to 'development', the nation would advance, it is said. This is one of the propositions of a type of ideological war, waged by international finance groups, corporate think-tanks, aid programs and local elites. These groups have used a number of modernist and economic arguments, which this book will address.

Yet there has been tremendous popular resistance to past demands (e.g. from the World Bank) for 'land mobilisation', to meet the needs of large corporate monocultures and mining operations (even though most mining is carried out without any real change to land tenure).

Due to the political defeat of several plans for land registration and commercialisation, in the 1990s and early 2000s, the context of this battle has changed. The financial and aid agencies have taken a back seat, preferring to fund 'local initiatives'. In 2005 the PNG government launched a 'land taskforce', to help drive a 'land reform' agenda. However 'land reform' in the Melanesian context means something entirely different to 'land reform' in countries where ordinary people were dispossessed under the colonial regime – as in Latin America and the Philippines. In Melanesia, 'land reform' means a commodification process, where family and clan land is registered and legally redefined, so that it is able to be leased, sold and otherwise capitalised. This, of course, also means that it can be alienated from those same families and clans. There are legal initiatives (such as new types of lease) which attempt to force the pace of land modernisation; and behind this the accusations that land-owning families are an 'obstacle' to development, that they are 'unreasonable' and need to be educated on the benefits of this 'land reform'.

But what if the land-owning families and their resistance were right? Perhaps they know more about the value of land, which underwrites many centuries of successful livelihoods. Where are the voices in support of their claims, and in defence of their traditional lands? That is where this book begins, as a non-Papua New Guinean's defence of customary land–owners, and a vindication of the possibilities of extending decent livelihoods through maintaining control of family and clan lands.

Using a critical, institutional approach and focussing on economic livelihoods based on customary land, this book makes use of the best available evidence and extends it with original quantitative and qualitative studies. It finds that the economic potential of many of PNG's 'hybrid' livelihoods, based on customary land, is already superior to most of the alternatives offered in the 'new' formal economies. Many economic returns in the rural informal sector are well ahead of the low wage labour of supermarkets, fish canneries, chicken farms and mining operations, and well ahead of the incomes provided by the large plantation industries, in particular oil palm. And most traditional uses of land are far more valuable to families than the pitiful rural rents, paid to those unfortunate few who have been induced to lease out their 'unused' lands.

Yet specific evidence on rural livelihoods is necessary to confront a number of 'modernist' myths at play. The myths include these ideas:

1. People in PNG 'must move from the subsistence to the cash economy'. Wrong. Most families have been engaged in both for some time. Very few live 'pure' subsistence livelihoods and most participate in cash economies. Families will continue to grow their own food, build their own houses and engage in cash economies. The more relevant question is: what particular composite or hybrid livelihoods offer the best prospects for rural PNG families?

2. Customary land owners must 'mobilise their land' to help the 'development' of the country. Wrong. PNG's rural livelihoods, based on customary land, are extremely vulnerable to land alienation. The government has plenty of income from royalties and equity in mining and gas; it already has more than enough to abolish school fees, establish a public health system and maintain a network of roads. However the political will has been missing. From an practical economic point of view, families would be best advised to maintain control of their customary land to protect their existing food security, housing and social support systems.

3. 'Large scale monocultures (like oil palm) are more productive than small farming'. Wrong. These monocultures might provide more export income, and some tax revenue, but they represent neither a more productive use of land let alone a superior livelihood option for participating small farmers. PNG experiences shed new light on the international discussions over the 'multifunctionality' and productivity of small farming. Chapter Six provides detail on PNG's oil palm experiments.

4. 'Economic options are better in the formal economy'. Well, only for a few. Wages for most unskilled labour, and some skilled labour, are less than the median incomes in much of PNG's rural informal sectors. Chapters Three, Four and Five set out comparative incomes. PNG's formal economy is less than impressive.

5. Customary land 'must be registered' to provide 'greater security of tenure, and these centralised titles will assist in agricultural productivity, rural credit and women's rights'. Baseless. These were

common themes from land registration processes in East Africa in the 1950s and 1960s, and in World Bank programs in more recent years. Yet neither the evidence of East Africa nor that of PNG supports such claims.

Here is a brief overview of the chapters, following this introduction:

Chapter Two, 'Customary Land and Land Modernisation', explains customary land, how it works and is recognised in PNG law, and how it underwrites rural livelihoods. It then discusses land modernisation, particularly from the East African experience and the (unsuccessful) attempts to transmit that model to Papua New Guinea. This foundation is important, because misunderstandings and conflicts over land not only derive from clashes of interests but also from modernist mindsets, and the consequent poor recognition of indigenous cultural achievement.

Chapter Three, 'Land Economics: the Old and the New', compares and contrasts what I call the 'old school' approach to economics – with its focus on growth, exports and the formal sector – with a 'new school', which values livelihoods, human development and ecological sustainability. It is useful to consider the 'old school' and its arguments (internationally and in PNG), from liberal modernists such as Boserup, Deininger and De Soto, as well as the corporate think–tanks and a few PNG economists. However, I argue, we learn little of real economic or developmental significance in PNG unless we replace the old concepts with a focus on the 'new school' themes. 'Economics' in PNG is meaningless without these newer ideas. The chapter introduces comparative data on rural livelihood options, which helps inform the discussion of the following chapter

In Chapter Four, 'from Subsistence to Hybrid Livelihoods', I challenge the popular myth that traditional communities like those in PNG are 'moving from subsistence to the cash economy'. I do this by pointing out the importance of the informal sector, and how it integrates with 'hybrid' rural livelihoods. To fully understand these 'hybrids', subsistence production and consumption, along with cultural exchange and informal cash economies, must be valued and added to the formal sector options. Only in the recent years have informal sector surveys provided data which allows us to more fully consider the breadth and productivity of these hybrids. The chapter characterises those hybrids.

Chapter Five, 'Roadside Sellers' draws on original surveys of mostly women roadside sellers in four PNG provinces, between 2004 and 2011. While there had been earlier rural informal sector surveys, none had studied the most visible, woman–dominated markets in rural PNG, allowing comparison with the other formal and informal sector livelihood options open to rural women. Such markets have not been afforded much importance elsewhere, but in PNG they assume greater importance because of the particular circumstances: a relatively even distribution of family land and at least some access to main roads. The survey results, in all four provinces, show that the income potential of these particular informal markets matches other informal sector activities (such as transport and small business) and surpasses most of the formal sector options available. How families combine a focus on these fresh produce markets while engaging in other activity, and the relative importance of each activity, helps us better understand the hybrid livelihoods they are constructing.

Chapter Six, 'Oil Palm', considers in some depth what role this dominant monoculture might have in helping build decent livelihoods in rural PNG. What emerges from the best available data and some focus group studies is that a highly profitable industry, dominated by a small group of foreign companies, offers only limited returns to farming families. The promises of the industry have been exaggerated, as average returns in the informal sector are higher. Not only are 'smallholder' oil palm incomes relatively low (due to the monopoly power of the 'nucleus estates'), the monoculture introduces serious environmental costs, in particular silted and polluted rivers and water tables. Further, oil palm plantations introduce an inflexible use of land, which prevents companion planting and competes both with subsistence gardens and other cash crops. The 'Mama Lus Frut' scheme for women, developed by the oil palm industry, does not improve matters much. These several drawbacks mean that oil palm does not present as a useful addition to superior rural livelihoods.

Chapter Seven, 'Village Cooperation', looks at some initiatives taken by communities that have rejected the idea of leasing their customary lands and of participating in oil palm programs, and have worked together to build their own programs. In particular, the chapter tells the story of the Sausi community, which has developed some unique forms of village finance, as part of their own 'poverty reduction' program. This is a type of cooperative which builds on existing family business operations and extends itself into new schemes (including food processing, transport and college scholarships) by use of the traditional principles of mutual support and reciprocity.

Chapter Eight, 'Customary Land: Reconciliation or Resistance', returns to the theme of land management and counterposes two actual trends. The first is the attempt by international agencies, and some extent within the PNG Government, to chart a 'middle way' whereby customary owners are persuaded to lease out their land, without losing their status as landowners. In rural PNG this is dispossession under another name. The second trend can be seen in the activities of rural communities, backed by some PNG groups, to reject the commercialisation and commodification of their lands. This chapter discusses some of the elements of this resistance: legal challenges, community organisation and farm management training.

Chapter Nine, 'Food Security in PNG and the World', is a cautionary tale, which charts the problems of other developing countries which have given up their subsistence capacity in favour of an export oriented agriculture, following the neoliberal model. The 2008 global food crisis helped highlight the high risks of agricultural liberalisation, and the value in conserving many of the elements of PNG's land tenure and small farming systems.

The concluding chapter brings together the main themes of the book, along with some final reflections on land and livelihoods in Papua New Guinea. I hope it provides some food for thought.

Customary Land and
Land Modernisation

❧

It is not possible to understand land and livelihoods in Papua New Guinea without some background in the principles and practice of customary land, and the ways in which notions of land custodianship are embedded in social relationships. Only then can we start to form a reasonable perspective on the relationship between customary land and processes of land modernisation.

I use the term 'modernisation' here in its sociological sense. It does not indicate an approach 'more relevant to contemporary circumstances', but rather a centralising logic of the modern era where distinct histories and circumstances were considered of little importance. Human society is seen to have a convergent and common form. (e.g. Berman 1983;

Giddens 1998). The 'one size fits all' approach of economic liberalism is a key part of such modernism.

Many outside observers simply assume that modernisation of land (mapping and centralised registration, individualisation and exchange) is desirable. They often tend to trivialise or are scornful of customary systems, even when some important contributions, e.g. to food security, are acknowledged (e.g. Hughes 2004: 4). Such approaches typically focus on the supposed limitations of customary systems and ignore the dangers of modernisation processes.

Others consider customary land systems more sympathetically, yet share the 'evolutionary' assumptions of both liberal modernism and historical materialism. The idea here is that land systems 'evolve' to address new problems, such as scarcity and agricultural productivity, ideas traditionally the province of 'market economics'. Fitzpatrick for example, citing an important World Bank report (Deininger 2003), concludes that 'in certain circumstances, communal forms of customary tenure are optimal arrangements because they provide tenure security to group members at relatively low cost'. However, he asserts that 'in the long run individual western–style ownership may provide the ideal environment for economic investment'. He proceeds to focus on a 'transitional' recognition of customary tenure, and sensitising state interventions that affect customary tenure (Fitzpatrick 2005: 450, 452).

Similarly, while Weiner and Glaskin (2007) stand aloof from the economic liberal assertion that customary land is 'a brake on wealth creation', they say their aim is simply 'to understand the mechanics of the translation process in which non–western cultural and social forms are incorporated and regulated by western legal and statutory bodies' (Weiner and Glaskin 2007: 1–2). Again we see the evolutionary assumption. Nevertheless, others have pointed out that customary land tenure arrangements are complex, and often co–exist with other systems (Brown, Brookfield and Grau 1990: 22).

This book sees greater contemporary relevance for the genius of custom. A land tenure system that has sustained communities for thousands of years seems to deserve more careful attention. The book mainly considers the economic opportunities available to Papua New Guinea families, without pursuing the complexity of customary practice in an extremely diverse country. Nevertheless, it takes customary tenure seriously: as more than a relic of the past, or a cultural ornamentation of local social relations. Customary tenure systems, I suggest, might better be seen as adaptive and functional social structures with important roles to play in the future. At a time when modern agricultural systems are facing severe problems – with food crises in more than seventy countries and ecological collapse (e.g. Shiva 1993) in many more – why should we not consider more fully the lessons of time–proven systems?

I begin by identifying some basic principles of customary tenure in PNG, then introduce the history of modernist interventions from Australia and East Africa to Papua New Guinea and Melanesia, noting the modernist principles, the stated objectives and some of the outcomes.

CUSTOMARY LAND

Customary land systems in Papua New Guinea, in part due the country's remarkable diversity, were not distorted by feudalism. No large land owners developed, either through indigenous processes or (as elsewhere) by collaboration with and emulation of the colonial powers. The main pressures on land tenure came from the need to co–exist with neighbours. Recognised in the constitution and law of the independent state of Papua New Guinea, customary land survived the colonial era more than 97% intact (Lakau 1991; Larmour 1991; NLDT–SCCLD 2006). Apart from the other Melanesian countries, this ongoing dominance of customary land tenure makes Papua New Guinea fairly unique in the world.

This particular history meant that the dominant mode of land management remained that of a locally controlled, oral tradition, with authority resting in clan leaders. Land rights and land use are administered by the communities. Land itself is inalienable; that is, it cannot be sold or otherwise taken away from the communities. Land is held in trust for future generations, to ensure their livelihoods; a principle also well known in many African cultures. In PNG it is common place to hear PNG intellectuals speak of the cultural, ecological and subsistence values of land, as additional to and underlying the potential commercial value of land. PNG writers also point to the sustainability and inter–generational equity values built into the customary ownership system. For example, Narakobi (1988: 8) writes: 'land is the link between the earth and the sky, the sea and the clouds, the past and the future; because land is eternal, it is held in trust for succeeding generations'. Similarly, the

African saying that 'land belongs to the few who are living, many whom are dead and the countless yet unborn', has been said to be 'relevant and deep–rooted' in PNG (Lakau 1994: 80). Customary land systems ensure survival of the community as well as reproduction of each communities' particular social system.

In most of PNG those with principal authority over land are the male leaders, while in many of the islands and some of the coastal regions (e.g. Bougainville, Milne Bay, East New Britain) the principal land authorities are women. Despite the fact that these gendered systems create primary and secondary rights, in both patrilineal and matrilineal systems all men and women have rights to land. The customary land systems of the Solomon Islands and Vanuatu are similar in also having both patrilineal and matrilineal systems. In Vanuatu it has been observed that 'customary law ... recognises the land rights of both men and women .. [and] the central function of customary land tenure has been to ensure social security and cohesion' (Naupa and Simo 2008: 77).

Fingleton (2004), contesting Gosarevski, Hughes and Windybank (2004), says customary land is often misunderstood as a simple communism where there are no defined responsibilities. He suggests PNG's customary land systems might better be seen as 'a balance between group and individual rights and obligations ... a traditional balance, but one which can when necessary be shifted in the direction of strengthening the rights of individual group members and relaxing group controls, to allow for the new demands of modern living' (Fingleton 2004: 97). These new demands notably include the pressures for children's school fees and for health services. He stresses the dynamism of these systems, adding that a major misunderstanding is 'the belief that customary tenures are static, non–adaptive, uncertain [and] backward–looking' (Fingleton 2004: 98).

While practice within customary land systems varies considerably, I suggest some common principles are: (i) that customary land systems retain a central focus on sustainable family livelihoods; in doing this (ii) they maintain strong currents of social inclusion; and (iii) in their survival through the centuries they have practised high degrees of local flexibility and adaptation.

The Chimbu land system of PNG's highlands, for example, has been characterised as one of flexibility, adaptation and change. Individuals and groups 'claim rights at several levels, from tribal to clan territory, through the right to access or share arable land ... to the individual and inheritable right to use specific plots' (Brown, Brookfield and Grau 1990: 23). These are familiar elements elsewhere in PNG. The study described the Chimbu system as adaptive, with historical processes of change, e.g. from the seventeenth century introduction of the sweet potato, to more recent overcrowding, to new commercial opportunities. The authors 'think it likely that there was no such thing as a pre–colonial equilibrium condition [but rather] that change has been continuous' for at least several centuries (Brown, Brookfield and Grau 1990: 46).

As opposed to modernist systems, which impose a defined and compartmentalised 'cadastral landscape' (Burton 1991), some PNG systems have developed a functionality in 'loose' borders. A study speaks of PNG highlanders seeming to be driven to 'obfuscate and dissemble boundaries'. Sillitoe said this was 'an integral aspect ... of containment in an acephalous context of power plays that might try to extend control over access to productive land resources'. The 'mobile' nature of land use and land rights related to 'conceptions of identity and boundary' (Sillitoe 1999: 331–332). That is, an egalitarian, inclusive system does not have the same need to impose exclusive and exclusionary boundaries. The centre will dominate the periphery of any bounded entity, in a structure of domination (Lamont and Fournier 1992); yet the urge of the highland system was 'to diffuse rather than concentrate economic and political power' (Sillitoe 1999: 355). The attempt to impose defined boundaries on a flexible and adaptive system was 'subverting the existence of social groups and communities as currently constituted' (Sillitoe 1999: 357). The general point here is that the technical elements of land tenure are subordinate to the social values of the community, in this type of customary system

As in African customary systems, those of Papua New Guinea have accommodated 'vernacular markets', where land is rented or transferred under customary rules (see Chimhowu and Woodhouse 2006: 346), as well as other forms of land use (e.g. for churches and schools). Land for churches and schools has been readily made available under customary 'leases', when those activities were seen to be part of the community, or of benefit to the community. More contemporary commercial activities, such as cooperatives, have also been provided for, on the same basis. However exclusionary use of land, cut off from the needs of local communities, has been seen an alien and conflictive process (e.g. Garu 2010). Hence the conflict with foreign–owned, large plantations. Outsider families and individuals have been readily included in communities, in a customary way. However attempts by outsiders to appropriate land and land use, excluding the community, are resisted.

Those with secondary rights to land, such as women in patrilineal systems, may be subordinated but not excluded. Indeed, new forms of land use which demand more clearly defined ownership threaten greater damage to the secondary title holders. Rodman saw customary land as 'not necessarily [providing] a hedge against the emergence of new forms of social inequality', such as gender inequality (Rodman 1984: 62, 77). Yet as Naupa and Simo (2008: 77) note in Vanuatu, rapid transformation of customary law, in particular to incorporate commodification of land, often more definitively excludes women from decision making processes.

The valuable features of customary land systems are often poorly understood by those proposing modernist interventions. While it is difficult to generalise customary practice internationally, some useful elements were identified by the FAO in a 2002 report on sustainable agriculture and resource management. In the face of modernist arguments that registration and individual titling would contribute to greater security of title and improved agricultural productivity, the FAO report made these points:

- The social value of land is often better preserved by 'rules of the community' rather than 'uniform systems of property law set by the state';
- 'Community–based rules may be better at providing security of tenure to individual cultivators than are state systems. Often what individual cultivators fear is dispossession at the hands of government or outsiders';
- 'Community based systems can often be better at reflecting the complex rights that individuals, families ands groups have over land, including secondary rights of access and use – rights that might be distorted or lost by titling according to a standardized format that is not adapted to local realities'; 'a community's relationship with land is more than just an aggregate of individually occupied and used plots; it is a system that includes land–base resources used in common, such as

13

pastures, water and forests'; these rights may not be well recognised in state–registered cartelization of land (FAO 2002: 230).

Fingleton (2004: 98) similarly points out, in the PNG context, that state controlled titling 'might itself contribute to insecurity of tenure, by raising the spectre of land being lost to outsiders and creditors'. The question of productivity, linked to livelihoods, is the subject of much of the rest of this book.

MODERNIST INTERVENTIONS

State-based interventions in customary systems form just one part of what has been called 'land reform', relevant to the particular Melanesian context where customary systems remained mostly intact. 'Land reform' in Latin America and parts of Asia (the Philippines, India) meant returning or redistributing land to poor communities, after a history of dispossession and concentration of ownership. On the other hand, in Melanesia and Papua New Guinea 'land reform', pushed by the large aid agencies, has come to mean processes of surveying, registration, titling and creating enhanced 'markets' in land. The state assumes control of these processes because, as Larmour (1991: 4) points out, 'registration is intrinsically centralising'. The main recent experiment with such modernist interventions was the large scale land registration and land titling processes in eastern Africa (Uganda, Zimbabwe, Kenya, the Sudan), beginning in the late colonial era (see Platteau 1996: 38). This late colonial experiment by the British was based on the notion that the privatisation or 'enclosure' of land was essential to successful agriculture, and that 'African traditional forms of land tenure were often incompatible with 'good farming', essentially because of their small scale (MAAHWR 1956: 1, 5). This African experience deserves some review here.

Early land registration in Africa was simply about colonists accessing indigenous land: 'Almost all land registration systems introduced in colonial Africa before 1950 .. were primarily intended to secure European rights to land' (Dickerman et al 1989: viii). In Algeria in the 1840s, the French passed laws to dispossess indigenous people on 'public interest' grounds, handing over their land to colonists. In Belgian occupied Congo and Rwanda–Burundi colonial laws banned

14

Africans from owning land in certain areas (Dickerman et al 1989: ix–x). Only later on did modernist 'general benefit' arguments attach themselves to land registration. Registration was also used for political settlements. In the conflict ridden kingdom of Uganda, for example, registration was introduced in 1900 to allocate lands to 'members of the royal family, nobles and 1,000 chiefs and leading private citizens' (Dickerman et al 1989: x).

Registration processes owed something to the British colonial experience in Australia. There, in the 1830s, parliamentarian Robert Torrens engaged in a debate with the British colonial office over the possible land rights of indigenous Australians. Robert Torrens believed 'they have none' (in Reynolds 1987: 114). The subsequent 'Torrens Title' system, introduced in South Australia in 1857–58 (see Esposito 2003), combined a system of registration with 'indefeasibility', a legal protection from almost all other claims except fraud. This was designed to prevent any resurgence of Australian Aboriginal land claims, under customary law. British and European systems, from old societies with their own customary law, were not as highly commodified or centralised as this. Australia's Aboriginal people were not able to reclaim any recognised land rights until Aboriginal–led campaigns forced some legislative changes in the 1970s and 1980s (see Foley and Anderson 2006). Until 1992, Australian common law maintained a legal doctrine ('terra nullius') which asserted that all indigenous customary land tenure had been wiped out by the act of colonisation (Brennan 1992). However, while Australia was the last colonial power of Papua New Guinea, the land outcomes for indigenous Australians and indigenous Papua New Guineans were quite different.

Kenya's Swynnerton Plan of the mid–1950s began colonial processes of customary land registration (Swynnerton 1955), but these carried on after independence in 1963. This colonial plan had the stated goal of 'developing African agriculture', by providing 'greater security to landholders, enhanc[ing] the freedom to transact land and serv[ing] as a basis for agricultural credit' and, in response to indigenous rebellions, 'to create a class of African freeholders, yeoman farmers' who would have a stake in the regime (Dickerman et al 1989: x–xi). The Swynnerton arguments are essentially those used today by the World Bank (e.g. Deininger 2003): the creation of modernised 'secure title' and an increased exchange of land which is said to help build agricultural productivity, enhance access to credit (allow 'capitalising' of the land) and will also (in some way) benefit marginalised groups, particularly women.

Kenya became the African country with the greatest extent of registered land, and therefore also the most promising field of study for the lessons from this sort of registration. Reliance on the development of freehold land continued after independence, in Kenya and several other African countries. In the Sudan, during a large World Bank agricultural expansion program (1969–71) all lands not registered were deemed (by the *Unregistered Lands Act 1970*) to belong to the government (Elhadary 2010: 214). This compulsory registration dispossessed a huge number of traditional users, who then had to work leased land. Apart from the predictable problems of incomplete registers, analysts have concluded that these changes 'brought an end to sustainable patterns of land use by local people, replacing them with mechanised shifting cultivation which has degraded the land and helped initiate desertification' (Dickerman et al 1989: xvi). The militarisation and extreme conflict in the Darfur region has been linked to land alienation, concentration of ownership and mechanised agriculture (Ahmed 2002: 77–95).

Lawrence, the chief British colonial expert on and administrator of land registration, came to the view that registration should be used only when the economic advantages justified it. That is, when there was a 'general demand' for registration, when the costs were not high and where there were likely gains in agricultural productivity (Lawrence 1970). More scathing were criticisms by Kenneth Okoth–Ogendo, former Dean of Law at Nairobi University. He concluded that the benefits of this land registration plan were outweighed by specific disadvantages: the redistribution of political power, creation of economic disparities, generation of a 'disequilibrium' in social institutions, failure to develop extension and rural credit, and a general failure to improve agricultural productivity. He noted that, of the new registered land owners, less than 5% were women; further, the new land regime was 'creating new forms of stratification and status differentials' amongst the small farming sector (Okoth–Ogendo 1982).

The focus of the World Bank in the 1970s had been mostly on formal title, land sales and large scale agricultural production (World Bank 1975). This is logical, as the World Bank is constitutionally dedicated to the promotion of private investment, and removing barriers (such as customary land) to such investment. However due to the unpopularity of formalisation, in countries where customary law remained strong, a revised approach was needed. The Bank produced a report in 2003 which sought to embed land policies in its broader joint aims of economic growth and 'poverty reduction'. This report (Deininger 2003) revised the bank's approach but kept major modernist elements intact. Through 'governance' ideas the bank also extended the political ambit of its land campaigns. Maintaining the evolutionary approach to land, the report recognised that 'poorly designed' (i.e. cruder) 'market interventions' on land had failed due to lack of popular and institutional support. It said less attention should be paid to pushing for land sales and more to the creation of auxiliary markets (rents, leases, taxation) and to the building of local institutional capacity. While 'indefinite property rights' (i.e. transfers by sale) were 'the best option', 'giving longer–term rights that can be renewed automatically' were the next best; a gradual movement towards individual rights was also desirable (Deininger 2003: xxii–xxiv). Limits on land sales markets were undesirable in the longer term (Deininger 2003: xxxv–xxxvi).

Echoes of Swynnerton can be seen in the World Bank's key emphases: 'greater tenure security' through registration, greater agricultural productivity, enhanced rural credit and benefits for secondary title holders, in particular women (Deininger 2003: xix–xxi, xxxi, 57–60, 116, 187). A key focus of this revised approach was on how formalisation could help poor and disadvantaged sectors. Informal markets were said to lead to conflict, while formalisation and rapid economic growth would benefit the poor (Deininger 2003: 107–108), the report claimed. The process of modernising and formalising land title, through enhanced local capacity, was seen as a long term project. As it had met such resistance in rural areas, an initial focus on urban and peri–urban areas would assist, 'because the same regulatory and institutional framework will apply to rural and urban land' (Deininger 2003: 186). The revised approach thus maintained the key modernist themes of colonial East Africa in the 1950s.

This was in the face of considerable evidence. Okoth-Ogendo's conclusions on the general failure of land modernisation in Kenya were confirmed by a number of others. One report quantified the earlier reported failures in tenure security, access to formal credit and crop yields. Land disputes continued, land title was 'not strongly related to the use of credit', nor was land title 'significantly related' to crop yields; titles were acquired to enhance rights, not to increase agricultural production (Place and Migot-Adholla 1998: 360, 368, 371). The registration program was found to have had 'relatively little impact on agricultural development compared with infrastructure development and easing of restrictions of cash crop growing by Africans'. The authors suggest 'other countries ... should be wary of undertaking nationwide registration programs' and urge greater attention to spending on 'rural infrastructure, health and education' (Place and Migot-Adholla 1998: 371–372). The FAO, in turn, had noted that 'the main sense of [land tenure] insecurity experienced within strong customary systems is caused by the behaviour of the state and external market forces' (FAO 2002: 222). Meinzen–Dick (2009) explains these failures 'to understand the complexity of property rights', as contributing to a reduction in poor peoples' security of tenure.

Researchers from London's International Institute for Environment and Development similarly concluded that, in eastern Africa, 'the hoped for benefits of registration do not accrue automatically and, in some circumstances, the effects of registration may be the converse of those anticipated' (Cotula et al 2004: 3). Registration could exacerbate land disputes, elite groups may claim land beyond their entitlements under the customary system, those without education or influence may find their land registered to someone else, secondary owners of land such as women 'often do not appear in the land register and are thus expropriated'. In Kenya, there was 'no significant correlation' between registered land title and rural credit, there were 'negative repercussions' on vulnerable groups and 'more generally, land registration reinforced class and wealth differentiation' (Cotula et al 2004: 4–5). A later report noted that the World Bank report (Deininger 2003) had made use of gender rhetoric but had made no practical suggestions for strengthening women's rights (Ikdahl et al 2005). Regardless of this extensive experience, modernist reports continued to assert Swynnerton–type benefits, while occasionally noting the problems of documenting them.

Attempts to obliterate customary systems and replace them with a single modernised system face some well recognised dangers. Nobel Prize winner Elinor Ostrom (2010) observes 'no single idealised structure of governance in successful …institutional monocultures are not robust .. [and there persists] a dangerous tendency to impose uniform rules' on common properties. These dangers are implicit in a rejection of the customary principles of sustainable livelihoods, social inclusion and social adaptation. The principles of the customary system, counterposed to modernist principles, as well as the latter's claimed benefits are set out in the table below.

Table 2.1 Principles and claims of customary and modernist land systems		
Customary principles	Modernist principles	Claimed modernist benefits
Focus on sustainable family livelihoods	Focus on individual appropriation	Greater security of title
Social inclusion	Exclusive and exclusionary boundaries	Improved agricultural activity
Community–controlled	Central regulation by the state	Enhanced rural credit
Flexibility and adaptation	Definitive rules based system	Improved status of secondary title holders (esp. women)

The above literature shows that, from the East African experience, few of the claimed modernist benefits materialised. On the contrary, new problems of dispossession and inequality emerged.

ATTEMPTS TO 'TRANSMIT' MODERNIST LAND SYSTEMS

There were colonial era attempts to 'transmit' the East African experiment to Melanesia, including Papua New Guinea. These failed, but were followed by an aid agency driven 'liberal wave', after independence, in the 1980s and 1990s. When this also failed, a PNG government initiative in 2005 put the modernist land drive back on track.

Larmour describes the 'first wave' of modernising influence on PNG from colonial Africa, in the 1950s and 1960s. It was to involve 'systematic adjudication' of the ownership and boundaries of customary land. This approach to land, from colonial Sudan and Kenya, was brought to the Solomon Islands, Papua New Guinea and Vanuatu by a group from the British Colonial Office: Rowton Simpson, Jerry Lawrance and Jim Fleming (see Simpson 1976). As early as 1957 they spoke of the

Kenyan system with Paul Hasluck, then the Australian minister with responsibility for PNG (Bredmeyer 1975; Downs 1980).

The result was that a somewhat less systematic form of the Kenyan model of formalising customary title was proposed, under the colonial regimes, for PNG, the Solomon Islands and Vanuatu (then called the 'New Hebrides'). A *Land (Tenure Conversion) Act* was introduced in 1963, to allow conversion of customary into commercial title; but the law proved unpopular and was rarely used. However a pre-independence legislative package for PNG, including the *Land Groups Incorporation Act* of 1974 (which provides for clans to form an incorporated land group, an ILG, for the purpose of land dealings) and the 'lease-lease-back' scheme (where the state acts as a facilitator for the leasing of customary land, usually by ILGs) suggested a framework for commerce in PNG's customary land (Larmour 1991; Larmour 2002: 155; NLDT–SCCLD 2006). Larmour describes a 'nationalist reaction' to these legal proposals, which influenced academics like Alan Ward, Jim Fingleton and Ron Crocombe to develop more heterodox advice, which drew on Maori and other pacific island land experience. The systematic registration model was said to have been eventually 'stopped in its tracks' (Larmour 2002: 155–157).

At independence in 1975, the *PNG Constitution* recognised customary law in its preamble, a principle to be respected in all subsequent legislation, including land law. Article 56 of this *Constitution* also specified that 'Only citizens may ... acquire freehold land' (NLDT–SCCLD 2006: 5). This reflected the broad-based, nationalist support for PNG law and values, at that time. Nevertheless, the post-colonial 'liberal wave' saw business interests (mining companies such as BHP), western analysts (the Institute for National Affairs, Michael Trebilcock and Robert Cooter) and aid agencies (notably the World Bank and AusAID) again pushing for land modernisation (Larmour 2002: 157–158).

Although this 'liberal wave' was also largely unsuccessful, the process and the thought behind it warrants some attention. Some land law was amended in the late 1980s, but the impact on actual land tenure was minimal. The *Land (Tenure Conversion) Act* (1963) was amended in 1987 to allow for business and incorporated land group title. The lease–lease back scheme and the *Land Groups Incorporations Act* (1974) were also amended in 1987, while the *Provincial Land Act* (regulating dealings in unincorporated customary land) was introduced (Larmour 1991: 51). Yet most prominent were the funded programs of the large agencies, which spelt out their aims quite clearly.

In the Asia-Pacific region, between 1985 and 2000, Australia's overseas aid agency AusAID (formerly ADAB) backed more than twenty projects at a cost of about $130 million. Most of this went into major projects in Thailand, Laos and Indonesia, co-financed with the World Bank (AusAID 2000: xiii). The thinking behind this spending was both modernist and neoliberal. AusAID said:

> 'When sound economic policies accompany functioning land markets, a prerequisite to development has been satisfied. Titling of land provides owners with security of tenure. Land becomes an asset, a tradable good in the market place, and capital can be raised from it. Titles provide owners with a secure ownership and a financial incentive to make capital investment, and improve environmental management' (AusAID 2001: 2).

In PNG, AusAID contributed to the World Bank's 'Land Mobilisation Project' of 1996–2001 (AusAID 2000: 4), which was in turn linked to the Bank's 1999 Structural Adjustment Program loan. The Australian projects were claimed to be 'effective in targeting rural poverty and increasing the security of landholders who might otherwise be at risk of being removed from their land'. In the South Pacific these AusAID projects were said to 'have an impact on poverty reduction if they encourage economic development ... [land administration] should be considered in the context of public sector reform' (AusAID 2000: xiii–xiv). This drive for a 'land reform' aimed at modernising customary tenure was backed by academics such as Tim Curtin, who consistently argued the need for tenure reform in PNG to enhance exports and back formal economy growth (Curtin 2003: 6–17).

The land projects were supposed to be of general benefit, not least for Australian companies with an interest in land. This potential conflict of interest was, at times, prominent. At first, the large Australian-based mining company BHP was involved in land projects. BHP had become directly involved in 1984, in land titling and administration projects in Thailand. Subsequently the company project managed land titling in

Laos, Indonesia and Papua New Guinea, amongst other countries. BHP saw land registration as:

'simply the means employed to achieve a land administration climate where land resources are more effectively managed, peoples' rights are secure, transactions are economically and fairly recorded and social conflict over land is minimised. In short an environment for effective and equitable national development.' (Burns et al 1996: 1.1, 4.2 ; Grant 1999)

Shortly after this BHP was effectively driven out of PNG, following complaints over the environmental destruction and contamination caused along the Fly River by the OK Tedi mine, in PNG's Western province (Hyndman 2001).

Registration of land proved unpopular in PNG because it:

'was popularly associated with alienation ... almost all registered land had, in fact, been bought from small amounts of money, or taken by the colonial government as so called 'wasteland'. Registration had already made it hard to get it back' (Larmour 2002: 154).

Strong resistance to 'land mobilisation' (Fingleton 2004: 98; Yala 2005: 1), had produced few results, and this forced a more pragmatic stance by the 'aid' agencies. In a 1999 report on PNG the World Bank admitted:

'Comprehensive land reform is unlikely to succeed. Still, the government could implement some reforms – improving the leasing system, developing mortgage insurance, rejuvenating the industrial estates program, allocating more resources to credit collection efforts – particularly where there is large demand for certain land for market–based use' (World Bank 1999: 114).

After a series of protests at the World Bank conditional loan program (linked to its 'land mobilisation') in the late 1990s and early 2000s (Healy 2001), the agency retreated to a 'behind the scenes' role, where it encouraged local organisations to take part in 'land reform' agendas.

Over 2005–06 both the Australian and the PNG governments developed a more complementary strategy (despite tensions in other areas), the former adjusting its language and the latter stepping up into a more prominent role. Canberra's 'White Paper' on aid (in 2006) showed a less confrontative approach, but also a commitment to the 'long haul' over land modernisation. The commitment to economic liberal principles had not changed. AusAID said:

> 'The issue of land tenure in the pacific, although controversial, cannot be avoided if sustained growth is to be achieved. However, any changes to land will have to come from within the Pacific, and such changes will take considerable time.' (AusAID 2006: 37).

The notion of a 'middle way' essentially meant support for the leasing of customary land. Canberra would also pursue this approach through two general programs: 'a Pacific leadership program and by building demand for better governance' (AusAID 2006: xii). This meant cultivating individual pacific intellectuals to assist with their plans.

An AusAID document produced across a change of governments in Canberra spelt out some 'pacific land principles', which seemed relevant to a set of aid projects under a 'pacific land program' (AusAID 2008). Although there was a more conciliatory tone towards customary tenure, the principles began with a familiar theme: 'make tenure security a priority'; then 'intervene only if it is necessary', make land policies 'relevant to local circumstances', be prepared for 'long timeframes', involve stakeholders, 'adopt simple and sustainable reforms', 'balance the interests' of landowners and land users and 'provide safeguards for vulnerable groups (AusAID 2008: 105–108). A \$54 million 'Pacific Land Program' backed up these ideas (AusAID 2009).

The 'Pacific Principles' were not said to represent government policy, but the general approach does seem to have become one of fomenting institutional change and grooming (or contracting) a sympathetic local elite. Such a long term plan might have been clever, but it would not easily show the short–term results which had come to be expected of aid projects. In early 2011, Foreign Minister Kevin Rudd suddenly suspended the Pacific Land Program (ABC 2011). It was not clear if this was a temporary move, or the sign of a review of strategy. Bachriadi says that, without its own land policy, AusAID 'follows the broad land policies of the World Bank'. AusAID's projects are conditioned by its 'national interest' aim, aimed at supporting corporate interests. The claim that 'land reform' assists poor pacific peoples depends on the 'trickle down' theory, and the evidence is against it. (Bachriadi 2009: 30–31).

Nevertheless, AusAID's wish for a locally developed modernist land plan was taking shape in PNG, for the first time. In face of the obvious unpopularity of such 'reform', the government set up a 'Land and Development' symposium in August 2005 and, following that, a 'National Land Development Task Force' in 2006. At the symposium Deputy Prime Minister Moi Avei called for a 'middle way' while Professor Lawrence Kalinoe and Lands Commissioner Josepha Kanawi claimed land registration would 'protect customary land'. Some National Research Institute academics argued that customary land was 'dead capital', and would aggravate poverty in the country (in Rusanen 2005). On the other hand, Patrick Harricknen, the lawyer for a group of NGOs, argued that economic interests lay behind the registration push, and that existing land laws needed to be protected, strengthened and enforced (in Rusanen 2005). The task force committees included a mix of people, but was stacked with pro–registration voices. A sub-committee on customary land nevertheless recommended: (i) voluntary land registration under the *Land Groups Incorporation Act* 1974; (ii) tightening of this law, to address past ILG frauds; (iii) a more rigorous process of actual registration; and (iv) abolition of the unpopular *Land (Tenure Conversion) Act* 1963 (NLDT–SCCLD 2006).

The rationale for these developments was spelt out by PNG academic Charles Yala. He noted that past initiatives to register and otherwise transform customary title had failed and led to serious conflict. Nevertheless, the government of PNG had decided to invest at least 100 million Kina (about A$40 million) 'in a process in which Papua New Guinean institutions and experts maintained complete control of the land reform process, from conception to formulation and implementation' (Yala 2005: 1). Despite the PNG Government assuming leadership on the issue, the agenda was an old one, and backed by powerful outside interests. Yala argued the need to overcome 'foreign domination of land reform discussions'. He claimed that 'foreign non-governmental organisations also played a role in stirring up protests against land reform' (Yala 2006: 130). Even more strident that many of the outside modernisers, Yala argued that 'traditional land tenure systems were unsuitable for a modern society' as the transmission of rights was linked to either patrilineal or matrilineal systems, both of which were 'discriminatory because either practice makes one gender landless' (Yala 2006: 132, 135). This was an oversimplification for, as we have seen, both men and women have land rights in PNG's customary systems. Yala even questioned the 'social safety net' benefit in customary land tenure. He called this a 'dangerous assumption', asserting that 'subsistence farming' could not support an increasing population. Adopting the liberal evolutionary approach he asserted that customary title could not deal with overpopulation and other pressures, that it would contribute to 'large scale ethnic conflicts' (Yala 2006: 133–135). The land modernizers had found at least one 'kindred spirit' in PNG.

CONCLUDING OBSERVATIONS

Customary land systems in PNG have been resilient over many centuries, but face new challenges. Their basic principles (support for sustainable livelihoods, social inclusion, community control and flexibility and adaptation) allow for new developments such as migration, schools and commerce; but they also conflict with many of the principles of modernist land systems (individual appropriation, exclusive and exclusionary boundaries, centralised state regulation and definite and universal rules). Fingleton and Larmour have contrasted the 'inflexibility and unfairness of tenure conversion with the dynamism and flexibility of customary land tenure' (Larmour 2002: 154).

There was a colonial era attempt to transmit the earlier Kenyan land registration process to system to Melanesia, including Papua New Guinea. This attempt mostly failed, in the face of nationalist resistance. Subsequently, the Kenyan modernisation and registration process was shown to have not delivered any of the major claimed benefits (security of tenure, agricultural productivity, rural credit and enhanced land rights for women). This did not deter a second 'liberal wave' push to reform PNG's customary land, in the 1980s and 1990s; yet this wave also failed, in face of renewed popular resistance.

A change of strategy saw a Papua New Guinea government pick up the land modernisation 'banner' in 2005, and the debate remains alive. Some local advocates have replaced the international agencies on the 'front line' of this debate, but the modernist themes remain much the same. Powerful interests clearly favour widescale abolition of customary tenure, to open up private investment opportunities; yet their arguments remain modernist and liberal, claiming benefits for all. PNG families feel more secure with the system they know and trust, but are regularly confronted with promises of great benefit if they 'give over' their land to 'development'.

High stakes are involved in the misleading promises and poor track record of land modernisation, in strong customary land regions. The reasons are not a secret, and are a common theme in Melanesia. The Canadian born Bishop of Malaita, Rev Terry Brown, after a political crisis in the Solomon Islands, observed 'The only reason the Solomons is not starving is because of its customary land tenure system' (in Richardson 2006: 47). On the customary side we see the same message: a man from Malaita (Solomon Islands) is quoted as saying: 'Your regista lands ye selfis ye no gut iu komu mekim rabis long custom land iu sahi'. ('Your land registration plan is selfish, you're no good; you'll make rubbish of customary land, you'll be sorry') (Tiffany 1983: x). Just how sorry they might be is a story that economic analysis is said to be able to tell; but which type of economics? That is the subject of the next chapter.

Land economics – the old
and the new

❧

In the broadest sense of the word, 'economics' can be important to help inform us about production, exchange, distribution and resource management. The problem is that the old and narrow (yet 'modernist') form of economics actively hides many relevant issues. Pushing an agenda of 'aggregate growth' in the national economy, and consequently privileging large corporations and export industries, this line of logic obscures many critical considerations of everyday life, not to speak of sustainable futures.

While Papua New Guinea's distinct economy mostly involves family livelihoods based on diverse agricultural production – with government revenues underwritten by mining and some other industries – the 'old school' economics barely notices the country's economic base.

For example, a recent booklet by the Bank of the South Pacific (BSP) wrongly asserts: 'agriculture (coffee, cocoa and copra) provides a subsistence livelihood for the bulk of the population (about 75% of PNG's population)' (BSP c.2010: 21). In fact, most agricultural production in PNG is focused on vegetables, fruit and other fresh produce. The three export crops mentioned have almost nothing to do with 'subsistence': people eat very little coffee, cocoa and copra. The BSP goes on: 'The driving force behind commercial agriculture in Papua New Guinea has always been the export crops' (BSP c.2010: 21). Wrong again. Even in commercial agriculture, for most PNG families export crops come a distant second to domestic crop sales. In surveys of sellers in domestic produce markets across four of PNG's provinces I have only found a handful (less than 5%) who say their income from export crops is greater than that from the local markets. Hardly any grow produce only for export. The best cash crops in domestic markets are usually peanut, betel nut, melons, taro and other fruits and vegetables. Families frequently supplement their incomes with export cash crops, but rarely do these crops earn more than produce sold in domestic markets.

There are some immediate and obvious problems with 'old school' economics. With its focus on finance and the formal sector:

- It does not take proper account of 'subsistence' production, or 'social exchange';
- It fails to adequately measure domestic, informal market activity; and
- It does not take into account the broader costs of formal market activity, such as the chemically intensive monocultures, like oil palm.

Yet the subsistence sector combined with domestic cash markets (supplemented, in third place, by the export crops) remains the core of rural livelihoods. If people have anything to do with economics, diverse rural production for sustenance, social support and domestic markets is the mainstream PNG economy. Furthermore, damage to local ecologies – from formal sector activities such as logging and monocultures – directly affects local production and livelihoods. 'Old school' economics sometimes stupidly characterise this debate as 'the economy' versus 'environmentalists'. In fact, as customary land managers know very well, production and livelihoods depend directly on the health of local ecologies, including soils and rivers.

It is no coincidence that banks, at the centre of the financialised world, ignore PNG's large scale subsistence production and do not properly count the productivity of the thriving microbusiness and fresh produce sectors. These sectors have little access to, and in most cases no need for credit; thus they pay no 'rent' in the form of interest or other charges to the banks. What matters most to the banks is the formal economy and financialised agriculture – that is, big companies making a surplus from the land. Following a similar logic, economists of the 'old school' sometimes claim that until land and rural production can be financialised (mortgaged, capitalised) it is unproductive or 'dead capital' (see some NRI views in Rusanen 2005; also Fairhead, Kauzi and Yala 2010). Never mind that such 'dead capital' is productive enough to sustain most PNG families. It is a very limited 'economic' understanding that fails to take account of the livelihood underpinnings of the vast majority of a country's citizens.

We need wider economic perspectives to see what matters to most people: the subsistence sector, the informal economy, the competition for resources and the maintenance of healthy local ecologies. The simple fact of families feeding and housing themselves, raising funds for school fees and health services – and then complaining about the absence of government services and roads, despite substantial state revenues from mining – mostly passes by the proponents of this 'old school' economics. Their focus is firmly on national income (GDP), aid programs, foreign investment and exports.

Nevertheless, while building wider perspectives, we need to understand some of the logic of this 'old school' economics, because it is influential and causes a great deal of confusion. We need to review this 'old school' before moving to a broader economic logic, which recognises the limitations of aggregate measures like GDP, re-focuses on livelihoods and ecological sustainability and makes use of the human development indicators (for example in education, health and the environment). I call such broader perspectives the 'new school' economics. It has special relevance to countries like PNG, with large rural populations and large informal sectors.

This chapter explains and contrasts the 'old school' with the 'new school'. It then considers the old school arguments in PNG over 'land reform', based on 'growth' oriented models. It brings the contradictions to a head by comparing rural livelihood options in both the formal and informal sectors, while looking at 'the economy' in a broader and more inclusive way.

FROM THE 'OLD SCHOOL' TO THE 'NEW SCHOOL'

The 'old school' relies on aggregate growth measures (such as GDP), privileges large formal sector activities and promotes 'market formation', including in land. The 'new school' – while recognising the role of the formal sector and public finance – has its main focus on human well–being and family livelihoods, takes seriously sustainable ecologies and considers the 'human development' indicators as of greater relevance than GDP. Let's look first at the origins, features and problems of the 'old school'.

The foundations of narrow economics can be found in the European neoclassical writers of the 1870s (Jevons 1871, Menger 1971, Walras 1875/1877). They tried to escape the worrying focus of earlier classical political economists (Adam Smith, David Ricardo and Karl Marx) on questions of value from production, social class and distribution (see Stilwell 2006). These theories tended to raise the profile of social power relations. Neoclassical 'pure economics', on the other hand, portrayed the world as comprising millions of 'economically rational' individuals acting in harmonious yet impersonal markets. This modeling attempted to eliminate questions of cultural difference – as also of domination and justice – in favour of a more mathematical consideration of 'purely' economic matters. These ideas suited the rising corporations, because they deflected criticism and recrimination over the corporations' social role and backed the rising formal sector economies. Unfavourable economic outcomes could be blamed on impersonal 'markets'.

This neoclassical project was amended in the mid twentieth century by the macroeconomic ideas best presented by the English economist John Maynard Keynes (1936). Using neoclassical language, Keynes drew attention to problems of capitalist stagnation and presented some new ideas on state economic management and public finance. The post–war 'neoclassical synthesis' (e.g. Samuelson 1947) adopted elements of Keynes' ideas, linking up 'market economics' with new concepts such as gross domestic product (GDP). The 'old school' draws on this tradition by returning to the themes of extending 'market forces' and a keen focus on aggregate economic growth. The implications for customary land are seen in expanding 'land markets' and building up the idea that land must be 'capitalised'.

During the 'Green Revolution' of the 1960s, where capitalist agriculture was given a technological boost, these 'old school' economic ideas began to be applied to traditionally managed lands. They linked up very well to the British 'modernist' ideas over land in East Africa, of the late colonial period. The logic was serving similar economic interests. Indeed, through these links we can see the strong symbiosis between neocolonial and economic liberal ideas: both aim at an institutional environment which favours international investors.

Economic theorist Ester Boserup saw the extension of formal agriculture as a means of escaping population pressures. This was an economic liberal version of the 'evolutionist' model, asserting that 'high population density and advanced agro-technology are correlated with individual land tenure, while communal or tribal tenurial systems are typical of extensive or long-fallow cultivation systems' (Boserup 1965). She argued for land tenure systems which supported the growth of the new large scale monocultures. Land 'modernisation' would thus be an induced response to the higher 'shadow prices' of land and was said to encourage longer term investments (Boserup 1965). Drawing informal sectors into the formal economy was said to be able to lift productivity and, of course, contribute to economic growth.

By the seventies, however, a series of criticisms of this type of approach – and in particular the reliance on GDP as a measure of socio-economic well–being – had sprung up. It was clear, even to economists of the 'neoclassical synthesis', that GDP did not include important aspects of the productive economy (such as domestic and subsistence work), yet included production which was not unambiguously about socio-economic welfare (e.g. the production of weapons). Growth measures were also blind to economic mal-distribution and did not take account of environmental degradation. Economic texts (e.g. Samuelson and Nordhaus 1948–2009) noted some of these limitations, but their macroeconomism retained a focus on GDP measures. Such criticisms were even more acute for the developing countries, with their large subsistence, domestic and informal sectors. It was no coincidence, then, that it was a group of broader minded economists from developing countries (notably Mahbub Ul Haq and Amartya Sen) who suggested more attention be paid to human development indicators. These alternative measures began to be promoted in the UNDP's Human Development Reports and the Human Development Index (HDI), from 1990 onwards, and then again in the UN's Millennium Development Goals (MDGs) of 2000 (UN 2006).

The limitations of GDP, as an economic indicator, could be spoken of in three main areas: problems of economic formalisation, distributional issues and environmental concerns. 'Growth' oriented strategies typically favour the rise of new, formal economies, private businesses with formal employees and, with the neoliberal emphases of the 1980s, export industries in particular. However this emphasis ignores, undervalues and often actively displaces promising 'hybrid' livelihoods, which build new and diverse strategies on a base of informal and subsistence economies. Growth strategies are also blind to key distributional issues, including the marginalisation of large populations and the development (or not) of critical shared services, such as in education and health.

Finally, it is notorious that environmental benefits and costs are perversely included or excluded by economic growth measures (Meier and Seers 1984). The loss of a natural resource, such as a forest, is not 'deducted' from GDP, precisely because it had never before entered the formal economy. Nevertheless, not only is a forest a 'stock' of timber which can be depleted, it is also a system of living processes with utilitarian value for humans: the capacity to filter water, to generate oxygen and to preserve a range of other biodiverse resources. The perversity of GDP measures does not end there. Economic growth is aided by environmental disasters and wars, as well as failing to incorporate the costs of degradation and unsustainable behaviour.

All this has important implications for 'land economics'. Boserup's idea of capitalising land was picked up by other economic liberal 'modernisers'. For example Deininger and Feder (1998: 35), following Boserup, back the liberal evolutionist 'transition from traditional to [individual] private property rights' to help 'productivity enhancing land–related investments'. They concede that 'traditional systems are associated with a wide range of equity benefits not all of which can normally be preserved in a system characterized by private land ownership'; but they nonetheless extend the 'evolutionary' logic, which suggests no real future for customary management.

In a similar way, yet claiming a developing country voice, Peruvian-born Hernando de Soto urged greater formalisation of property rights (De Soto 2000). He argued that failures in such formalisation held back capitalism in developing countries. Clearly documented property rights were an essential foundation for systems of credit, share ownership, contracted services and so on. 'Capitalism requires the bedrock of the rule of law, beginning with that of property', he argued (De Soto 2002: 349). These ideas were not new. De Soto followed the British in East Africa, Boserup, Deininger and others in claming that the 'greater security' of (registered, individual and transferable) land tenure would stabilise investment and help increase agricultural productivity and the growth of formal economies.

As with the East African case, there has been substantial empirical refutation of De Soto's ideas. It has been pointed out, a number of times, that imported models of formal rights are 'too often ... not grounded in local realities' and can make things worse for ordinary people (Meinzen-Dick 2009: 5; see also Lavigne Delville 2006: 18–19; Hunt 2004: 174). A South African study observed that greater formal property rights had not increased tenure security, nor promoted greater lending to the poor, and had instead been expensive, exposing many poor people to homelessness (Cousins et al 2005: 4).

Similarly, land modernisation in the Pacific persists, based on similar arguments and backed by powerful interest groups. For example, the World Growth Institute (WGI) and International Trade Strategies Global (ITS Global), contracted by logging, wood pulp and oil palm industries, present arguments on the value of giving over Melanesian land to those 'high productivity' industries (see ITS Global 2011). These studies have not thought it necessary to demonstrate how, for example an oil palm plantation is 'more productive' than the diverse production of small farmers. They just assume this. Their own formal economy frameworks are too limited to allow such a comparison.

Similarly an Australian corporate 'think tank', the Centre for Independent Studies – backed by banks and mining companies – regularly produces reports asserting the need to convert customary land systems into individual property rights regimes. For example, Helen

Hughes (2004:4), backed by the CIS, simply asserts that customary land is 'the primary reason for deprivation in rural Pacific communities'. She does not attempt to prove such a claim. Referring to the Solomon Islands, Gaurav Sodhi, also backed by the CIS, likewise argues 'Agriculture is the key ... without land surveys, registration and long term leases there can be no progress' (Sodhi 2008). The assumption here is that the only 'agriculture' that matters in the Solomon islands is corporate plantations. Yet these export oriented monocultures (mostly oil palm) neither feed nor provide the majority of income for the most Solomon Islanders.

AusAID in recent decades has supported this 'modernism' and 'old school' line. The agency has run land titling and administration projects for many years, and has long claimed that its projects enhance the security of land rights and target rural poverty (AusAID 2000). The agency urges updating land registers but – in face of the many failed land modernising projects – has looked for what it sees as a 'middle way', mostly through leases (AusAID 2006), which are said to be able to 'assist' customary land owners get better value from their land (AusAID 2008). Some Papua New Guinean academics and officials (e.g. Yala 2010) have joined in this chorus.

From colonial East Africa to the 'Green Revolution' to Melanesia we have seen repeated modernist claims, backed by the logic of 'old school' economics. These themes are characterised in the table below, alongside some similarly characterised themes of what might be called the 'new school'.

Table 3.1: Measuring productivity and achievements: which economics?	
'Old school' economics	'New school' economics
Growth of a national economy	Inclusive human well–being, livelihoods
Large corporations, formal markets	Diverse economy, includes small farming
Export sector privileged, future and ecological costs 'discounted'	Consolidate domestic economies, protect social systems and local ecologies
Financialised measures (GDP, profits, foreign investment, aid, taxation)	Human development measures (education, health, participation, clean environment)

The 'new school' themes both address deficiencies in the 'old school' and reconceptualise the economic problem. In the first place there is the idea of a more inclusive economy, where people, their livelihoods and their 'capabilities' (Sen 1983; Sen 1999) are at the centre. Second, the demands of a broader and more diverse 'economy' means that the focus is on addressing domestic needs first, including the requirements of social systems, domestic markets and local ecologies (e.g. Shiva 1993). Finally, this new more inclusive and human–focused view of an economy needs other measures, a need which is to some extent met by the human development indicators of the UNDP, popularised since the early 1990s (UNDP 1990) and now to some degree incorporated in the Millennium Development Goals (MDGs).

The newer economic approaches, looking beyond modernist assumptions, are more able to recognise the contributions of customary land systems. At least they might be able to see that these systems remain vehicles for food security, housing, widespread employment, social security, biodiversity protection, ecological stability and a store of natural medicines, as well as a source of social cohesion and inclusion and cultural reproduction (see Lee and Anderson 2010). These are social systems which address a number of the 'capabilities' referred to by the human development indicators, and which embody elements of what elsewhere has been called the 'multifunctionality' of small farming: where small and diverse rural social and productive relations make multiple economic and social contributions, many of which lie beyond the scope of formal economies (Rosset 2000; Moxnes Jervell and Jolley 2003). In fact, fuller studies of customary systems can illustrate and test out the new productivity arguments over small farming.

Nevertheless, modernist 'land reform' programs persist, driven by commercial interests and modernist mindsets. These programs insist on the economic benefits of registration, individual property rights and commercial land markets. The enthusiasm for such 'reform' seems barely dampened by the serious environmental and social problems catalysed – in PNG and elsewhere – by land rationalisation and chemically–intensive monocultures (see e.g. Shiva 1993; Kimbrell 2002; Altieri 2004). Let's turn now to some of the applications to PNG of this narrow economic logic.

'LAND ECONOMICS' IN PAPUA NEW GUINEA

Contemporary arguments for formal land markets in Melanesia come from the international aid agencies, companies with direct interests in resource extraction, foreign academics and some Melanesian government officials. The arguments address economic growth, government revenue and development finance; only occasionally and in a very limited way do they touch on family livelihoods.

For example ITS Global, an Australian company contracted by the peak logging group in Papua New Guinea (which is dominated by Malaysian companies), has prepared a series of reports that argue the case for logging and oil palm plantations. These arguments focus on the contribution of those land-intensive industries to PNG's gross economy, their contributions to public finance (in the case of logging, through export taxes) and consequent revenue for development spending. In the case of oil palm there is a limited discussion of livelihoods, through 'smallholder' incomes: those few small farmers who have joined a scheme to sell oil palm fruit from their own land to the corporate mills.

ITS Global calls for an expansion of PNG's wholesale log exports, on the basis that logging generates a substantial amount of income (about 300 to 400 million Kina per year). Even though most of this accrues to the logging companies, it is said that the PNG government reaps almost one third (about K100 million) in export taxes per year, while local landholders receive 'substantial' royalties (ITS Global 2006: 12). On top of this, there are said to be 'significant benefits' to local people from infrastructure spending (airstrips, roads, health centres) although it is acknowledged that such works 'are constructed primarily for the purposes of the project' (ITS Global 2006: 39, 41). This report denies the claims of environmental damage, unsustainability and limited benefit to landowners, made by many other reports (e.g. IFRT 2004), and boldly asserts that 'there is no economic case against fostering a vibrant and productive forestry industry in PNG' (ITS Global 2006: 27). This is, however, a partisan argument, compromised by its direct links to interested parties.

In addition to the constant environmental criticisms of wholesale logging (e.g. Laurance et al 2011), the economic returns to customary landowners are very poor. For example, local communities are paid $11 per cubic metre of Kwila wood, less than 1/20th of the typical returns of $240 per cubic metre in China (EIA-Telapak 2005; Bun, King and Sherman 2004). Meanwhile, the roads and bridges built by the loggers are not maintained and do not survive much beyond the logging operation (CELCOR and ACF 2006), while the importance of logging taxes is falling rapidly as mining and gas revenues rise. Many agencies now accept the need to support more sustainable timber alternatives, such as eco-forestry.

Yet logging survives in league with large plantation developments, which in South East Asia and Melanesia has meant oil palm. Logging permits have been made conditional on 'back end' oil palm development, and all the major international financial agencies in the region (AusAID, the Asian Development Bank, the World Bank) have subsidised oil palm development, often in the guise of supporting 'community participation' and enhancing the 'productivity' of smallholder agricultural development (e.g. World Bank 2007). Here we see some departure from the more general, modernist arguments about growth and government revenue into a limited engagement with livelihoods and family incomes.

The World Bank, for example, claims that incomes for landowners who give over part of their land to oil palm are equivalent to 2,793 Kina per hectare per year, a figure greater than an estimated K1,136 for cocoa cultivation. On this basis the Bank (wrongly) claims that 'oil palm currently provides small holders with higher returns on their land and labour than most other agricultural commodities' (World Bank 2011: 2). Notice the 'old school' assumption – it is only export crops that matter; no other crops are considered. The industry consultant ITS Global seizes on this claim, calling for a removal of the 'restraints' on land availability for logging and oil palm (ITS Global 2010; ITS Global 2011). As the World Bank itself is effectively a private investors' lobby group, there is no independent voice in this chorus.

There are several problems with the World Bank's calculations. First, the returns on oil palm are gross income, and oil palm is a more expensive crop to maintain, using a great deal of fertiliser and other chemicals. Second, oil palm is a very productive but greedy plant, which cannot be companion planted. It competes with and reduces the diversity of other local crops, unlike cocoa, coconut and coffee and the many other more lucrative crops grown for the domestic market. Third, the comparison made is mainly with export crops, without real reference to incomes in domestic markets. Yet returns on crops like peanut and betel nut can be much higher, and without chemical inputs (Anderson 2008). Fourth, the environmental damage from oil palm is stark: rivers are silted up and algae clogged from fertiliser run-off. Like other large chemical-intensive monocultures (see Kimbrell 2002), oil palm has a range of costs that reach well beyond the price calculations of the plantation industry.

Limited and selective engagement with livelihood issues does not seem to dent the enthusiasm for generalised growth arguments. Three academics (two Papua New Guineans and an Australian) present a modeling exercise which purports to show a several billion dollar addition to PNG's GDP by extending formal tenure over just another 2.5% of land, over a decade (Fairhead, Kauzi and Yala 2010: 29). While they abandon the old idea that land registration will enhance rural credit for small land owners – because of the consistently negative evidence (Fairhead, Kauzi and Yala 2010: 26) – they maintain the modernist and 'old school' notions that private, individual title will allow capitalisation, investment and thus a generally more productive agriculture.

This is a cultural argument, too, and one that is not too sympathetic to Melanesian culture. They suggest that only those who individually invest in land, engage in projects separate from the needs of the clan or family, are to be considered 'productive'. Individual investment and benefit – contrary to the customary ethos of land as a shared community asset – is implied as these 'productive' people (whether clan members or outsiders) are said to be denied (by customary law) 'exclusive access' to 'optimal amounts' of the clan's best land, as well as 'exclusive access' to the income that might be generated from that land. Thus individuals who make exclusive business for themselves through clan or family land are said to be 'superior' economic agents. Yet the pre-condition for such 'success' is that the clan is specifically excluded from sharing the benefits of land development. This would amount to an anti-social act, indeed probably a criminal act under customary law. The reference to 'productive' and 'non-productive' people is backed by reference to 'the bankability of land' (Fairhead, Kauzi and Yala 2010: 3). This is the idea that land is productive only when it becomes a financial asset. This is a familiar 'old school' argument: customary land is not 'valuable' until it can be financialised, and thus separable from its community. These concepts make it certain that the model which follows both undervalues the current productive functions of customary land, and constructs a 'productivist' argument for land commercialisation.

The computer generated model used was a modification of the Australian ORANI and Austem techniques, even though Australia's land tenure system is entirely different to that of PNG. Cash crops are important inputs to the model, but the first problem is that model shows no estimate of non-market production (i.e. subsistence, cultural exchange and ceremonies). Yet the authors should have been aware of at least one AusAID funded study, which had estimated that Melanesian staple food production (of sweet potato, cassava, taro, banana and coconut) was about 0.92 tonne per person, with a money equivalent of between A$693 (wholesale) and A$876 (retail) per person (Bourke et al 2006: 24). That is before we talk about other agricultural produce. Second, there is little indication that Fairhead and the others considered productive exchange in informal markets, including domestic produce markets. They rely instead on an old Rural Development Handbook which claimed that '93% [of rural residents] ... earned less than 200K per year from the cash economy' (Hansen et al 2000: 25). In fact, that estimate was based on 1990s data, a highly valued Kina and only on incomes from '21 agricultural cash crops', mostly export crops (Hansen et al 2001: 2, 296). It was an extremely poor 'baseline'. There was no reference to more contemporary rural incomes, yet there had been published work on this (Sowei et al 2003; Anderson 2006; Anderson 2008).

This failure to include an economic value of subsistence production and 'social exchange', and the apparent failure to properly incorporate exchange in domestic markets should, by itself, render the model's results worthless. Yet there is a third serious flaw, this time to do with land valuation. The authors explain:

'Given the significance of land for this analysis, the PNG CGE database has been expanded to include land as a separate primary factor for each industry ... [by using] the weighted sum of the land price in each industry' (Fairhead, Kauzi and Yala 2010: 12).

But how do they calculate a price for land in a country which has virtually no rural land market? If it were on the western basis of previous land sales, the value could be zero. Alternatively, also based on practice, it might be the tiny 20 Kina per hectare per year (plus 10% royalties) that is charged as rent for oil palm 'mini-estate' leases in Oro Province (Gou and Higaturu 1999). On the other hand, if it were on the basis of the 'opportunity cost' of productive land lost, it could be 17,000 Kina per hectare per year (Anderson 2006: 146).

Which method do they use? None. Without any attempt to develop or apply a PNG–based method of land valuation, they borrow some land prices from Fiji, another Melanesian country, but one with a quite distinct land tenure history. They say: 'Given that forestry and subsistence agricultural practices across the Pacific are not dissimilar, this [Fijian] data is used in the PNG database' (Fairhead, Kauzi and Yala 2010: 13). The whole model, therefore, is made dependent on whether land valuation in Fiji had any reasonable and comparable basis or, better said, whether such prices reflected values that might enhance rather than undermine rural livelihoods.

The model goes on to set a baseline estimate for GDP growth in PNG, without land reform, then a model giving three possible growth outcomes (low, medium and high impact) with land reform. The overall conclusion – predictable, given the assumptions and input valuations – is that the economy will grow strongly with land reform. They assert there would be additions of between six and sixteen billion Kina to national income, if only a few percent more customary land would enter the formal system (Fairhead, Kauzi and Yala 2010: 29). For the reasons given above, I suggest these calculations are worthless.

The 'sting is in the tail' of this paper because, while it is not made clear who might benefit from the suggested economic growth, it is the customary landowners whom, it is said, must surrender their land rights. The authors say that investor demand for land must be met 'by customary landowners bringing their land into the cash economy' (Fairhead, Kauzi and Yala 2010: 27). Well, there is no doubt this is what foreign investors want, However the authors make the modernist claim that customary owners might also benefit, as it would:

> 'open up alternative income earning opportunities for rural residents, leading to a strong shift away from subsistence to market based agriculture, employment and income generation' (Fairhead, Kauzi and Yala 2010: 25).

However, they do not refer to any particular 'alternative income earning opportunities' for those PNG landowners who might lease or otherwise alienate their land. The major benefits are said to be an expansion of the formal economy, large agricultural projects and other land based investments, and an associated, but unspecified, increase in formal sector jobs.

There is great deception in these land 'modernisation' arguments, backed by narrow and exclusionary 'old school' economics. The arguments privilege the claims of foreign investors, holds out flimsy promises to customary landowning families and brands small farmers as 'unproductive', while ignoring the substance of their production. The economic analysis is weak and carries barely disguised contempt for Melanesian cultural achievements. The best way to shed some economic light on these confused and confusing claims is to look at some actual livelihood experience.

COMPARATIVE RURAL LIVELIHOOD OPTIONS

Let's compare the returns on various rural livelihood options in PNG. We should do this bearing in mind that families with customary land can engage in several forms of income earning activities, and that some activities have greater 'opportunity costs' (i.e. excluding more valuable alternative options) than others. Table One below shows a range of income (or income equivalent, in the case of subsistence consumption) options, based on fairly recent PNG experience. A fuller explanation of this data will be provided in the following chapters. For now, notice that we are comparing economic options associated with the formal sector, as stressed by 'old school' economics (corporate plantations, smallholder oil palm, the 'mama lus frut' program, and wages in factories and mines), and informal sector options, more often associated with the 'new school' (subsistence production, sales in local fresh produce markets, and associated small businesses). In practice, PNG families often combine several options, to form 'hybrid' livelihoods.

Table 3.2: Formal and informal sector incomes in PNG	
	AWE (Kina)
Formal sector incomes –	
Ramu Sugar basic wage, 2006 (Madang Pr, 2007) A8	42
RD Tuna factory wage, 2006 (Madang Pr., 2007) A8	34
Ramu Nickel construction wage, 2006 (Madang Pr, 2007) A8	50
VOP/LSS (oil palm) growers (Oro Pr., 2002 / 2009) WAB, WB	60 / 107
Mama Lus Frut (oil palm) income (WNB, 2000 / 2006) WAB, KB	29 / 49
Chicken factory workers (Morobe Pr.,2011) A11	102

Cont.

Private store workers, Kokopo (ENB, 2011) A11	45
Papindo store workers, Kokopo (ENB, 2011) A11	100
National minimum wage, (2006 / 2011) – IB	37.20 / 91.60
Leasing family land to OP company (per ha, K20–100/year) A6	2
Informal sector incomes –	
Family subsistence production (7 people, Kina *equivalent*) A6	[258]
Informal sector business (Central Pr.) S3	158
Informal sector business 2003 (ENB Pr.) S3	124
Informal sector business 2003 (Morobe Pr.) S3	130
Informal sector business 2003 (Western Highlands Pr.) S3	138
Roadside sellers (mainly women), 2006 (Madang Pr) A8 [weighted]	286 [138]
Roadside sellers (mainly women), 2011 (Morobe Pr) A11 [wtd]	285 [144]
Roadside sellers (mainly women), 2011 (Eastern Highlands) A11 [wtd]	230 [230]
Roadside sellers (mainly women), 2011 (East New Britain) A11 [wtd]	198 [144]
Sources: A6=Anderson 2006; A8=Anderson 2008; A11=Anderson 2011; S3=Sowei et al 2003; WAB Warner and Bauer 2002; KB=Koczberski 2007; WB=World Bank 2010; IB=Matbob 2011; **Notes:** AWE = average weekly earnings in Kina	

The main division in the table is between formal and informal sector incomes. In rural PNG the latter (and sometimes the former) form elements which often supplement subsistence production for consumption. The income equivalent figure for subsistence production, explained in the next chapter, is based on estimates of what it would cost a family to purchase the food and housing they currently gain from their own land in local/regional markets. The Kina value represents the 'opportunity cost' of existing without productive subsistence land.

The first thing to note is that rural rents in PNG bear little relationship to the productive capacity of land. Rents return only 1% or less of the value of subsistence production for family consumption; between 1% and 50% the value of marketing garden produce; and 1% to 5% the value of a range of other formal and informal sector activities. These fractions grow even smaller for the more economically active families engaged in livelihood 'hybrids'. Why anyone would agree to lease out their land in these circumstances deserves consideration.

The second matter that merits attention is the great variability in informal sector incomes, in particular in the marketing of garden produce, which can draw in just a few hundred Kina per year, or many thousands. Typically, we see those lower incomes coming from an unplanned marketing of surplus production, while the higher incomes are seen amongst those who focus on specific crops for market, and in particular for domestic markets (Anderson 2008). The top domestic cash crop earners (200 Kina or more per week) in the four provinces surveyed were as follows: Madang (peanut, betel nut, melons and mangoes), Morobe (taro, peanut, cooking banana, oranges, tobacco, cucumber), Eastern Highlands (sweet potato, various vegetables, fried food and peanut) and East New Britain (peanuts, tobacco, oranges, cooked food and vegetables). Many of those surveyed also grew export crops (coffee, cocoa, copra and vanilla) but hardly any earned more from these than from the locally sold crops (Anderson 2011).

The third feature of note is that the formal economy options listed (Village Oil Palm, Mama Lus Frut, various basic employment options) typically have lower incomes than the other informal and small business options and, in particular, they were less than the incomes of those who market fresh produce. In my survey of women roadside sellers in Madang, the weighted average income (for three days a week at market) was significantly higher than the highest reported incomes for Village Oil Palm (Anderson 2008a; World Bank 2010). Furthermore, there seem to be 'ceilings' on these formal sector schemes, as wages are set by employers and oil palm fruit prices for growers are set by a single local company. That is, the potential of formal sector options for families is limited by other powerful players who dominate those markets.

Finally, the opportunity costs are greater, and there is less flexibility, in the formal sector options that involve leasing of land or turning one's own land over to oil palm cultivation. Oil palm allows no companion planting and ties up good quality land for many years (e.g. Wilcove and Koh 2010; Danielson et al 2009). On the other hand, land use for high return domestic crop options such as peanut, taro, betel nut and melons can be adjusted from year to year. Export crops such as cocoa and vanilla can be companion planted, and do not consume the fertiliser that oil palm demands.

Table 3.2 shows another interesting feature of the roadside seller surveys (2007 and 2011). Most local fresh produce sellers also participate in growing and selling export crops; however in very few cases do the incomes from export produce equal or exceed the cash income from local markets. This tells us that domestic markets are usually much more important to these small farming families. Further, a very high (but variable) proportion of roadside sellers have family participation in other businesses (like small stores and poultry businesses) as well as in formal sector employment. This data suggests the need to rethink the emphasis given to export crops, and to pay more attention to the multi–faceted livelihood options being adopted by small farming families.

Table 3.3: Roadside sellers: additional livelihood activities							
	Also participate in?			Highest income from?			
	exports	Other business	Family member employed	Local markets	unknown	exports	Other business
Morobe	24 (48%)	18 (36%)	9 (18%)	37 (74%)	7 (14%)	4 (8%)	2 (4%)
EHP	34 (62%)	9 (16%)	8 (15%)	40 (73%)	9 (16%)	1 (2%)	1 (2%)
ENB	41 (73%)	7 (13%)	27 (48%)	41 (73%)	6 (11%)	7 (13%)	0 (0%)
[Madang]	36 (82%)	27 (61%)	5 (11%)	33 (75%)	10 (23%)	0 (0%)	1 (2%)
Sources: rural surveys by this writer in June 2011 (Anderson 2011); further to the Madang rural surveys of 2007 (Anderson 2008a)							

The 'land modernisers' (e.g. Fairhead, Kauzi and Yala 2010; Hughes 2004) have put the case for the 'growth and state revenue' contributions of land–using formal sector activities, like logging and oil palm, often ignoring family and community livelihoods. Where it has been suggested that landowning families would benefit from these activities (ITS Global 2006; ITS Global 2010; World Bank 2010), the evidence neither matches the assertions nor considers the full range of options. Overall, the evidence makes it plain that neither rural rents nor engagement with formal economies in rural PNG provide either the range of options or the income earning potential of the better hybrid livelihoods. In these hybrids, families retain their customary land and subsistence production, while engaging in various supplementary informal and formal sector activities, some of them quite successful, yet incompatible with land alienation.

CONCLUDING OBSERVATIONS

The 'old school' economics is notable for its narrow focus on crude economic growth, on formal economies and the export sector. It is an exclusionary view, particularly in developing countries, as it ignores large subsistence sectors and social exchange and then fails to properly account for the commerce of large informal sectors. Having thus privileged formal sector operations it further fails to account for their social and environmental costs ('externalities', those elements that are not included in a industry's pricing structure). All this means that the 'old school' ignores an often highly productive small farming sector. This is, however, consistent with land 'modernisation', developed in the late colonial era. An associated evolutionary theory claimed, without evidence, that traditional sectors were effectively doomed to extinction. In both cases a 'universal benefit' was claimed for modernisation and formalisation processes, while the claims of special interests were advanced.

Nevertheless, a 'new school' economics has both responded to the failures of the old school and re-conceptualised the economic sphere. This school has re-focussed on family livelihoods, using human development indicators while elevating the concept of 'ecologically sustainable development'.

In PNG the implications of this new approach should be a better informed and more inclusive view of the economic sphere, including better understandings that small farming (which sustains the great majority of the population) is in fact the mainstream economy of the nation. It is supplemented principally by the mining sector, which has become the main source of government revenues and (potentially) services and infrastructure. Protecting and helping develop the potential of this mainstream small farming sector must then be at the centre of any serious discussion of 'land economics' in PNG.

Nevertheless, the 'old school' ideas have the backing of powerful interests, and persist in their attacks on customary land. In the name of aggregate economic growth they privilege corporate plantations, like oil palm, which come in the wake of logging. There is little regard here for mass livelihoods. Nor is there recognition of the many promising 'hybrid' livelihoods, based on clan and family control of customary land.

Comparing data on current formal and informal sector livelihood options can provide some clearer perspectives. The fact that the most formal sector wages and rural lease values do not even come close to existing and common informal rural incomes should be decisive. Why would any well informed customary land owner listen to the 'old school' arguments? Well perhaps only if they were not so well informed, or if they were misled, or if they were quite desperate for some money. So where are their best options? We need to look at the combinations of subsistence production and social exchange with other flexible informal and formal sector livelihood options. That is the subject of the following chapters.

From subsistence to
hybrid livelihoods

॰৶

One of the most persistent myths in development is that people linked to traditional lifestyles must be in a process of 'moving from subsistence to the cash economy'. This expression comes not only from finance agencies (e.g. World Bank 1962) and aid administrators (e.g. Downer 2006) but also from analysts with greater sensitivity to livelihoods (e.g. Falconer and Arnold 1988: 3). Whatever the source, the idea is a piece of didactic nonsense which neither describes current livelihood realities nor the better future possibilities. Most Papua New Guinean families have engaged in cash economies for many decades, so as to purchase fuel, supplementary foods, clothing, and school and college fees. Yet this has not reduced the general reliance on family land for basic food, housing, natural medicines and many other needs. In fact, subsistence production and cash economies are both elements of more complex hybrid livelihoods, which are resilient precisely because of their various, adaptive combinations.

'Hybrid' livelihoods are widespread. Amongst small farmers in Thailand, for example, researchers have shown that 'subsistence' in its limited sense barely exists, because rural households have diversified into 'hybrid' livelihood activities which include various farm and non–farm activities (Rigg and Nattapoolwat 2001: 955). Looking at indigenous Latin American experience, Bebbington (1999) suggests that shifting and more complex rural livelihoods make use of a range of assets, resources and markets. Similarly, Warren (2002: 11) says that 'enterprise-based diversification' (as opposed to wage labour) may better help build sustainable rural livelihoods, particularly when there is a basis in assets, supportive structures, access to markets and resilience against market failure. Warren was writing for the UN's Food and Agriculture Organization (FAO), which supports rural livelihood diversification. Similar lessons could be drawn from Melanesian livelihoods, which most often combine a range of economic activities, with their base on customary land.

The modernist or common idea of 'subsistence' as 'bare survival' barely exists in PNG. It is commonplace to find Papua New Guinea families engaged in: subsistence production and consumption, social exchange, local cash crop markets, small businesses, employment and export crop production. If they are not engaged in all six of these, they will be involved in several. This is what is meant here by 'hybrid' livelihoods.

Nor are traditional, indigenous modes of living frozen in time or in technology, as is often imagined in western cultures. The western idea of the native trapped in 'bow and arrow' technology, or in simple 'hunter-gatherer' mode, is a myth; but not an accidental myth. There were particular reasons in colonial history why the technological adaptation and agricultural achievements of indigenous peoples were denied. Developed custodial relationships with the land had to be ignored when indigenous land was being stolen, as in North America and Australia. For that reason, for example, indigenous corn cropping in North America (e.g. Smith 1989) and indigenous fish farming in Australia (Gunditjmara 2010: 18–22) were ignored or denied. In Papua

New Guinea, advanced agricultural systems were introduced in the Highlands nine thousand years ago (UNESCO 2011), with irrigation only abandoned some hundreds of years ago (Brown, Brookfield and Grau 1990), with the introduction of the more easily-grown sweet potato. Indigenous societies survived by their adaptive and flexible nature (FAO 2002; Sillitoe 1999), and by making new technologies and new ideas serve their own socio–cultural systems. Viable livelihoods were not preserved by simply exchanging one entire mode of living for another.

In Papua New Guinea the ongoing control and management (not just 'ownership') of customary land remains the basis of current hybrid livelihoods and the substance of powerful adaptive responses to changing needs and conditions. For example when the prices of globally traded food rose sharply in 2008, many farming families had their attention drawn to the new marketing possibilities this might open up, in a country which produces a large food surplus.

The productive value of the subsistence component of hybrid livelihoods deserves attention, as does the character of those hybrids, including emerging hybrids. This chapter will consider value produced in PNG's subsistence sector, by way of some provisional calculations at the family level using an 'opportunity cost' method. This value must be added to the other productive activities practised on customary land by small farming communities. The chapter will then characterise current hybrid livelihoods, built on the family management of customary land. The strengths and vulnerabilities of these hybrids will be suggested.

THE VALUE OF SUBSISTENCE

'Subsistence' in the Melanesian context, I suggest, is better understood as the foundational element of a range of hybrid livelihoods. It is built on an essential base of customary land management and control, including the management of a stock of 'unused' land to help deal with population pressures, commercial ventures and contingencies. The dismantling of customary land relations through commercially oriented 'land reform' would cause tremendous social disruption as well as undermining the basis of these practical livelihoods.

In any inclusive economic assessment in PNG, we must take account of the productive output of customary land, including the subsistence component. It is foolish to pretend that such value does not exist, or to simply ignore it in economic assessments. What is the best way to value subsistence production? There have been some estimates of the variety in such production, and of aggregate food production, and I will start by noting these. However to put an equivalent value on this non–monetised activity I will use an opportunity cost method, based on some 'pilot' interviews and simulations. The final aim is to sum these estimates of subsistence production with the value produced from other elements of hybrid livelihoods.

It has been said that about 30% of PNG land is arable (UNDP 1999: 12), and about half of that is under cultivation (Rere 2004). This farming produces a large range of indigenous and imported crops. Van Helden (1998: 163) noted the main north coast crops as sweet potato, taro, cassava, yams, cucumber, corn, pumpkin, pitpit, rungia, various beans and greens, ginger, tobacco, chillies, spring onions, peanuts, oranges, bananas, passionfruit, pawpaws, pineapples and melons, amongst a total of 46 cultivated food crops, plus 34 wild foods, 23 mammals and 44 birds hunted in this area (Van Helden 1999: 163–186). Birds were also hunted for their feathers and for live sale, chickens were an occasional food source and pigs were killed as food for special occasions. Fish form part of the diet in coastal areas. Another study has listed 180 traded crops across the whole of PNG (Bourke et al 2004).

Much of this production simply does not register in the 'formal' economy. In 1995 the Fresh Produce Development Corporation estimated total PNG fruit production at 58.35 million kilograms (valued at 88.08 million Kina) and total PNG vegetable production at 47.32 million kilograms (valued at 53.53 million Kina). However, using 1996 national survey data Gibson estimated that the total value of household food consumption was 2.253bn Kina, while total domestic production was estimated at only 1.3bn Kina. Locally produced food was also estimated as providing '80% of available calories' (Gibson 2000: 41–42). That is, subsistence production accounted for the bulk of food consumption but less than 60% in money terms. Bourke similarly estimated that 4.5 million tones of staple foods (roots and grains) were grown in PNG every year, 'a little more than one tonne a year for every rural villager'. He valued this at K2, 850 per capita in 2004, based on the cost of substituting that food with the cheapest equivalent imported food (Bourke 2005: 7). Being underrepresented in the National Accounts, subsistence food production is poorly recognised in economic policy debates.

If we are to assess the value of non-traded productive activities on customary land, we must start with food and housing. However in addition to this we have to recognise that customary land also provides access to natural resources used as medicines, fuels, fences, weapons, tools, canoes, textiles, string bags, cords, musical instruments, artworks, articles of personal adornment and articles of ritual and magic (Powell 1976). To this list of commodities we should add value provided by customary land relations in terms of social security, employment, cultural reproduction and environmental management. However, compared to food and housing, the equivalent value of these other elements is more difficult to calculate.

Nevertheless, at the family level, we can at least estimate the value of food produced for consumption, and housing equivalents, through an 'opportunity cost' method. That is, we calculate the closest equivalent cost of replacing the food and housing if it were not delivered from subsistence production methods based on customary land. This is, after all, what would happen if families were to be dispossessed of their good productive land, the basis of their capacity to effectively feed and house themselves. For the moment we can leave to one side the value from such other goods and services as medicines, tools, resources for crafts, social exchange and environmental management from customary land. To make the basic calculations we need to know the food consumed by the family, each day, and its cost in local markets; and the cost of housing rentals in the region.

I carried out two lots of pilot surveys, in 2004 and 2011, across several provinces, on family food consumption. The handful of interviews in 2004 (see Table 4.1) centred on the basic foods typically consumed daily by families, at the village level. Some additional marginal items were occasionally hunted, grown, baked and bought (Paol 2004); but for the purpose of this analysis, the diet has been simplified to items produced for consumption. People from villages in three different regions gave a preliminary idea of the range of diets and detailed descriptions of typical daily meals (Paol 2004, Sindana 2004; Sinemila 2004). FPDC (2002) data was relied on for most fruit and vegetable prices, supplemented by 2004 market prices for chicken, pork and fish prices, as estimated by the interviewees (Paol 2004; Sindana 2004). The notional 'ordinary' household comprised two adults and 4–5 children, roughly the national average.

The results suggested a range of 9.4 to 16.9 Kina per day in equivalent local currency for food consumed by the family, according to regional town markets prices; and from 19.9 to 31.2 Kina per day, according to capital city (Port Moresby) market prices. Daily consumption figures can be aggregated to annual figures. In this way, the annual cost of otherwise purchasing the food, normally produced and consumed by such families, was estimated to range from 3,431 to 6,169 Kina (in regional markets) and 7,260 to 11,388 (in Port Moresby). This could be rounded to a range of 3,400 to 11,400 Kina per year.

Table 4.1: Estimates of the value of a typical daily family village diet from subsistence production (two adults and 4–5 children), 2004

	Madang coastal	Madang inland	Highlands (Simbu)
	(a=mad; b=pom)	(a=mad; b=pom)	(a=goroka; b=pom)
Morning meal	Cooking bananas, 3kg; Greens, ½kg a. 2.16+1.44; b. 4.29+0.52	Cooking banana + taro (boiled or roasted); fruits (several), sago a. 2.16+1.60; b. 4.29+3.80	Kaukau 1.5kg; local tea+sugar; **fried banana ½kg a.1+0.50+0.60; b.1.86+0.50+0.90
Daytime snacks	Either pawpaw, ripe bananas or pineapple, 2kg; Coconut 3½* a. 1.60+1.32; b. 3.80+1.54	Bananas, various fruits, nuts (galip, okari, peanuts), coconuts, & beetles a. 1.60+ 1.44+1.32+?; b. 3.80+2.10+1.54+?	Kaukau ½kg, one of bananas/pineapple/ sugar cane/sugar fruit 1.5kg a.0.33+1.20; b.0.62+3.00
Evening meal	Taro ½kg; kaukau 1kg; cooking bananas 1½kg; tomato ¼kg; onion ¼kg; carrots ¼kg ; plus some ginger/chillie/tumeric a. 0.36+0.80+1.08+ 0.52+0.83+0.55+1/; b. 1.10+1.24+2.15+0.66+0.75+1.75+1	Soup (greens, coconut, banana, taro), mix of banana/ cassava/ yam/ kaukau/ tapioca, also tomato, onion, greens, various spices a.1.44+0.80+1.08+0.36+0. 80+0.52+0.83+0.55+1; b.0. 52+0.92+1.24+2.14+1.10+ 0.66+0.75+1.75+1	Kaukau & banana 2kg; Greens 1kg; tomatoes ¼kg; onions ¼k; beans ½kg a.1.50+0.98+0.30+0.32+0.65; b.2.60+1.05+0.66+2.50+3.40
Weekly foods	Either medium fish 1kg, ½ chicken OR ½kg pork (K5–10) a. 1.1; b.1.6	nil	Chicken ½, # Pig ¼ kg a.1.3+0.4; b.2.5

Cont.

Monthly foods	Bandicoot OR Tree Kangaroo (K10–20) a. 0.5; b. 0.8	fish (4x year), chicken, goat and pig (2x year) a.0.80+0.40+0.20; b.1.20+0.60+0.30	Cuscus – three times a year ? est. 0.3/0.3
Total daily, in Kina	a. 13.26; b. 31.20	a. 16.9; b.27.71	a.9.38; b.19.89

Sources: Diet estimates and meat prices: Madang coastal (Paol 2004); Madang inland (Sindana 2004); Highlands (Sinemila 2004); **Prices:** October 2002 prices in Gordon's (Port Moresby), Goroka and Madang markets (FPDC 2002); *one coconut per person every second day; ** fried banana perhaps every third day; # Some pig might be shared once every two weeks, ## quantities estimated as for Madang coastal; **Notes:** based on 2004 interviews and 2002 regional and capital market prices

This was not a representative study and the sample was small. However as an indicative study it illustrates actual experiences (as opposed to simple neglect or abstract modelling) and suggests the possibility of similar experience elsewhere. The actual differences in food prices between regional town markets (Madang and Goroka) and the capital (Port Moresby) (see table 4.2) suggest an inflation that would grow with urbanisation, widespread land alienation and reduction in scale of the subsistence sector. On an unweighted price average for the twelve highest traded volume sales of fruit and vegetables, Port Moresby prices (Gordon's Market) were about double those of Goroka and Madang (see Anderson 2006).

Table 4.2: Fruit and vegetable prices, Port Moresby, Goroka and Madang markets, Kina/kg, 2002

	Gordon's (Port Moresby)	Goroka	Madang	Prices: POM/ Gor–Mad av.
Sweet potato (Kaukau)	1.24	0.67	0.8	168%
Cabbage	2.87	0.98	0.65	350%
Tomato	2.64	1.2	2.06	162%
Carrot	7.01	2.02	2.21	331%
Broccoli	5.9	3.17	2.69	201%
Capsicum	6.41	4.77	4.63	136%
Aibika (greens)	1.02	1.68	1.38	67%
Banana (ripe)	2.21	0.77	0.82	276%
Pawpaw	1.79	0.47	0.65	320%

Cont.

Coconut (green)	0.44	0.53	0.33	102%
Lemon/lime	4.54	0.74	2.06	324%
Mango	1.21	2.99	0.77	64%
Unweighted average price ratio for 12 common vegetables/fruits				208%
Source: FPDC 2002, pp.15–18, * October 2002 mean prices, largest volume traded items				

Rental equivalent values are difficult to apply, as town housing is limited and expensive, while village housing is constructed cooperatively, mostly from local materials, and is rent free. School teacher rentals in villages in Madang and the Highlands seems to range from zero (where housing is simply provided for the teacher) to 20 Kina per fortnight (Sinemila 2004; Paol 2004). But teachers' accommodation is a special case. A more likely alternative housing option for landless families would be settlement housing, on the fringes of the towns. However as squatting in this way neither offers neither the security of tenure nor the relative comfort of village housing, I chose 'basic' town rental housing as the most reasonable equivalent. The annual cost of housing in Madang town in 2004 (rentals have risen considerably since then) was 1,500 to 2,000 Kina per month for a 'decent' house; however a 'basic' house in town would rent for 500 Kina per month, or 6,000 Kina per year (Chitoa 2004). This seemed the closest substitute for secure, village housing. On this basis, the equivalent value of food produced and consumed and basic housing for a family in the Madang region could range from 9,400 to 12,200. This is a regional calculation, ignoring the much higher costs of food and housing in the capital.

In a second pilot study in 2011, I maintained this 'opportunity cost method' but with a 'simulation' approach. I asked some women with families to do the shopping for the daily food of a family of two adults and five children in the town market. The idea was for them to choose and price items and quantities they would normally eat from their own 'gardens' in the village. The question was this: 'If you have no land and no gardens, and you go to buy garden food in the market, for a man, a woman and five children, what would you buy and how much would you spend?'

Two women from Madang and one from Kokopo (East New Britain) responded with their priced shopping lists, as shown in Table 4.3 below. The figures were considerably up on 2004, probably to some extent reflecting the generally higher prices of food in recent years. Equivalent value of one family's subsistence production for consumption ranged from 29.50 to 52 Kina per day, or 10,767 to 18,980 Kina per year. This value, by itself, was in all cases well above a national minimum wage.

Table 4.3: Women shopping for a typical family's daily food, 2011			
	Breakfast	**Lunch**	**Dinner**	**K/day**
Elizabeth (Kokopo)	CBanana – 3 Tomatoes – 1 Onion – 1.20 Choko – 3 Singapore – 2	Greens – 3 Tapioca – 1 CBanana – 3 Pawpaw – 4 Tomatoes/ ginger– capsicum– 1	CBanana – 3 Kaukau – 2 Singapore – 2 PumpkinTips – 3 Pitpit – 2	34.20 [12,483]
Annie (Madang)	CBanana – 2.5 Kaukau –2 Greens –1 Broccoli –1.50 Carrots–1 Onions–1	SEBanana – 4 Pawpaw –2.50 Lettuce – 1.50 Tapioca – 1	Taro bunch – 5 Fish (m) – 15/3* Grn/Aibika –1 Coconut – 0.5	29.50 [10,767]
Rosa (Madang)	CBanana(K) – 1 Pawpaw – 3	Rice – 7.5 Kumul/gr – 1 Fish – 5 Kulau (4) – 2.40 **Snacks:** Peanut – 5 Galip nut OR orange – 3 SEBanana – 5	Kaukau – 1 Taro – 5 CBanana – 5 Veges – 2 Chicken – 15/3* Coconut(2) – 1	52 [18,980]

Source: This author's pilot surveys in Kokopo and Madang; **Notes:** (i) *= not every day, so e.g 15/3*= 15 Kina about every three days; (ii) Cbanana=cooking banana; K=kalapua; SE=sweet eating banana (iii) snacks=food between meals

Once again, this was an indicative and not a representative survey. To my knowledge there has not yet been any representative surveys in PNG along these lines. A fair question is then: what is the value of such small, non-representative surveys? I suggest there are several purposes. First, the data indicates a real production value which is mostly ignored.

Second, the pilot surveys put us in a 'zone' of likely real loss, in the case of loss of farm land and gardens. Third, elements of this data can stand as reference points until better, representative surveys are carried out and published.

CHARACTERISING HYBRID LIVELIHOODS

Subsistence value must be summed with that from other productive activities to get some perspective on the value of hybrid livelihoods. However, as these livelihoods are so diverse, we cannot speak in simple quantitative terms. It seems more useful to look at the character of hybrid livelihoods, illustrated by some examples which show their possibilities, and limitations.

We have to note that, in terms of land use and economic activity, many of the customary land-based hybrids can be threatened by modernist projects. Looking at Tonga, Storey and Murray (2001) warned against 'growth oriented strategies which undermine or marginalise traditional social institutions' and diverse livelihoods. In Papua New Guinea Grossman (1981: 220) warned that cash focussed activities in PNG can undermine subsistence systems, 'even when surplus land and labor exist', as dependence on export focussed commercial systems like cattle and coffee 'reduces the resilience of village systems'. In a similar vein, Benediktsson (1998) pointed to the need to focus on actually existing markets in PNG, rather than stylised and general 'market' development.

Examples of hybrid livelihoods – where cash economies supplement rather than replace 'subsistence' production – have been noted in PNG, as in Melanesia more generally. Allen (2000: 100–111) discusses the improved food security prospects of the community of Malo Island in Vanuatu, who have developed some cash cropping options. Some of this income was used to supplement their home–grown diet with imported foods. However only 20% of their food was gained from imports. Similarly, Mosco showed a Central Province community taking advantage of the Port Moresby markets, with average households making 5,000 to 24,000 cash income per year, mainly by marketing betel nut products (areca nut and pepperfruit). This had a marked impact on living standards in their villages, in terms of consumer durables purchased and the ability to fund secondary education for their children (Mosco 2005: 16–21). But staple foods still come from their gardens. Much the same applies to families engaged with the plantation oil palm industries. Koczberski et al note that about 80% of the diet of Kavui and Popondetta LSS farmers was from garden food, and that most women (100% on LSS blocks and 52% on VOP blocks) regularly sold market food, many relying on the market as their main source of cash income (Koczberski, Curry & Gibson 2001: 50 & 57–58). LSS and VOP farmers are smallholders who grow oil palm either on a leased block (LSS) or on their own land (VOP).

More exceptional cases tend to capture attention, but hybrids are more common that this. In my own research it quickly became apparent that many people in formal sector work were also productively engaged in subsistence, informal and export activities. One Madang man I interviewed (L) in 2006 worked part–time in a community group, while his wife baked and sold bread; their farm produce income was no less than others in their area. Similarly one Highlands woman (S) held part-time employment while her husband worked full–time in the public service; their farm income was similar to others in their area. Another Madang man (H), also holding part-time work, said he earned as much as 11,000 Kina per year on a variety of cash crops (cocoa, peanut, coconut, vanilla, betel nut). All continued to produce fruit and vegetables for family consumption, from their own gardens.

Roadside seller surveys carried out in four provinces (Madang, Morobe, Eastern Highlands and East New Britain; these surveys are described in more detail in the following chapter) give a representative idea of hybridity, at least in relation to those rural populations with good land and reasonable access to main roads. In the first place it became clear that these mostly women sellers were earning on average well above ordinary wage rates paid in the local formal sector industries, such as fish canneries, mines, plantations and shops (Anderson 2008; Anderson 2011). Equally importantly, a large majority reported family engagement in other income earning activities. A majority (48–82%) across the four provinces were engaged in growing and selling some export crops, though a strong majority of these said exports provided less income than sales from domestic markets. A substantial minority (11–48%) had one or more family members employed; and an even larger minority group (13–61%) were engaged in other business, such as poultry sales, transport and store trading (Anderson 2011). All this suggests that multiple livelihood activities have become common, in much of rural PNG, perhaps apart from the very isolated areas.

We might thus conceptualise hybrid livelihoods as including three elements: production for non–monetised family consumption and cultural exchange; production for cash crop marketing, in both domestic and export markets; and other (often non-farm) informal and formal sector activity. Each element makes a valuable contribution and each also has its own vulnerabilities. These elements are set out in Table 4.4, below. Each element is vulnerable to displacement or erosion by shifts in land tenure and patterns of agriculture. If traditional lands are eroded, leased or otherwise taken away, garden production will be restricted. Similarly, expansion of monocultures (like oil palm) is likely to reduce the diversity of local production.

Table 4.4: Basic elements of Hybrid Livelihoods	
Production for:	Vulnerable to:
Family consumption and cultural exchange	Erosion of traditional lands
Cash crop marketing	Monocultures reducing diversity of local production
Other informal and formal sector activity	Variable

Production for family consumption, for example – which my 2011 pilot surveys show can amount to a value equivalent of between 10,000 and 19,000 Kina per family per year in regional PNG – forms the foundation of rural hybrid livelihoods, across all manner of family engagement in other activities, such as informal sector, export crop, oil palm and formal employment. If the pilot surveys are backed up by wider, representative studies on subsistence production, the value equivalent from the subsistence sector would also outstrip almost all other productive activities. That is before we count the additional value contributed by cultural exchange; which can range from food for visitors through to substantial contributions of animals, vegetables and fruit on special occasions. Yet the richness of PNG's subsistence sector would certainly be undermined by any erosion of traditional land tenure.

Second, there is the marketing of produce from family gardens, which can range from a simple surplus in production (e.g. staple foods such as sweet potato) to market specific produce (e.g. peanut, cucumber, melons); in other words, items grown specifically for sale. The latter seems to generates most income, as the following chapter will explain. Cash income from fruit and vegetable marketing can be as low as a few hundred Kina per year (for those who market a simple surplus, often at a time when others also have a surplus) to many thousands of Kina per year. My surveys of roadside sellers in four provinces showed average incomes of between 140 and 280 Kina per week, or 7,000 to 14,000 per year (Anderson 2011). While the great majority of fresh produce sellers get more cash income from domestic sales rather than exports, the latter remain popular and an important source of supplementary income (see the following chapter). Nevertheless, cash crop production is also vulnerable to land loss and competition with encroaching monocultures, which also affect the diversity of local production and, consequently, of sales in local markets. Alternatively, fresh produce sales could be enhanced by the improvement of rural roads.

Third, there is family engagement in various informal and formal sector activities, often not related to family gardens. This can include small stores, transport services and other full or part time work in the formal sector. Informal sector surveys across four provinces found incomes at between 120–150 Kina per week (Sowei et al 2003), or 6,000 to 7,500 Kina per year – three times the nation's minimum wage, at that time. Incomes in the formal sector vary considerably, but much basic unskilled work in regional areas is paid at, or only slightly higher than, the minimum wage; at 2011 this was 92 Kina per week, or 4,600 per year (Anderson 2011). While professional and skilled employment pays higher wages, some of these people also remain engaged in subsistence and cash crop work. After work hours, some of the office workers in Kokopo (East New Britain) go to the town market to sell produce. Despite some better options in the highly skilled work, customary land owners face generally poor options in the formal sector.

Beyond the basic elements, arising from my surveys we can see what I will call an 'education effect' within along with 'adaptive responses' from these hybrid livelihoods. Both seem capable of contributing to the development of superior hybrids. An 'education effect' here refers to a more sophisticated approach to livelihoods and family farm management, through a more focussed plan, sometimes supported by a higher level of formal education. The 'adaptive response' describes a defensive movement in face of threats, usually threats to from large corporations to assume control of customary lands.

An 'education effect' might be seen simply in the taking advantage of a strategic circumstance, such as the Central Province betel nut sellers, fairly close to the capital (Mosco 2005); or the peanut sellers at Watta Rais, who can earn several thousands of Kina per week by producing and selling at the junction of two major highways (Anderson 2008). More generally, it is the focussed market sellers who concentrate on superior value crops, such as taro and melons, rather than common place crops in massive surplus, such as retail bananas and sweet potatoes. There seems to also be, perhaps amongst those with greater formal education, a more efficient and focussed pursuit of farming and marketing, which compensates for the time 'lost' in other employment or other small business activities. This allows multiple activities within the 'hybrid'. In other words higher income earners, with livelihoods based on family land, seem to have developed a good sense of their market opportunities. Others appeared to have well developed livelihood strategies, dividing their time between local markets, export crops and other small business, in context of their traditional and cultural lives.

Confirmation of this 'education effect' comes from a small agricultural college on the outskirts of Goroka, where a experienced educator took on young people who had dropped out of school. A two year course was provided in farm management, technology and marketing, at the end of which the students had to prepare detailed accounts of returns from their family farm land. The first group of graduates reported an annual income of between 2,000 and 11,000 Kina (Rere 2004). The highest income earner in this group was a young woman who secured vegetable contracts with a town supermarket. Others did well with more diverse production. More recently, the college has been taking larger groups, including professional people and others who have returned to working their family land. The emphasis in this college is on steady, year-round production and supply to wholesale markets (Rere 2011). This college and the community below are discussed a little more in Chapter Eight.

'Adaptive responses', which I suggest can also contribute to superior hybrid formation, can be seen in a rural community in Madang Province. The Sausi community began large scale planting of cocoa, to demonstrate to the government and an oil palm company that they could manage and 'develop' their own land. The cocoa supplemented their already strong local crops such as peanut and melons, and helped spur diversification into rice cultivation and fish ponds, initially just for local consumption. After several years of this diversification the Sausi community now enjoys higher than average incomes. Following this commercial success, they have developed their own village finance scheme and a small scholarship program for local college students (Aipapu Marai 2009). While cocoa is taking over a deal of land, unlike oil palm it can be companion planted (for example with banana, vanilla and legumes). Most of their income, however, still comes from domestic crops.

Table 4.5 below shows a typology of hybrids, from basic to focussed to 'diverse and efficient'. The latter group, I suggest, would most likely have the benefit of some 'education effect' and perhaps the impetus of an 'adaptive response'.

Table 4.5: Varieties of Hybrid Livelihoods	
variant	features
Basic	Subsistence production, sale of surplus garden produce, perhaps additional employment
Focussed	Subsistence production, sale of market specific domestic and export produce, perhaps other business or employment
Diverse and efficient	Subsistence production, sale of market specific domestic and export produce, other employment or business, effective management of hybrid

One outstanding question over hybrids is: 'what place might there be in a valuable hybrid livelihood for engagement with the corporatised monocultures'? In PNG this means 'small holder' engagement with oil palm estates. I deal with oil palm in more detail in a Chapter Six. For now, it is worth noting some particular problems. Oil palm continues to be promoted and subsidised (by government and aid agencies), as a strong source of corporate and export income. Yet, as Table 3.1 in the previous chapter showed, its contribution to family incomes is low to middling, and not nearly as high as most of the informal sector average incomes. That still leaves open the question of whether it might supplement other activities. The problem here is that oil palm has additional costs. First, there is the need to buy chemical inputs, mainly fertiliser. Second, fertiliser and land clearing contributes to the pollution and siltation of local rivers and streams. Third, oil palm is a voracious plant that cannot be companion planted, so crop diversity is reduced. Finally, there are the economic disadvantages for small–holders selling to a price–fixing, 'monopsonist' company, which purchases all local fruit, takes the bulk of the surplus and so limits 'village oil palm' incomes (Koja 2003). Small farmers have no real bargaining power in this relationship. I will return to these issues in a Chapter Six.

CONCLUDING OBSERVATIONS

Beyond the misleading 'subsistence to cash economy' clichés, and from the family and community point of view, it is the integrity of evolving hybrid livelihoods based on customary land that matters. Most rural families in PNG engage in subsistence production and also rely on cash income from marketing a mixture of crops for both domestic and export markets. Many families also engage in small business activities and take on some formal sector employment. These multiple income streams seem quite widespread

Yet the base of these hybrid livelihoods remains customary land, which is subject to constant attack. It is important to recognise that, with rising food and housing prices, the equivalent value of subsistence production is substantial, and increasingly so. Families can produce 10,000 to 19,000 Kina equivalent in non-monetised food and housing equivalents, not to speak of the other non-monetised value in such commodities as medicines, crafts and clothes, and services such as social security and environmental management.

Then there is income from informal sector activities, particularly fresh produce marketing, and particularly domestic markets. Most families that sell into local markets also produce export crops; but very few of these families will say they get more income from the latter. Many families also engage in non–farm small business and employment. The starting point of such hybrids is a 'basic' model which supplements subsistence production with sale of surplus garden produce and perhaps additional employment. Next is a 'focussed' hybrid, which is also based on subsistence production but sells more specific domestic and export crops, perhaps combined with family participation in other business or employment. Finally there is a 'diverse and efficient' model, probably enhanced by an 'education effect' and sometimes by an 'adaptive response' to threat. Here there is also the base of subsistence production, focussed domestic and export crops, other employment or business and effective management of the family 'hybrid'. Higher income earners are those who exploit specific commercial opportunities or combine employment with intelligent marketing.

Yet PNG's rural families, who are required to pay for health and education services, are asset rich, cash poor and often poorly educated. This makes them vulnerable to formal sector schemes and nice sounding corporate proposals. In face of this, families deserve some better quality information and management training, some means of helping them maintain control of their own lands and the option of creating superior 'hybrid livelihoods' by gradually supplementing their more traditional activities with new and intelligent cash economy options.

Roadside
sellers

ℰℑ

The 'old school' economics, with its emphasis on financial aggregates, neglects cash income from informal sector activities as much as it neglects production for subsistence and social exchange. Yet informal markets play a key role in family livelihood strategies. In rural PNG, where families grow much of their own food, some family members also seek formal employment, whole families participate in export cropping (such as coffee, copra and cocoa), and others engage in informal sector 'micro-business'. This latter category includes such things as preparing and selling cooked food, poultry farming, transport services, running small stores and the sale of fresh garden produce. In that last sub-sector we have a substantial group which sells fresh produce by the side of the country's main roads. These are overwhelmingly women, generally bringing their own fruit, vegetables and other produce directly to market for sale. The 'value chain' here is very short, there are virtually no middlemen, and (at least for those who live close to a main road) the costs are minimal. Many thousands of women participate in these roadside markets, which form a key but neglected element of PNG's mainstream economy. The contribution of these roadside sellers to family and hybrid livelihoods deserves attention, particularly as many of their incomes are higher than formal sector wages.

With this in mind I began to develop surveys of roadside sellers. The idea was to consider their performance, potential and possible competition with the larger, formal-sector activities such as logging, factory work and oil palm monocultures. My attention was drawn to some high income earners in the Upper Ramu region of Madang Province, then to the problems of small farmers engaged with the oil palm industry in Oro Province. I carried out pilot surveys of family incomes from small farming in these two provinces. After this, representative surveys were carried out of roadside sellers in Madang, then later on Morobe, the Eastern Highlands and East New Britain. The surveys were of rural roadside markets on the main roads, thus excluding both the town markets (as it is not always easy for rural populations to get to town) and markets in the remote areas (as these have special limitations). Many tens of thousands of people participate in these markets, and there is potential for greater participation, especially when roads improve. The particular conditions applying to participants in these markets were: (i) given PNG's current land tenure system, they almost all have access to good quality land, and (ii) they have reasonable access to main roads.

This chapter will briefly set the context for women's livelihood options in rural PNG, before explaining the results of the roadside market surveys and discussing the implications for rural livelihoods and related policy. The surveys provide support for a re-examination of priorities in PNG's rural and agricultural policy, to recognise and support the livelihood options for women and rural families. Greater attention should be paid to domestic markets and rural infrastructure and less to the new monocultures, which have higher costs and generally less to offer rural families.

WOMEN, LAND AND DOMESTIC MARKETS

Several broad assumptions confront any discussion of women in informal, rural and agricultural sectors. The first is that the development of formal markets, while displacing informal activity, might create ongoing employment or sub-contracting opportunities (e.g. Jarret and Anderson 1989). A second suggests that exports must be a priority, because these expand accessible markets and, therefore, employment and livelihood possibilities (e.g. ADB 2002). A third notes that informal economic activity is often marginal, using few skills, limited technology and capital. Its opportunities are often constrained by lack of land, credit and limited markets (ILO 2000; Sandaratne 2002: 22). Women may also be marginalised and vulnerable in informal agriculture, through traditional subordination (e.g. Sachs 1997) as well as the displacement process of formal development. On top of this the ILO notes 'a general bias against women in formal employment, together with their typical preference for working closer to home', which results in their high numbers in the informal sector (ILO 2000: 1–2). Here is a conundrum: while the informal sector might appear to present limited economic opportunities for women, the options presented by new formal sector activities might be no better, or worse.

All such general notions, however, deserve re-examination in their particular institutional and cultural context. Not all informal activity is a dead end, and small domestic markets are often important for local communities. They can provide rapid access to market income, with few middlemen, allowing exchanges for important domestic needs and creating a home-grown and relatively autonomous and sustainable social environment. This is particularly the case where, as in Papua New Guinea, rural women and their families retain fairly equitable access to good quality, productive land. And in both the patrilineal and the matrilineal areas of PNG, women maintain access to land, either in a primary or a secondary sense.

Rural food markets are numerous in every province, though they are said to be 'a relatively recent institution' in PNG (Bourke et al 2004: p.2). They play a particularly important role for women, including those engaged in formal sector activities, such as in the oil palm areas. For example, PNG women are said to have:

'identified more closely with marketing than with oil palm ... [this is] a historical legacy of women's marginal status in the oil palm industry ... [but also] reflects the immense social significance women attach to marketing and the marketplace' (Koczberski, Curry & Gibson 2001: 63).

Food markets (sometimes combined with craft and clothing markets, particularly in the urban areas) are a place of women's social interaction, outside the home, and it is clear that many women enjoy the company and the social environment. These markets are important for large rural populations, and deserve 'special attention because [women's] activities are crucial to the survival of the family, especially children' (Adedokun et al 2000: 197).

Domestic food markets in PNG have great potential. Some time ago it was recognised that the country's food production was seriously underestimated. Barry Shaw argued that subsistence food production in PNG was 'far in excess of national human requirements' and that subsistence production had 'considerable' overlap with the cash economy. In the 1980s rural families were said to be able to 'produce sufficient food within 20 hours or less labour per adult per week for humans, pigs and commercial purposes and still probably have a surplus for insurance or sale' (Shaw 1985: 15, 18, 23). Later studies showed that national accounts underestimated the contribution of farming (Gibson 2000: 41–42), and that PNG's staple food production could amount to 'a little more than one tonne a year for every rural villager' (Bourke 2005: 7). While many of the more lucrative cash crops are often more specialised than staple foods (e.g. cucumber, melons, peanut, betel nut), there is nevertheless a strong link between subsistence food production and fresh produce for local cash economies. They are most often grown side by side in small rural 'gardens'.

Some years back, rural informal sector incomes were charted in National Research Institute (NRI) surveys across four of PNG's provinces. Women were prominent across a range of activities, including the higher income activities. Men dominated by 80% or more in each of: passenger motor vehicle transport, coconut and cocoa production and sales, coffee cultivation, construction, fishing, small scale mining, forestry/logging. The women-dominant activities (80% or more) were noted as: betel nut cultivation; collection of shellfish; manufacture of baked products; and manufacture of handbags. Women were also dominant in sugar cane cultivation (67%); fruit and nut cultivation (63%) and were more regular informal sellers than men (69% compared with 58%) (Sowei et al 2003: 104, 108). It is quite obvious that, in retail fresh produce markets, whether in the towns or the rural areas, women dominate. The major problems noted by informal sector women in the NRI survey were: high operating costs 13% (though this was less than for men); transport 13% (the same as for men); knowledge and skills 9%; law and order 9% (more than for men); and the demands of wantoks (relatives) for credit 5% (a little more than for men) (Sowei et al 2003: App Table 16). In many of these informal activities, according to the NRI surveys, incomes were two to three times higher than low wage formal sector work. Table 5.1 below shows these activities and their average incomes. These average incomes can be compared to those listed in Table 3.2 of Chapter 3.

Table 5.1: Informal Sector incomes in four PNG provinces			
Province	Highest income activities (and range of income)	Most common activities (and range of income)	AWE
Central	Fish buyer, PMV, trade store (K350–1,800)	Food crops, fish, betel, coconut (K50–250)	K158
East New Britain	PMV, trade store (K500–1,200)	Cocoa, copra, food crops (K100–300)	K124
Morobe	PMV, cattle, trade store, fish buyer (K500–4,000)	Coffee, food crops, fish (K30–160)	K130
Highlands	Potatoes, kaukau, coffee, trade store, PMV (K400–1,500)	Potatoes, Kaukau, coffee (K20–1,500)	K138

Source: adapted from Sowei et al 2003: pp.11–39; **Note:** PMV = passenger motor vehicle (mini–bus); **Note:** AWE = average weekly earnings

While this survey indicates some relatively superior livelihood activities in the informal sector, a question arises as to the possible competition between these activities and the newer formal sector activities that make use of substantial arable land. In many provinces there are pressures on families to give over some or all of their land to formal developments, in particular logging and leases for oil palm plantation. In some provinces (e.g. Oro and West and East New Britain) oil palm companies have set up sub–contracting schemes for rural women who collect scattered oil palm fruit for the local mill (the 'Mama Lus Frut' program). Despite the very low incomes (29 Kina per week average in 2000, 49 Kina per week in 2006: see Table 3.2), this program has been hailed by some a 'resounding success' (Koczberski, Curry & Gibson 2001: 193). This program is discussed further in Chapter Six. In Madang, a foreign owned fish cannery (R.D. Tuna) harvests local marine resources and offers low paid employment to hundreds of women. And a large oil palm development has been proposed for inland Madang Province (Korugland and Santana 2007: 4), on either side of the very large estate of what used to be known as Ramu Sugar. None of this formal employment offers wages which even come close to the informal sector income averages (see Table 3.2 of Chapter 3); yet diminishing land for traditional production and informal sector markets is likely to adversely affect the latter. Indeed, from observation it does seem that the variety of produce in domestic markets in the oil palm areas (for example in the Popondetta plains in Oro Province) is lower than that in those areas where there is no large, land consuming plantations (e.g. coastal Madang and the Eastern Highlands). With these concerns in mind, I began roadside seller surveys in 2004.

ROADSIDE SELLER SURVEYS

The first pilot survey in 2004 in Madang noted the land, production and income of 18 small farmers. The results are noted Table 1 of the Appendices. As the sample was small and no sampling error was calculated, the results cannot be said to represent a particular population. However a number of high incomes (between 10,000 and 36,000 Kina per year) were observed, and the incomes from crops sold in domestic markets were often above those for export crops. Particular high incomes were observed in the sale of peanut and buai (betel nut) and, amongst the export crops, cocoa. The pilot survey does demonstrate the livelihood possibilities in such activities. The second pilot survey in August 2005 was of 21 small oil palm farmers in Oro Province. I discuss this more in the following chapter.

The first representative survey of rural roadside sellers was conducted in December 2006 on the road north from Madang to Alexishafen, and south from Madang through Usino to Watta Rais, at the junction of the Okuk (Highlands) Highway. The northern road includes traffic from Madang to Bogia (south of the Ramu River), while the southern road links Madang to PNG's second city Lae, as well as to the highly populated Highlands region. The markets sampled ranged in size from 10 to 200 sellers. Sellers were selected randomly, from the front and back of the larger markets, and with 5 to 8 sellers chosen in the larger markets and 2 to 4 sellers chosen in the smaller markets. An identical method was used for surveys of three additional provinces (Morobe, Eastern Highlands and East New Britain) in June 2011. The markets chosen were generally at least 5 kilometres out of town, and then heading for some way towards the interior, along the main roads (the market locations are listed in Appendix Tables 4 and 6–8). By this approach, the surveys excluded both the markets in more remote areas (where road access and transport is a major constraint) and the thriving town markets of Madang, Goroka, Lae, Kokopo and Rabaul. These large town markets do attract a lot of rural people, but the surveys set up as a conditioning factor access to a main road, and not to the large provincial towns.

Samples in each market ranged between 5% and 25% of all sellers. Markets with less than 10 sellers (micro-markets) were generally not surveyed, as these were thought perhaps to have had less than a 'critical mass' to attract buyers. Self-report style interviews were conducted in the Tok Pisin language by Papua New Guinean research assistants, men and women. The interviewers collected information on items sold, daily and weekly incomes, days per week at market, items providing best returns, and some other matters including costs and problems faced (the questions are listed in Appendix Table 3). In the four provinces, about half the markets of the chosen area were sampled, with the estimated vendor populations ranging from several hundred to over a thousand: Madang (about 1,000), Morobe (about 1,400), Eastern Highlands (about 260) and East New Britain (about 700). Samples of about 50 were taken to give a sampling error of plus or minus 7.4% – that is, a relative standard error of about 15%.

In an earlier published version of the Madang survey (Anderson 2008) it was suggested that the markets might be considered as segmented and so a weighting of each market (where the weight of a market = % total population / % total interviews) was called for. I did this in that paper and have included weighted averages for the data provided for the other provinces, in this chapter. However, on reflection, I do not think weighting adds anything to these surveys. The markets are remarkably similar across and within the provinces, even while local and seasonal produce varies. The vendors are overwhelmingly women selling produce grown from gardens on their own family land, they mostly carry all this produce to market and there is no real state support in any of the markets. Greater differences may be noted within each market than between markets, even across the different provinces. For example, in most of the markets surveyed, there were vendors earning 4 to 5 times more than others. This reflects, in my view, more the different strategies applied by the vendors, than any great circumstantial difference. I will say a bit more on this, later on in the chapter. Some cross-provincial differences were observed. In Madang Province the women sellers spent an average of 3 days per week at market; while in the Eastern Highlands the average time at market was close to 5 days per week. However a solid three-quarters of vendors in all four provinces got their best returns from these local markets (Table 5.2). That is, neither formal employment nor other small business nor export crops returned as much cash income.

Women were not singled out, but formed 89–98% of those surveyed (see Table 5.2). The few men surveyed (two in Madang, five in Morobe, six in EHP and one in ENB) had average incomes. Most vendors were growers of the produce they sold – the exceptions to this rule were those selling cooked food and those engaged in buy and sell of store goods and fish. Items that attracted the greatest returns differed across the provinces and are shown in Table 5.4. These high value crops are sometimes staples (like taro), sometimes intoxicants (buai), sometimes high energy food (peanuts) and sometimes snack foods (like melons, mangoes and cucumber). Most often, they are crops grown specifically for market. The markets also have their social functions. As others have observed (Koczberski, Curry & Gibson 2001: 63), as well as providing economic opportunities, local markets form significant spaces for women's social interaction.

Putting the markets in seasonal and geographical context we can observe that both buai (betel nut) and peanut are less seasonal in Madang than in Morobe or in Goroka. Coastal buai (areca catechu) is also more highly valued than the highland betel nut (areca macrocalyx) (Bourke et al 2004: p.43–45). The Madang survey was conducted in December 2006, a time when betel nut prices typically reach their peak in Goroka. It was also the watermelon and mango season in many parts of Madang and Morobe Provinces (Bourke et al 2004: p.182, 197, 201). In East New Britain in 2011 a cocoa borer plague had wiped out much of that crop, leading to increased dependence on local market produce. Generally, however, the diversity of crops is such that seasonal factors would seem to not play such a great role. No province was dependent on solely one or two high income earning, seasonal crops (see Table 5.4).

Table 5.2 Roadside seller populations, in four PNG provinces				
			Highest income from?	
	% female	Av. days per week at market?	this market	export crops
2006 Madang	95%	3	75%	0%
2011 Morobe	90%	4	74%	8%
2011 Eastern Highlands	98%	4.9	73%	2%
2011 East New Britain	89%	3.4	73%	13%
Surveys 2007–2011 (see Appendix Tables 4, 6–9)				

In the Madang survey, men seemed to maintain their dominance on wholesale trade. While the retail growers and sellers of betel nut were almost entirely Madang women, the wholesale buyers were mainly Highlands men – family groups from Chimbu and the Eastern Highlands, and by observation about 90% men. This is a similar pattern to that observed in West Java, where rural women dominate local vegetables and fruit sales, but transshipment to the urban centres is controlled by groups of mostly male middlemen (Hayami et al 1991: 55). The Highlands men at two of these markets (Four Mile and Mambu) were engaged in continuous bargaining with the entirely female betel nut sellers. Retail buyers were a mixture of men and women. In East New Britain, on the other hand, there was an ethnic aspect to the wholesale peanut trade. The Baining people – original landowners who have been pushed into the inland by waves of migration on the eastern part of the island on New Britain – seemed to have worked cooperatively to dominate the wholesale trade in and around Kokopo (ENB's major town, after volcanic eruptions reduced the dominance of Rabaul). Most retail peanut sellers in ENB seem to be women who buy large bags from the Baining communities. In the Eastern Highlands there is a strong wholesale trade in vegetables and sweet potato, a great deal of which is exported to Lae and then on to the capital Port Moresby. No road yet links the productive highlands to the capital, and the logistics of such exports present substantial costs and some risk. However while we heard anecdotes of big money here, this survey did not look in any detail at that wholesale trade.

Perhaps a central feature of these surveys was the consistently high incomes of the roadside sellers (one element of family livelihoods, and usually the dominant cash element), especially when compared to formal sector wages and the national minimum weekly wage (MWW). Table 5.3 sets out the vendors' self-reported average incomes, those incomes as a proportion of the 2011 minimum wage (91.60 Kina) and the proportion of vendors whose daily income surpassed the 2011 MWW in either one day or two days. Even though the Madang survey was carried out a few years earlier (when the MWW was much lower, see Table 3.2), and even though compliance with the 2011 MWW is by no means universal, the same benchmark is used. These comparative indicators help provide some perspective on the informal sector options. Weighted figures (based on the notion that there is some 'segmentation' in the character of these roadside markets) are given alongside the unweighted averages but, as I explained above, I do not think much is gained from this weighting process. It is included for the sake of completeness

The provincial average incomes of the roadside vendors are set out in Table 5.3. They show that the average weekly earnings of the vendors (many of whom work considerably less than 5 days a week, except in the Eastern Highlands) ranges between two to three times the 2011 national minimum wage, or 1.5 to 2.5 times that minimum wage with 'weighted' data. Further, significant numbers of these women are earning that minimum wage in one day, and more than half are currently earning that minimum wage in two days. This helps explain the anecdotal evidence we encountered (particularly in East New Britain) of some women leaving wage labour to return to the markets, and of others going to town markets (e.g. in Kokopo) to sell produce after work.

Further discussion of the high income earners is desirable because, while these groups always lift the averages, they also indicate the possibilities for others. In this case, I suggest, there is substantial room for expanded market participation. That is, far more could learn from the high income

Table 5.3 Roadside seller average incomes in four PNG provinces				
	AWE (Kina)	AWE as % of 2011 minimum weekly wage	% of sellers earning More than MWW	
			in one day	in two days
2006 Madang [weighted]	286 [138]	312% [151%]	30%	48%
2011 Morobe [weighted]	285 [144]	311% [157%]	20%	48%
2011 Eastern Highlands [weighted]	230 [230]	251% [251%]	4%	51%
2011 East New Britain [weighted]	198 [144]	216% [157%]	7%	63%
Notes: (1) AWE = average weekly earnings in Kina; weighted figures in [square brackets]; (2) 2011 minimum weekly wage (MWW) of K91.60, per Matbob 2011				

earners amongst the roadside sellers, and thus improve their livelihoods. Unlike in developed industrial economies, these markets have hardly any 'barriers to entry', nor has any corporation or cartel been able to 'capture' and control the market.

What are the factors that contribute to vendor success? Several elements suggest themselves: good location, specialising in high value foods (peanut, melons, mangoes, cucumber), or addictive crops (tobacco and betel nut), selling a diverse range of products and value adding through cooked and locally processed food (scones, fried food, flavoured ice). At first it seems that specialisation was the key, but on further analysis this was more often than not combined with offering a diverse range of products. Most of the high income earners (100 Kina or more a day) in all four provinces who made good money from crops grown specially for the market also had a fair degree of diversification in their offerings. This suggests an 'education effect', not necessarily in terms of schooling, but in being able to develop an effective composite strategy.

A group of very high income earners at Watta Rais (at the junction of the Madang-Lae and Lae-Highlands highways) showed such a strategy through taking advantage of their unique location, selling high value products that stop traffic and also maintaining a diverse range of products. The Watta Rais sellers (two of whom worked 7 days per week) made their money mainly from peanut and buai (betel nut). Five of the six sellers were women. As this small market was so well located, from the point of view of travelers, most of the vendors (earning between 1,000 and 2,000 Kina per week) had given over large tracts of land (between 0.5 and 1.0 hectares) to cultivating peanuts, which were then sold retail and wholesale. Their industry thus depended on the availability of good quality land, strategically located. Their major cost had become feeding the relatives who were enlisted to help them intensively work these peanut fields. They also sold coconut and watermelon. In season watermelon is so popular (being very refreshing in the tropical heat) that it was commanding eight Kina per melon (2007) and ten kina (2011). Ten kina was the equivalent of a day's wages working in a tuna cannery. Yet the success in peanut, betel nut and melons had not undermined diversification. The top three income earners at Watta Rais were selling seven or eight fresh products each (melon, mango, betel nut, daka/mustard, banana, coconut/kulau, cucumber and peanut).

Almost all the Madang higher income earners had their success through some combination of betel nut, peanut, melons and mangos. 20 of the 21 sellers who earned more than 50 Kina per day were selling one or more of betel nut, peanut, melons and mangos. One of these was also selling coconut, and another brus (tobacco). The other higher income seller was earning over 140 Kina per day selling ice blocks and cordial. At 4 Mile and Mambu markets, groups of Highland men could be seen bargaining down prices with the women grower–sellers. Women sold the betel nuts for less than 10 toea retail, but the Highlanders got lower prices, buying whole branches, stripping them down and bagging them. From anecdotal evidence, they expected to make 300% to 400% on sales of these bags, in the Highland towns.

In Morobe Province, higher incomes seemed just as prevalent a long way from the capital as close to it, except for the Sunday market, which was crowded and obviously lucrative. Two of the higher income vendors (100 kina or more a day) were completely specialised, and in staple foods: one women sold just taro, every day of the week, while a man sold just cooking bananas, five days a week (see Appendix Table 6). However the other higher earners had diversified crops. They had their best income from peanut, cucumber, betel–nut, oranges and coconut, but usually along with other items (vegetables, ice, fruit, cooked items). Quite a number of the higher income earners came to market six or seven days a week.

In the Eastern Highlands, along the highway on either side of Goroka, there were smaller markets with less vendors; this may be at least partly because the Goroka town market is huge, accessible and popular. The higher earners at the rural roadside market were selling various vegetables (carrots, cabbage, potato, greens, corn, etc), cooked food, oranges, betel nut and peanuts. Most of these had a range of products (Appendix Table 7). As mentioned, these sellers worked an average of almost 5 days a week, higher than in the other provinces (see Table 5.2). While only two earned more than 100 kina per day, their weekly incomes remained respectable.

In East New Britain (ENB), the higher earners in roadside markets had their best returns from cooked food, peanut and vegetables, but many kept a range of other items. Returns on selling fish appear high, but in most cases surveyed this was a buy-and-sell operation, where the women faced substantial expenses, amounting to as much as 75% of their income. By contrast, the transport and other expenses of those selling garden produce are very small, often just a few kina per day. Raw tobacco (brus) sellers were common, and the betel-nut market was strong. The rural markets around Kokopo were quite small, again probably partly because the town market at Kokopo (not surveyed) is huge and very well maintained. Indeed, from observation, the Kokopo town market probably has the best facilities (shelter and concrete floors, bathrooms, cafes, landscaped, sanitation, etc) in PNG. In the rural roadside markets a strong majority of sellers were also engaged in copra and cocoa cultivation, but most got better returns from the local markets (Appendix Table 7). However, lower returns on cocoa were also due to the cocoa borer plague, which had forced the destruction of many trees. Roadside sellers in ENB were much more likely than those from other provinces to have family members in employment. Almost half (48%) reported family members (including at the times the vendor herself) with jobs, compared to 11%–18% in the other three provinces (see Table 3.3).

As indicated in Table 3.3, across the provinces most roadside sellers and their families also cultivated one or more export crops (48–82%), ran other small businesses (13–61%) and/or had formal sector employment (11–48%); yet a consistent 73–75% across all four provinces said (or demonstrated by their calculations) that domestic fresh produce markets earned them more cash income. In Madang the additional sources of income were from: trade stores or sale of other items (meat, eggs, cooked food, kava, prawns, cigarettes, dresses, second–hand clothes) (sixteen vendors); chicken rearing and sale (nine vendors); manufacture and sale of cooked food (bread, buns, donuts) (five vendors); pig rearing and sales (three vendors); employment (self or husband) (five vendors); timber royalties and/or sales (two vendors); transport business (husband) (two vendors). This level of detail of the other sources of income was not collected elsewhere, but other small business was noted as Morobe (36%), EHP (16%) and ENB (13%).

Vendors were asked about the main problems or costs associated with their market operations (See Table 5.4). The main source of complaint in all provinces was theft, particularly of betel nut This theft was by relatives, neighbours, settlers and sometimes police. In the Eastern Highlands, after theft, marauding pigs which entered their gardens were cited as the next most significant problem. Transport costs were the third mostly highly cited problem. Several women mentioned high school fees as a 'problem'. This was one of the main reasons cited for their need to sell at market. Other problems cited were: waste of money by their husbands, and other domestic problems, strong bargaining pressure from buai traders (in Madang), input and fertiliser costs (Eastern Highlands), crop pests (East New Britain). Not one vendor cited lack of credit as a problem.

Transport fees (and sometimes market fees) were cited but were mostly quite small. Of course, most of those with a serious transport problem simply did not come to market. The sellers at market mostly had the advantage of living near the Province's major roads. Only the very successful peanut vendors at Watta Rais noted significant costs in feeding the relatives who helped plant their peanut fields. This minimal financial constraint on market sellers is consistent with the findings of Shand and Straatmans. In a 1960s–1970s study of communities in four PNG provinces, they noted that neither labour nor finance appeared particular problems for PNG families participating in cash cropping (Shand and Straatmans 1974: 185–186). This seems due to availability of good quality land and the communities' capacity for work cooperation. Table 5.4 shows the higher income earning crops from each province surveyed, along with the principal problems reported by vendors.

Table 5.4 Roadside sellers in four PNG provinces: best sellers and problems		
	Highest income from?	problems?
2006 Madang	Peanut, betel nut/mustard, melons, green and mixed veges, taro	Theft, school fees, domestic
2011 Morobe	Taro, coking banana, green and mixed vegetables, cucumber, peanut	Theft, transport costs, domestic
2011 Eastern Highlands	Various veges and potatoes, cooked food, oranges, peanut	Theft, pigs (damage gardens), transport
2011 East New Britain	Veges, tobacco, fish, store food, peanut, oranges, betel nut	Theft, pests (cocoa borer), transport
Surveys 2007–2011 (see Appendix Tables 4, 6–9)		

Sellers were also asked if they received any assistance 'for your farming'. Most had not. However a significant minority had received some assistance, almost entirely for export crops, and mostly from government agencies (the CCI, NARI officers and the DPI). These agencies provide some extension services, including advice and sale of chemicals, for coffee growers (in the highlands) and cocoa and coconut growers in the coastal areas. The numbers of those who had received some assistance with their farming were as follows: Madang (15 or 34%), Morobe (11 or 22%), EHP (9 or 16%) and ENB (16 or 29%). (These figures are subject to the same sampling errors as the incomes, that is about ± 7.5%.) In Madang some of the assistance (9 of the 15 cases) had come from NGOs, mainly World Vision. In only four cases (amongst the 205 surveyed) was there any mention of support for non–export crop farming. The family of one Morobe woman had received assistance from a local MP with their poultry farm; two sellers in the Eastern Highlands had received some government assistance with vegetable growing; and the husband of one woman in East New Britain had been to some classes on gardening. Clearly farming for domestic markets has not been a government priority.

DISCUSSION: WOMEN AND ROADSIDE MARKETS

These surveys confirm that domestic, informal sector markets, and the women farmer-vendors that dominate them, play a key role in Papua New Guinea's hybrid livelihoods. Roadside selling, as a part time or full time activity, also has a social aspect that is clearly appreciated by many women. The relative economic success of these roadside vendors has a lot to do with access to good quality customary land and proximity to the main roads. Barriers to participation are low and, as most families had access to good land, the main immediate constraint was location. Most of the vendors in this survey had the good fortune to live near a major road.

Women in the informal sector are not always at the 'bottom of the heap'. Indeed it is plain from the results that roadside markets are amongst the better rural cash economy options, and better than most of the alternative formal sector options on offer. These surveys of women vendors show an average income two to three times that of the national minimum (formal sector) wage as at 2011, or 1.5 to 2.5 times that wage, if the data is weighted for each market. Most of this domestic market activity is carried out alongside and without prejudice to the more traditional subsistence and social exchange production, which remains the basis of PNG rural livelihoods. Further, not only does fresh produce selling not exclude other livelihood activities (such as small business, export cropping and formal sector employment), most of the sellers surveyed were already engaged in one or more of those activities. Nevertheless, three quarters of those surveyed in each province said and demonstrated that their income from domestic markets was higher than that from their other businesses or from export sales.

Women did not identify finance as a significant constraint on selling at market. There was thus no real demand for credit in respect of their farming and marketing activities. They identified their major problems as theft of goods, transport, gardens pests, high school fees, domestic problems and bargaining pressures. Despite the bargaining and competitive pressures, women vendors benefit from the short value chain of their local markets, by selling directly and avoiding middle-men. This may help explain their apparent preference for, and better income from, domestic markets. Nevertheless, a clear majority of families in all four provinces surveyed also participated in export cropping, as a secondary income activity.

The higher income earners (those earning 100 kina or more a day) had several elements, often combined, to their success. Specialising in high value foods (such as peanut, melons and cucumber), in popular addictive crops (tobacco and betel nut) and in prepared foods (such as scones and fried food) was central, but many of those that had success with such crops also maintained a diverse range of offerings. Another factor was location, whether by luck or design. Achieving a good combination of such elements is suggested to be an 'education effect', in the sense of understanding superior market opportunities. There seems considerable room for higher and more successful participation in these roadside markets, as barriers to entry are virtually non-existent and demand is very strong. The major constraints are proximity to a major road and continued access to their family land.

However, access to good quality customary land could be threatened by land leases or diversion of land into oil palm operations. The rich diversity of local crops could be compromised (as in Popondetta and New Britain) by the introduction of large monocultures. Not only do these large plantations compete with the land for healthy domestic markets, the incomes from Village Oil Palm and the Mama Lus Frut program do not even come close to many of the informal sector options. Many do not want to participate in such schemes. In their 1970s study, Shand and Straatmans (1974: 184) noted that many families did not participate in new cash crop initiatives. This seems to underline the wish to maintain control of customary land related activities.

The advantages women experience through direct control of their family land and their own enterprises would be compromised by diversion into lower paid formal employment or into subordinate schemes such as 'Mama Lus Frut'. This problem has been observed elsewhere. Economic success for women in the informal sector in rural Nigeria was similarly said to be linked to their access to 'critical resources' and 'direct access to the benefits of their own enterprises' (Adedokun et al 2000: 197).

On the other hand, problems of location could be alleviated by investment in better roads. Gibson and Rozelle (2002) have pointed out that poverty in PNG is 'primarily rural' and 'strongly associated with lack of access to services, markets and transportation'. Sowei et al (2003: xi–xiii) reinforce this point. This survey, by highlighting the superior opportunities of roadside markets along the main roads, is consistent with the observation that poverty may increase strongly with distance from roads, and with school levels (Gibson and Rozelle 2002: 9). On this basis, it may be that economic opportunities for women would be better enhanced by investment in widespread rural roads, rather than new industry subsidies, or the promotion of monocultures.

Theft of goods might be lessened by improved support systems for women at the major markets. The excellent facilities of the Kokopo town market are a useful reference point. Finally and importantly, in rural PNG, where most families have land and food and the demand for credit is not pronounced, the pressing demand often seems to be for improved access to education and health services (i.e. relief from high education and health fees) as well as for basic infrastructure, in particular roads. With this support rural women would be able to make even better use of their own resources.

Oil
palm

❧

Few developments in Papua New Guinea better illustrate the contradictions between the 'old economics' (with its focus on growth, exports and the formal sector) and the 'new economics' (with a focus on livelihoods, human development and ecological sustainability) than the oil palm industry. From the former point of view, oil palm can be a great opportunity; from the latter, it can bring few benefits and terrible costs.

The fruit of this West African palm tree now produces 30% of all traded edible oils and fats globally, and prices have been strong in recent years (MPOC 2010: 16, 18). For the small group of large companies that dominate the industry, oil palm production is highly profitable, its prospects seeming even brighter with the strong demand for edible oils in the wake of the 2008 global food crisis. Influenced by the World Bank and other foreign investment lobbies, governments in Papua New Guinea have supported oil palm development since the 1970s. Promoted as a back-end to unsustainable industrial logging, oil palm plantations combine corporate industrial estates with 'small holder' peripheries, mostly villagers who have been induced to grow oil palm on their own land and then sell to this 'nucleus estate'. Some additional customary land may also be leased to the company for its plantations. The estate is designed to be self-sufficient, profitable without the additional contributions from surrounding small-holders.

The PNG government view, across various administrations, seems to be that oil palm is highly profitable and can deliver returns to local communities as well supporting foreign exchange and adding to government revenues. However, despite the backing of the state and the eagerness of foreign companies, expansion of the crop has been slow. PNG contributes only about one percent to global oil palm production. Landowners have been reluctant to turn their land over to oil palm, and the small groups which have done so present many complaints.

Reasons for this landowner reluctance are not to hard to find. While oil palm is a strong industry for the corporations involved (mainly Malaysian, British and North American), PNG small-holding farmers get very low returns. They are at the competitive end of a long value chain which is dominated by a tiny group of large companies. Even though world oil palm prices have risen strongly in recent years, the small farmer share is limited by monopoly power.

Some academics assert the supposed livelihood importance of oil palm. For example, James Cook University researchers say: 'Palm oil is the cash crop with the greatest economic importance to Papua New Guinea, directly supporting about 20,000 small-holder families' (JCU 2011). However, as already indicated in Chapters Three and Five (e.g. Table 3.1), average incomes for oil palm small-holders compare unfavourably to average incomes in a range of informal sector activities, including roadside selling. Further, the 'Mama Lus Frut' program, touted as a formal sector advance for women (where the companies create separate accounts for women for picking up spilt fruit), offers the lowest of all incomes. Land disputes characterize the industry, both in relation to estate and leased land. These disputes are fed by the knowledge that the large sums extracted by the companies are not being shared in any real way with local landowners. On the other hand, the environmental costs of this chemically dependent monoculture are passed on to local communities, particularly through contamination of river systems and water tables.

Those directly involved in the industry have played up the suggested benefits to small farmers. For example, a spokesman for the Roundtable on Sustainable Palm Oil (RSPO) asserted that, in 2005, oil palm farmers and their families were paid K110 million from revenue and that the industry was at 'the forefront of positive environmental action' (CSR 2005). Similarly, a manager of Britain's CDC group, formerly a major shareholder in PNG oil palm, said that his company in Oro Province:

> 'buys produce from over 5,000 smallholders [and] generates an estimated 60% to 70% of the province's GDP as well as providing substantial tax revenue to local and national government. It has provided 700km of roads, 9 schools and 11 medical centres' (Twite 2005).

In fact, a great deal of this infrastructure has been funded by the World Bank and AusAID, while the GDP figures tell us next to nothing about livelihoods. Further, most economic and environmental studies carried out have been commissioned by the industry; few have been independent.

In view of the prevalent mis-information, this chapter applies the perspectives of 'new economics' to examine the livelihood possibilities associated with PNG's oil palm industry. It draws on existing studies, the best available livelihood data and some original surveys in Oro Province, to consider the economic possibilities offered to small farming families. The chapter begins by looking at the global oil palm industry and the role of the international finance agencies, before moving to the core considerations of economic returns to, and the wider concerns of, small farmers.

THE GLOBAL OIL PALM INDUSTRY

To understand the prospects for small farmers, several aspects of the oil palm industry must be recognised. First, its relative position in the global vegetable oil market has improved, under a largely Malaysian-dominated management of supply. Second, prices are quite volatile, as with most simple, non-oil commodities. Third, and taking into account volatility, strong demand for palm oil has held up prices, despite increasing supply. These strong prices are maintained by the same forces behind the 2008 global food crisis: high energy prices, commodity speculation, rising incomes in East Asia and global limits on land. Fourth, there are serious environmental problems associated with the expansion and entrenchment of palm oil monocultures. Fifth, the long value chain and monopoly mill and marketing structures place very severe constraints on the opportunities for small growers. This latter point is a most important economic consideration for communities in Papua New Guinea.

Palm Oil (when combined with Palm Kernel Oil) has moved ahead of Soybean Oil, in the highly important vegetable oil market. It comprises around 30% of total vegetable oil production, by weight, reflecting the high productivity of this West African palm, when well cultivated and fertilised. Other oils such as corn, peanut, coconut, olive, sesame are valuable but smaller in terms of productive output. Further, palm oil is a versatile product and is used in a very wide range of foodstuffs, as well as soaps, lubricants and cosmetics. Table 6.1 shows palm oil production in 2010, alongside the other major edible oils.

Table 6.1: Worldwide production of edible oils and fats, 2010		
	m. tonnes	Percentage
PO and PKO	51.18	30
Soy Bean Oil	38.74	23
Animal fats	23.8	14
Rape Seed Oil	23.8	14
All other	32.3	19
TOTAL	170	100
Source: MPOC 2010: 18		

Although the tree is of West African origin, the main producers of palm oil these days are Malaysia and Indonesia, with 46% and 45% of world exports, respectively (MPOC 2010: 18). Major importers of palm oil are India, China and Europe, each of which doubled (or, in the case of India, more than doubled) their imports over the decade of 1994–2003 (MPOPC 2005: Tables 6.9 & 6.10). Malaysian companies dominate global production and processing.

The strong demand helps explain why prices for palm oil have held up in the face of increasing supply, mostly from new crops in Indonesia but also from increased productivity in the Malaysian plantations. The volatility of prices (Table 6.2) is a typical feature of major commodities, and who bears the risk of this volatility is an important issue. Concern over volatility has led, in other countries, to floor prices and government marketing bodies. Australia, for example, has had public wheat and wool marketing bodies for many decades. Nevertheless, the price trend is clearly upwards, especially after the 2008 food crisis.

Table 6.2: Average annual prices of crude palm oil (local Malaysian prices), 1980–2010

	RM/tonne		RM/tonne
1980	919	1996	1191
1981	964	1997	1358
1982	829	1998	2377
1983	991	1999	1449
1984	1407	2000	996
1985	1045	2001	894
1986	578	2002	1363
1987	773	2003	1578
1988	1029	2004	1610
1989	822	2005	1394
1990	700	2006	1511
1991	836	2007	2531
1992	916	2008	2778
1993	890	2009	2245
1994	1283	2010	2704
1995	1472		

Sources: MPOB 2005 and MPOC 2010: 16; – prices are in RM (Malaysian Ringgit) per tonne

The counter trend in commodity prices has been a longer term decline in *relative* prices (that is, the 'terms of trade' of palm oil) against other goods, especially manufactured imports. The reasons for this are common to many primary commodities (except oil and gas). First, a homogenous commodity able to be developed in many countries faces strong forces of competition. No grower can dominate the market. Second, palm oil is subject to forces of substitution so that, if prices rise strongly, purchasers can switch to soybean oil, or other vegetable oils. Third, commodities suffer price decline as the demand for manufactured goods is more 'income elastic': individuals and countries buy proportionally more manufactured goods (than basic commodities) as they increase their income. The longer term decline in relative prices of such commodities is well documented (Singer 1950; Prebisch 1962; Radetzki 1990). In practical terms, over time, more and more oil palm might have to be produced and exported to buy the same amount of manufactured goods (cars, computers). Such forces have commonly run down the relative prices for undifferentiated commodities such as coffee, fruits, minerals and many other basic, unprocessed commodities. However, the strong rise in food prices over the past decade may have shifted some key foods into a special class of commodity, like oil and gas. High grade foods, like edible oils, may be escaping this longer term 'commodity trap', not least because of the links between energy and food prices. These are important considerations for the oil palm industry, but less so for the small holders, for reasons that will be discussed below.

Major environmental problems are associated with the spread and entrenchment of palm oil monocultures. The global picture is not a happy one. Oil palm development has devastated communities and forests across Indonesia, following the financial pressures from the 1997 Asian Crisis. Globally, oil palm cultivation areas increased by more than 40%, to 10.7 million hectares, between 1990 and 2002 (Casson 2003: 4). More than 3.5 million hectares in Indonesia were cleared for oil palm (mainly logged and burnt out rain forest areas in Sumatra and Kalimantan), rapidly converting Indonesia into the world's second largest exporter. The World Rainforest Movement brands the industry and its rapid expansion as yet another 'destructive monoculture' which has devastated land rights as well as tropical rainforests around the world (WRM 2001). Similarly, the WWF says that oil palm expansion 'not only pose(s) a threat to high conservation value forests, but also to freshwater ecosystems, the livelihoods of forest dependent peoples, biodiversity and the habitats of endangered species' (Casson 2003: 6). Some of these impacts certainly affect the daily lives of families in PNG's oil palm areas, as shown in the section below on 'small farmers' voices'.

European activists have looked at the business links and consumer boycott possibilities (eg. Van Gelder 2004), to obstruct the industry or draw attention to these damaging ecological developments. On the other hand, some international NGOs such as the Worldwide Fund for Nature (WWF) have begun a process of 'positive collaboration' with the oil palm industry, attempting to introduce some environmental safeguards and raise the notion of a 'sustainable palm oil industry' (WWF 2003). Such moves could well help legitimise existing operations. Whether they will have any substantial impact is another question. This chapter will refer to, but not examine in any depth, the environmental impact of oil palm.

OIL PALM AND THE INTERNATIONAL FINANCE INSTITUTIONS

The World Bank and the Asian Development Bank have pushed the PNG Government into taking out large loans to support oil palm development in PNG, through 'nucleus estates' and linked communities of villagers using both their own and leased land to grow oil palm. Combinations of foreign investors and small local groups maintain strong self-interest in backing the industry and in presenting it as bringing wider benefits.

There is a longer history to these plantations in PNG. The Germans planted oil palm on the Rai Coast in the 1890s, and there were more plantings near Popondetta in the 1920s. However the first substantial plantings were in 1966, in a World Bank–backed scheme at Hoskins in West New Britain. The Bialla scheme followed in 1972, then Popondetta in 1976 (after independence), Milne Bay in 1985 and New Ireland in 1998 (Koczberski, Curry & Gibson 2001: 1–10). West New Britain set the pattern for all these developments, that is: a central ('nucleus') private (or joint venture) estate with land 'purchased' from the state, surrounded by small farmers on 99 year lease land (Land Settlement Scheme: LSS) and customary owners growing oil palm of their own land (Village Oil Palm: VOP). The LSS blocks were generally 6 hectare lots of land that were originally prepared for returned soldiers, in the colonial period. The VOP blocks were encouraged in 2 or 4 hectare lots. Later on, 'mini-estate' land was leased from groups of customary owners and added to the core estate land. All categories of leased or 'purchased' land (i.e. estate, mini-estate, and LSS) have been subject to disputes, due to the unsatisfactory nature of transactions in the colonial and post-colonial periods.

The World Bank and the ADB share a neoliberal approach to agro-industry which sees greater commodification and deeper penetration by foreign investors. This is presented as an opportunity for investors to access the resource base of PNG, under the general argument that such operations are more productive. Yet, apart from the important question of 'who gains?', international experience does not always support the argument that large, chemical-intensive cash cropping produces more from the same land. Some small farmers can be very efficient, and small farming in developing countries always has a wider range social purposes, including food security, social security, the maintenance of culture and environmental custodianship. Those benefits are not captured in simple export figures. The idea that rural productivity must be considered more widely is the 'multifunctionality' concept of small farming (Rosset 1999; Mazoyer 2001). Initially, the World Bank supported oil palm, committing almost US$100 million in loans into agricultural, cash cropping projects, between 1983 and 1992. In the 1990s the ADB took over this role, committing over US$35 million in loans; and in the mid-2000s the World Bank resumed responsibility (Table 6.3). AusAID has also contributed to some infrastructure support for the oil palm areas.

In PNG in the mid 1990s, following in the footsteps of the World Bank, the ADB put over US$22 million into an Agricultural Research and Extension Project, which focussed on the commercial development of oil palm, coffee and cocoa. The ADB had greater regard for the productive potential of oil palm than for coffee, noting oil palm's increased use of fertiliser (ADB 1998). The ADB's next scheme, announced in late 2001, the Agro–Enterprises Technical Assistance Loan, did not express very clear objectives. It was to provide loans with interest rates of only 1% (for the first 8 years) and 1.5% for the next 24 years, but 60% of this (US$4.5 million) would be used as foreign exchange for the ADB's international consultants. Another US$1.5 million was to be raised by the Government of PNG, including from its 'private sector proponents' (ADB 2001b). The ADB said this Project was about developing:

> 'feasibility studies for nucleus enterprise–based development
> projects in agriculture and agro–processing ... [and] pilot activities
> in and around potential nucleus enterprises' (ADB 2001b)

Table 6.3: Multilateral bank cash cropping finance, PNG 1985–2002			
Financier	Started	Project	US$m
WB	1983	Agricultural Support Services	14.1
WB	1984	West Sepik Provincial Development Project	9.7
WB	1985	Nucleus Estates and Smallholders Project (mostly oil palm, but also cocoa)	27.6
WB	1985	Agricultural Credit project	18.8
WB	1992	Oro Oil Palm Development Project [later extended by AusAID grants]	27
ADB	1995	Agricultural Research and Extension Project [oil palm, coffee and cocoa]	22.11
ADB	1999–04	Smallholder Support Services Pilot Project	7.6
ADB	2000	Agro–industry Development	0.5
ADB	2002	Preparing the Agriculture and Rural Development Project	1
ADB	2002–04	Nucleus Agro–Enterprises Technical Assistance Loan [oil palm]	5.8
WB	2007–12	Smallholder Agriculture Development [part only on oil palm]	27.5
Sources: World Bank 2003d; World Bank 2007; Asian Development Bank 2003c, ADB 2002			

The ADB has often stressed the breadth of its projects, and the inclusion of small farmers in its projects, for example 'to increase small holder incomes and national output' (ADB 1998). However it is fairly clear that this type of 'commercially oriented agriculture' (ADB 2001) is not principally aimed at small farmers. The idea of a 'nucleus enterprise' agro-industry is centred on private corporate development: 'that provides small holders and outgrowers with market outlets, technical and financial support, planting materials and social services that cannot be provided by either the public sector or the small holders themselves' (ADB 1998). This is a privatisation scheme. Using indirect language the ADB is effectively saying 'we will use public money (most of the finance is a low interest loan to the Government) to create facilities that will be privately owned, and which will then condition the surrounding farming activities of small players'. The outcome of such projects, unsurprisingly, is to link small holders into a large monopsony facility, such as the mills in Popondetta and Hoskins.

How has oil palm helped livelihoods? It has helped provide extra income to some small farmers. However, there have also been a range of harmful environmental impacts, and small holders have been at the economic mercy of price–fixing companies, getting limited returns for their fruit. There are other problems. In many places oil palm projects have been a front for illegal logging operations. Oil palm requires clear-fell logging (PNGSPS 2003). The large mills are most often the main beneficiaries of World Bank, ADB and AusAID subsidies. For example the road works in Oro Province, funded by the World Bank, help Higaturu trucks collect fruit from small farmers.

Nevertheless, PNG governments have maintained their support for oil palm development. In 2002 the PNG Government allocated five million Kina (linked to the ADB loans) for 'nucleus agro-enterprises' which 'seek to expand the model that has operated successfully here, particularly in relation to our oil palm industry' (Philemon 2002). Rural Development Minister Andrew Umbakor said that oil palm was a success with 'the potential for further expansion' (PTQ 2001: 2), while Prime Minister Michael Somare said his Government had 'identified the oil palm industry as a vehicle and growth strategy to enhance the economic and socio–indicators of Papua New Guinea' (Somare 2003). A shifting group of regions were targeted for palm oil development (see table 6.4). However, following community resistance, including one major court case which stopped the Collingwood Bay proposal (see Tararia and Ogle 2010), the emphasis seems to have shifted to consolidating and expanding the existing palm oil areas.

Table 6.4: Proposed new Oil Palm development areas in PNG, 2003		
Existing Oil Palm Areas	Areas PM Somare said ADB studies have identified as 'suitable' (June 2003)	Areas from 'government sources', based on studies (The Independent, July 2002)
West New Britain	Amazon Bay (Central)	Amazon Bay (Central)
New Ireland	Arowe (West New Britain)	Arowe (WNB)
Milne Bay	Turubu/Sepik Plains (E. Sepik)	Sepik Plains (E. Sepik)
Oro–Popondetta	Bewani (West Sepik)	Vailala (Gulf)
		Ramu Plains (Madang)
		Open Bay (ENB)
		Morobe–Gulf Border
		Collingwood Bay (Milne/Oro)
Sources: Somare 2003b; Peni 2002; NB. In 2002 the Collingwood Bay proposal was legally blocked by Maisin landowners (Ben Ifoki and others v The State and others 1999)		

In late 2003 the World Bank returned to the game, announcing a US$25 million package for expansion of oil palm in the four main existing plantation and mill areas (Oro, West New Britain, New Ireland and Milne Bay). US$20 million of this would be a World Bank IDA loan (low interest, but strict conditions) with the other $5m from the European Union, PNG and 'project beneficiaries' (World Bank 2003: 3). A series of general assertions about the PNG economy back up the Bank's argument in support of this new plan, with the central aim being:

> 'To promote rapid growth in the rural areas in four oil palm
> growing provinces, by strengthening the small holder oil palm
> sector through capitalising on existing infrastructure, and by
> establishing replicable mechanisms for community driven
> development' (World Bank 2003: 3).

This eventually turned into the 2007–2012 project, with additional funding from the PNG government (7.4m), the provincial governments of Oro and West New Britain (10.7m), the PNG Sustainable Development Program (10.2m), Smallholders (7.3m) and the oil palm milling companies (5.7m). Total funding was US$68.8 million, and the aim was to: 'increase smallholder oil palm productivity while also improving local governance through greater community oversight and increase overall economic activity in the project areas' (World Bank c.2007).

No evidence is provided by the World Bank to suggest these plans are 'community driven'. In fact, communities in New Britain and Oro (eg. Mamoko 2003) have been complaining for years about land disputes and environmental damage from existing oil palm operations. Communities in Madang have also opposed oil palm development on their land (eg. Yambai 2003; Paol 2003). Whatever might be the national economic benefits from oil palm, it is customary landowners and local communities which bear most of the costs.

Why does the World Bank appear so partisan? We must recognise that it is not an independent development advisory body. The very first constitutional aim of the Bank is:

> 'To assist in the reconstruction and development of territories of
> members by facilitating the

investment of capital ... to promote private foreign investment ...
to supplement private investment ... to promote ... international
trade ... to arrange ... international loans.'

Article One concludes: 'The Bank shall be guided in all its decisions
by the purposes set forth above' (World Bank 1989: Article One).
Although the contemporary literature of the Bank includes a lot of nicer
sounding phrases, we can best understand the Bank as a lobby group for
private foreign investors. The interests of its directors and its neoliberal
ideology reinforce the constitutional aims. That is why the World Bank
neglects livelihoods and privileges private foreign investment.

Were oil palm simply an 'option' for small farmers (like cocoa, coffee, or
vanilla), and not one linked to a socially and environmentally damaging
monoculture, subject to domination by a single, large, price-setting
company, its appeal to small farmers might be stronger. However, unlike
many other cash crops (coffee, cocoa, vanilla, most fruit trees), oil palm is
a nutrient-hungry plant which cannot be companion planted. It competes
for space with other crops. Construction of monoculture industries, each
focussed on a private 'nucleus' (i.e. a large private company) seems likely
to tie small farmers into an unequal system, and one from which it may
be difficult to escape. The disadvantage is not so much a function of world
prices, as the weak market position given to small farmers.

The focus on resource-based, export-oriented agriculture has been
driven by the IFIs, AusAID, some foreign corporations and successive
PNG governments concerned with foreign exchange and government
revenue. These concerns are not the same as those of customary
landowners and small farmers, who typically want to maintain the quality
of their land and enhance their income possibilities. Neoliberal ideology
regularly seeks to conflate these differing interests. Those interested in
livelihoods must note the differences.

SMALL FARMERS AND THE OIL PALM ECONOMY

Small farmers in PNG are at the highly competitive end of a long
international value chain, and their economics prospects are limited. I
will explain why and to what extent, in this section. The domination of
the PNG oil palm industry by large companies, which purchase all the
oil palm fruit in their area, is central to this problem.

The advantages of oil palm for small farmers have been suggested as including the following considerations: (i) controllable pest and disease problems; (ii) that oil palm is very productive, and adapts well to different soils and conditions; (iii) that the trees can be neglected, if prices fall, and resuscitated later on; (iv) that oil palm trees produce fruit (and therefore also income) all year round; (v) that the produce of small farmers can be completely bought up by the 'nucleus estate' mills in their area; and (vi) that world prices seem strong (Koczberski, Curry & Gibson 2001: 18). These arguments, however, do not really address the issues of (i) small farmers' weak market position in a long value chain, (ii) the economic power of the monopsonist mill, (iii) the 'crowding out' of other cash crops by a commitment to oil palm, and (iv) the serious environmental damage caused by oil palm. On top of this, the relative returns on oil palm have been greatly exaggerated.

This section looks at the economic experience of small farmers, particularly those in the Popondetta plains of Oro Province. It draws on interviews and surveys in 2003 and 2005, as well as the best available data (as at 2012) on smallholder incomes. It discusses their economic returns, the division of value within the industry and oil palm cultivation compared to the alternatives.

THE PLACE OF SMALL HOLDERS IN THE PNG OIL PALM INDUSTRY

In November 2001, Koczberski, Curry & Gibson (Australian academics from Curtin University and ANU) published a detailed report on 'small holders' and oil palm in PNG, looking particularly at the West New Britain and the Oro/Popondetta schemes. Small farmers, oil palm companies and support agencies were consulted, and fairly detailed surveys of smallholders were carried out. This academic study was co-sponsored by PNG's Oil Palm Research Association, and the main aim was 'to help improve small holder oil palm productivity' (Koczberski, Curry & Gibson 2001: xvi). That is, the report was directed to the industry. It might be useful to summarise the report's main findings here.

This study found, firstly, that oil palm was one of many economic activities pursued, and that alternative income sources were important for household needs, especially in the leased LSS blocks. About 80%

of food for meals for families on LSS blocks came from gardens, compared to 50% for those on VOP. That is, LSS families were more dependent on garden food, despite their more intense focus on oil palm. The incentive to participate in oil palm for those on VOP blocks was said to be not so much for consumption or investment income as for 'redistributing wealth through kin exchange' (Koczberski, Curry & Gibson 2001: xvii–xix). Secondly, population growth was creating pressures and conflict for those on the leased LSS blocks. Population density had increased in the 20–30 years of the schemes, most LSS blocks were now multifamily, and sources of social instability included resentment at the 'outsider' settlers involved. Population pressures had led to an increase in reliance on garden food, though the Mama Lus program for women (see below) may have offset some of this pressure (Koczberski, Curry & Gibson 2001: xx–xxi). Thirdly, there were diverse forms of family engagement with the oil palm industry. These included, single families, work groups (*wok bung*), rotation systems and varying levels of labour engagement. All these had implications for an industry aiming to increase participation and efficiency. Finally, there were land conflicts in relation to 'sold' and leased land, in relation to the estates and mini–estates, the LSS and the VOP blocks. Land conflicts were particularly serious in Popondetta. These conflicts were 'undermining small holder commitment to oil palm, and the long term viability of the industry'. Several industry interventions had been made to improve participation and efficiency, the most successful of which was said to be the 'Mama Lus Frut' scheme, for women (Koczberski, Curry & Gibson 2001: xxiii–xxiv).

Table 6.5 below shows the variety of combinations of plantation and small farmer oil palm cropping in PNG, back in the year 2000. The ownership structure has changed since then (e.g. the US agro–business giant Cargill took over Oro's Higaturu Oil Palm from the British Commonwealth Development Corporation in 2005, but then onsold it to the Malaysian state–owned company Kulim, in 2010), but the nucleus companies remain much the same. In West New Britain (at Hoskins and Bialla), and in Oro on the Popondetta plains, small farmers on their own customary land or on leased land form a major part of the industry. However, all small farmers supply to, and are price dependent on, the single large company mill in their area.

Table 6.5: Estate and small holder oil palm in PNG, 2000					
	Hoskins, WNB	Bialla, WNB	Popondetta, Oro	Alotau, Milne Bay	Lakuramau, New Ireland
Company	New Britain Palm Oil	Hargy Oil Palms	Higaturu Oil Palms	Milne Bay Estates	Poliamba
Estate area, ha	23,927	5,600	7,785	6,990	6,000
Estate production, tonnes FFB	555,680	82,374	147,141	197,885	103,739
LSS area, ha	3,021	2,161	1,045	nil	nil
VOP area, ha	1,634	1,067	4,448	536	648
LSS/VOP production	277,642	119,730	113,665	9,609	10,616
Mini–estate area, ha	7,128	nil	2,051	1,975	309
Total production, 2000	833,323	202,104	260,806	207,494	114,355
Source: Koczberski, Curry & Gibson 2001: 6					

The experience of oil palm around Popondetta in Oro province is instructive, for the rest of PNG. The benefits of oil palm for the small growers were argued to me back in 2003 by Mr Leo Ruki, a Highland man and Project Manager for OPIC. He claimed that people in the villages were wealthier and healthier, with better access to goods (Ruki 2003). In addition, the 'Mama Lus' system allowed women collectors of fallen and spilt fruit (over 2500 were registered as at December 2002) to gain some income. In 2003 there were over 40,000 hectares of 'village oil palm', comprising 5,825 growers, (most of their holdings are between 2ha and 4ha), and some land settlement schemes (LSS blocks) for tenant farmers (Ruki 2003). All these small growers sell their fruit to the Higaturu mill which, due to the failure of earlier privatisation attempts, was still 40% state owned. Although it had been estimated that the VOP oil palm plots might be no more than 20% of the VOP villagers' total lands (A. Koja 2003), oil palm is expanding in the region. The Oil Palm Industry Corporation (OPIC), which services the region's oil palm industry, takes subscriptions from growers but has also received substantial finance from the World Bank and AusAID, mainly for developing feeder roads which help trucks from the Higaturu mill go out to collect palm fruit from outlying areas.

However Higaturu, as the only buyer in the area, sets the prices. Small growers complain bitterly about low prices. The Growers' Association told me their portion, in the grower-company split on the value of growers' fruit was 55% (A. Koja 2003). Many growers earned about 100 Kina a fortnight, but this was a family operation and was said to be very hard work, particularly compared to coffee or cocoa. In addition, the company did not pay separately for the palm kernels, even though they were sold separately. The growers believed they should be paid separately (A. Koja 2003). Some would like to see a new grower-run mill, but this was beyond their means. Contrary to the OPIC Manager, the head of the Growers Association had not seen much improvement in living standards over the previous 20 years. He believed growers had been kept at a subsistence level (A. Koja 2003). Higaturu would not collect fruit from small growers if the roads were run down, and this led to the pressure for foreign loans to maintain feeder roads to the mill. Insecticides were used, as oil palm attracts hordes of rats and flies, and the plantation, settlement and village crops used substantial amounts of fertiliser (Ruki 2003).

HOW IS THE SMALL HOLDER SHARE DETERMINED?

Small farmer participation in the industry is largely conditioned by the regional mills which buy all the local fruit and fix the prices for small farmers. In recognition of this problem, and of the many complaints, there have been several attempts to improve the relationship, through reviews of the mills' pricing fixing decisions (the 'payout ratio'). These reviews have made some modest suggestions for an improvement in the small farmer share, but their recommendations have not been binding on the companies and have in many cases been ignored. The World Bank has tried to discourage government involvement in the price reviews, in line with the neoliberal view that 'markets' should be allowed to set prices.

Despite the very limited impact of the price reviews, analysis of their method gives us some insight into the rationale of value distribution within the industry. Following is an outline of the price review process, and its reasoning.

In 2001 two consultants (Burnett & Ellingsen 2001) prepared a report for the Commodities Working Group of the PNG Government on a price regulation formulation, to protect small holders from the economic power of the mills. This was the fourth report in a series. The first price review came after an earlier report (Heaslip and Maycock 1990) had drawn attention to conflict over profit sharing between the mill and smallholders. This price review led to negotiations between the PNG government and milling companies, to develop a 'new and fairer pricing formula' (Burnett & Ellingsen 2001: 23). A second report in 1996, commissioned by the World Bank (seeking a lesser role for the PNG Government and backed by the companies' association, the Palm Oil Producers Association or POPA), simplified the pricing formula and introduced the 55% payout ratio (POR) for smallholders. The 1998 report (also by the 2001 consultants, Burnett & Ellingsen) urged (i) a shift from the 55/45 POR ratio to 60/40, (ii) a reduction in 'sales costs deductions for Palm Kernel from US$80/tonne to US$70/tonne, (iii) a shift in extraction rates (from fruit to palm oil) from 22.88% and 4.97% to 22.66% and 5.27% (CPO and PK), and (iv) a more commercial costing of transport for fruit, so that smallholders further from the mill would pay more. Only the second recommendation was taken up by the companies (Burnett & Ellingsen 2001: 24).

In their 2001 report, Burnett & Ellingsen formulated a 'break even' analysis for both smallholders and the oil palm milling company (the 'nucleus estate'). They presented a formula which deducted a collection of company 'sales costs', then compared the relative costs of small holder production with the costs of mill production. Fresh Fruit Bunch (FFB) values were converted to Crude Palm Oil (CPO) prices by a calculated extraction rate of 22.66%; similarly, Palm Kernel was converted to Palm Kernel Oil (PKO) by an extraction rate of 5.27% (Burnett & Ellingsen 2001: 24). They came up with a total cost of production figure of K110.58/Mt–FFB, split into small holder costs (K65.40 Mt/FFB, or 59%) and milling company costs (K45.18Mt/FFB or 40.86%). On this basis they slightly revised their 1998 findings, to suggest a 59/41 revenue split – in other words a recommended increase from 55% to 59% (Burnett & Ellingsen 2001: 48).

While in its conclusion the report recommended a 4% increased share for smallholders, two broader issues were notable from the method of the report: (i) explicit benefits, outside the 'break even' rationale, were identified as accruing only to the company, and not to the small farmers; and (ii) there was a fuller accounting of company break-even concerns, and a more limited calculation of small farmers 'costs'.

The report draws attention to several benefits, outside the 'break even' and subsequent 'payout ratio' cost calculations, which are available only to the milling company:

- Benefits from European Union duty exemption
- FFA ('free fatty acid') quality premiums
- Gains from the devaluation of the Kina (devaluation lowers costs of production; farmers are paid in Kina but revenue is raised in dollars)
- Non–payment to small farmers for company use of shell fibre and compost materials
- Benefits from hedging and forward sales (Burnett & Ellingsen 2001: 3).

Farmers in Popondetta also complain of no separate payment for palm kernel (A. Koja 2003). The report endorses the company claim of a lump sum deduction of US$80 in 'sales costs', before the Payout Ratio calculation. This sum is said to cover company costs in 'freight, insurance, brokerage, sales commission and overseas port charges'. However the figures are largely taken on faith, as detailed accounts could not be scrutinised due to 'commercial confidentiality' claims (Burnett & Ellingsen 2001: 36).

A further category of problems, not mentioned but implicit in the pricing review, arises from the choices made in calculating company and small farmer costs. The items included in company costs seem to comprise a fairly full commercial costing. For example, full labour costs (including high managerial salaries), depreciation of capital and various separate overhead costs were included (Burnett & Ellingsen 2001: 33–34). On the other hand, labour costs for small farmers were set at the minimum rural wage (previously they were 70% of this) and, while some land rent was added to the 2001 calculations for LSS farmers, no land rent at all is included for VOP farmers (Burnett & Ellingsen 2001: 31). The implications of these omissions are that (i) the costs of small farmers include only bare minimum subsistence wages, while the mill calculations include actual premium salaries (New Britain Palm Oil Limited, for example, notes in its annual report that 40 of its employees are paid more than 100,000 Kina per year, and (ii) no opportunity cost calculations are made for the land contributions by most customary owners (this discounts potentially profitable alternative uses of land). Further, no depreciation of land (eg. through soil depletion and chemical pollution) is added – in contrast to the depreciation allowances included for the companies' capital investments. The end result of this is to assign no value to the contribution of customary and to severely limit the returns to small farmers.

RETURNS ON OIL PALM FOR SMALL FARMERS

While the Higaturu mill injects cash into the Popondetta plains economy, a more careful study is needed to assess the benefits, costs and opportunity costs for small farmers. In 2003 the late Anderson Koja, former Chairman of the Popondetta Oil Palm Growers Association, estimated that VOP and LSS growers in the Popondetta area only received an average of about 100 Kina per fortnight for production from their average 2–4 hectare plots of oil palm. Gaining this sort of family income required quite a deal of work, at certain times of the year, and growers were constantly upset at the poor prices paid for their fruit (A. Koja 2003). His estimates can be tested by data from Warner and Bauer (2002), my own pilot survey of 2005 and more recent data from the World Bank (2010). The results appear in Table 6.6 below and show, while that average weekly earnings have risen in recent years (along with world prices for oil palm; see Table 6.2) they have never approached average informal sector incomes (see Chapter Three, Table 3.1). Smallholder incomes from oil palm are not impressive, given the combined family commitment of land and labour.

Table 6.6: Smallholder (VOP and LSS) Oil Palm household income		
	Average annual income (Kina)	Average Weekly Earnings (Kina)
Warner and Bauer 2002, VOP Oro Province (av. single household block, includes Mama Lus)	5,476	105
Warner and Bauer 2002, VOP Oro Province (av. dual household block, includes Mama Lus)	2,952	57
Warner and Bauer 2002, LSS, Oro Province (2.9 households per block)	2,167	42
Anderson pilot survey 2005, VOP Oro Province (average single household block) * pilot only	3,045 *	59 *

Cont.

World Bank 2010, PNG wide (average single household 2ha block)	5,586	107
Sources: Warner and Bauer 2002; World Bank 2010; ITS 2011		

Warner and Bauer's (2002:10) data on VOP and LSS farmers in Oro seems to have been obtained from Higaturu, via George Curry. They put average annual single household income from oil palm (including Mama Lus income) at 5,476 per block, 2,952 Kina for two household blocks and 2,167 Kina for the average LSS block of 2.9 household. My pilot survey in 2005, of 19 oil palm farmers in Oro, showed an average oil palm income of 3,045 Kina per family per year (Anderson 2006a). The World Bank (2010) data, showing an average income of 5,586 Kina per year from an average 2ha oil palm block, seems to come from the combined mills of PNG. The Bank has engaged with mills in all four oil palm provinces, in their most recent project (see Table 6.3).

Combining this data with the informal sector surveys, we can draw the following conclusions. The average cash crop income of Popondetta plains oil palm farmers (VOP, let alone LSS) has not approached the average incomes of the informal sector activities, including the roadside sellers, at any time in the past decade. (Even this comparison is loaded in favour of oil palm, as this crop commits a combined family effort and substantial land.) This unfavourable comparison is despite the strong prices rises from 2008 onwards. In the early 2000s, combined informal sector average incomes in four non–oil palm growing provinces (Sowei et al 2003) were in all cases higher, sometimes twice as high, as the VOP family incomes in Oro Province, and three times as high as the average LSS incomes (Warner and Bauer 2002; compare Table 3.1 with Table 6.6). By 2010–2011, rural roadside seller average incomes in four mostly non oil-palm growing provinces (Tables 3.1 and 5.3) were more than twice as high as PNG's average smallholder family incomes from oil palm (World Bank 2010).

So, while oil palm figures highly amongst crops producing foreign exchange, it is quite misleading to suggest that oil palm is 'key' to PNG's agricultural sector, and that it provides 'very favourable returns' on land and labour (World Bank 2010). There is simply no basis to conclude that the foreign exchange contribution from oil palm is matched by its contribution to livelihoods. Even worse is the claim by industry consultants that oil palm provides 'higher rates of return than other smallholder investment opportunities', and 'above average' incomes to smallholders (ITS Global 2011). Why this misinformation? In the case of the industry consultants, the conflict of interest is obvious. With the World Bank, we must recognise that this body is constitutionally bound to privilege the role of foreign investors.

What are the other relevant livelihood aspects of oil palm in PNG? Apart from average incomes we should look at the institutional constraints on oil palm smallholder income, the relationship to ongoing reliance on 'garden' (or subsistence) food, the impact on crop diversity, the opportunity costs and the environmental impacts.

Average incomes apart, the superior cash returns are not to be found in oil palm. My 2005 pilot study showed a clustering of seven of the more successful Popondetta oil palm farmers in cash income levels of 4,000 to 9,000 Kina, with a median of 5,000 to 6,000 Kina. While these are medium income levels, they may also represent a 'ceiling' that is difficult to surpass. Many oil palm farmers comment (see Section 4 below) that a disproportionate effort goes into their oil palm crops. None seem to have reached the income levels of the top earners in the roadside seller groups, who gained most income from local crops and then supplemented these crops with export options such as cocoa, coconut and vanilla. We can see much higher incomes from the local market sellers in other provinces. The 13 roadside sellers in Madang Province who earned 100 Kina or more per day (in 2007, at an equivalent full time rate of 25,000 Kina per year), were mostly selling some combination of peanut, buai, daka and fruit. The 13 roadside sellers in Morobe who similarly earned over 100 Kina per day (in 2011), were either focussed on one high value crop (taro or cooking banana) or a variety of peanut, cucumber, betel-nut, oranges and coconut, usually along with other items such as vegetables, ice, fruit, cooked items (see Chapters Three and Five). Sales of these crops in local markets involve very short 'value chains', where the grower is often also the seller, and so is not 'taxed' by middlemen.

A likely 'ceiling' on cash income from oil palm seems related to the problems of a longer value chain in many other commodity export crops, including coffee (ignoring for the moment niche markets such as organic and fair trade coffee). The subordinate relationship that small farmers experience with the local 'nucleus estate' puts them in a dynamic, regulated relationship with other powerful players, especially the corporate estates. This asymmetrical relationship builds in substantial labour commitments. For example, reviewers of the pricing formula estimated that VOP farmers with 2ha of oil palm require 110 to 146 'man-days' of labour per year, in the first three years of oil palm farming, and 41 to 53 man–days per year after that. LSS farmers on 4 ha blocks required 220 to 289 man–days in the first three years, and 70 to 106 man-days per year after that (Burnett & Ellingsen 2001: 9, 11). This is a heavy and long term commitment to a single crop and, given that each day in these calculations was specifically accounted for, it is likely an underestimate. People are usually less efficient than exacting models.

The pricing formula locks in disadvantage. Data from Higaturu Oil Palm Limited (HOP) in 2004 tells us that small farmer output in the Popondetta plains expanded to match the Higaturu estate's fruit output, over the years. However, when the world price of oil palm was high (as in 1998, and to a lesser extent in 2004) the fraction of FFB payments to the CPO world price declined (HOP 2004). That is, farmers received a smaller fraction of the overall value when prices rose. Despite a constant payout ratio, the nucleus estates managed to effectively capture most of the benefit of higher prices.

Maintenance of healthy gardens is important, especially in the face of land loss to the oil palm monoculture. Despite the income from oil palm fruit, farmers remain heavily dependent on their gardens for subsistence food as well as other market income (Koczberski, Curry & Gibson 2001: 50). Others have noted that women farmers generally rely on diverse cropping (Jenkins 1996). In my own pilot studies, most of a Madang group expressed a 75–85% reliance on their gardens as a food source, while most of a Popondetta group expressed a 75–90% reliance. However a limiting factor is that oil palm does not allow for companion planting. The palm tree draws heavily on the soil (CELCOR 2005; Koja 2005) and deprives other plants of nutrients. The competition between oil palm and other crops can have serious consequences, through undermining both subsistence and other commercial crop options.

This leads to a general and observable lower diversity of cash crops in oil palm areas, such as the Popondetta plains. Despite a thriving buai market in town, supplied from surrounding areas, the limited wider crop production is due to the intensive plantations, the voracious nature of the monocultures and the substantial labour involved. In my pilot studies the diversity of cash crops was lower in the Popondetta group than the Madang group. Seven in the Madang group of eighteen had substantial income (1,000 or more) from three or more crops. Only three in the Popondetta group of twenty had substantial income (1,000 or more) from three or more crops. Further, the highest annual returns per family in the Popondetta pilot survey (9,940 Kina per year) were from a family which had (for an oil palm grower) unusually high diversity of cash crops.

Opposed to the modest cash income possibilities of oil palm are two important opportunity costs, that is, costs involved in excluding alternative activities. First, oil palm cultivation tends to reduce the diversity of production, by occupying land that becomes closed to companion planting. Oil palm trees, being highly productive but also voracious, then deplete the soil of nutrients. Others have observed that:

> 'Growers of other crops can survive price drops more easily because
> they can plant a variety of different crops together (like coconut
> and cocoa). This way the growers always have another source of
> income ands protection from market price changes .. [however]
> oil palm will not allow any other crops to grow alongside it'
> (CELCOR 2005).

This is a common complaint amongst oil palm growers (K. Koja 2005).

It is well to say that oil palm trees can be neglected when prices are low (Koczberski, Curry & Gibson 2001:18), and that alternative crops (coffee, cocoa, copra) can 'provide an alternative income source when oil palm prices are low' (Koczberski, Curry & Gibson 2001: 42–45). However neglected hectares of prime land are a wasted resource, and alternative crops compete for space with oil palm. Small farmers do not have unlimited land, nor should we regard their land as having zero opportunity cost.

Finally, an easily observable cost of the oil palm monoculture is the degradation of water and river systems on the Popondetta plains, from land clearing, erosion and nutrient–rich fertiliser run–off. Local farmers often comment on the changed physical features of the rivers, and it is plain to see that many rivers have silted up and are full of green algae. Oil palm trees require complete land clearance, after logging, and this has important implications for erosion, topsoil depletion, and the siltation of rivers. The principal chemical pollution from oil palm (and this does not seem to apply to other PNG crops) is the extensive use of fertiliser which (a) to some extent compensates for the oil palm trees' depletion of soil nutrients, (b) adds to the productivity of the trees, and (c) runs off into the water table and river systems, causing algae blooms and damaging natural biological processes. Others have noted the impact of oil palm on endangered species, waterways, coral reefs and the oceans (Tan 2004: 4.10–4.11).

The environmental costs of oil palm plantations and the large mills need to be fully considered with particular reference to: (i) the impact of this particular form of monocultural agriculture on crop pests (eg. rats, flies) and the local ecology (including soil erosion and biodiversity impacts); (b) water and soil pollution by chemical and other wastes (eg. rat poison, tree killing chemicals, weed poisons, fertiliser run–off, oil mill waste, general mill/plantation sewage). At least ten types of fertiliser and ten types of other chemicals (surfactants, herbicide, insecticides) are used by the Higaturu Mill. An understanding of the impact of these chemicals is necessary for a full accounting of the opportunity costs associated with oil palm.

THE 'MAMA LUS FRUT' SCHEME

There have been exaggerated claims that an oil palm company scheme for women represents a great breakthrough, both in livelihood terms and for gender relations. It has been said that the 'Mama Lus Frut' scheme might help reduce household conflict, domestic violence and even slow the spread of HIV infection (Koczberski 2007; Seeley and Butcher 2006). This is mostly speculation. I suggest the scheme is better seen as a very limited formal sector option.

The scheme was started by oil palm companies in West New Britain and the Popondetta plains as an attempt to improve 'smallholder productivity' and draw in women's labour. It sets up women–only accounts for the women collectors of loose oil palm fruit, scattered by the processes of harvesting and hasty road side collection. Prior to that, women had been reluctant to join in oil palm work; it was mainly seen as men's work. Koczberski et al (2001: 63) observed that women 'identified more closely' with local markets than with oil palm. However they also calculated that the Mama Lus Frut scheme at Hoskins (since

1997) had delivered an independent source of income to women, who spent this money far more according to family needs. The average weekly income in 2000 for those with a 'Mama Card' at Hoskins was 28 Kina per woman, which they note was '93% of the [very low] average weekly wage for low skilled rural workers'. There was apparently strong support for this scheme, which gave women greater financial autonomy, and 'only a few women mentioned the strain on the back from bending over and collecting loose fruit and none mentioned the time or work conflicts between lose fruit collection and their other work roles'. The program, they concluded, had been a 'resounding success' (Koczberski, Curry & Gibson 2001: 174, 178, 193).

There were qualifications. The scheme had in many ways formalised the gender division of labour, with the main family account now being termed the 'Papa Card', which drew four times as much income as the Mama Card, and was used more as discretionary income. Many women spoke of 'the meagre contribution' made by their husband to the household budget (Koczberski, Curry & Gibson 2001: 174). The Mama Lus Frut scheme had been less successful in Popondetta, they said. Introduced in 1999, the income had been lower than at Hoskins, and the Higaturu mill had made loan deductions from the Mama Card, where it believed family loan repayments were being avoided on the primary card. The Mama Card had initially been shielded from loan repayments to the Mill, for supplied fertiliser and tools, but this was changed when it was thought the Mama Card was allowing debt avoidance. Higher levels of debts avoidance were linked to very low incomes and insecurity of tenure on the LSS blocks (Koczberski, Curry & Gibson 2001: 195).

However a focus on gender equity, linked to a belief that large companies might somehow help reconstruct familial gender relations, tends to hide greater issues of equity in the oil palm industry. Oil palm companies make a great deal of money, largely through the land and labour of customary land owning families in their areas. New Britain Palm Oil, for example, has gained substantial financial strength from the land and people of West New Britain. In 2004 the company anticipated profits of over 126 million Kina, after paying its six directors one and a half million Kina, and after paying more than 100,000 Kina per year to 41 of its executive employees (NBPOL 2004: 6). The income also helped the company invest in cattle farming, treasury bills, a new oil palm business in the Solomon islands and an 80,000 ha expansion of its oil palm operations in West New Britain. New Britain Palm Oil also became a member of the 'Roundtable for the Production of Sustainable Palm Oil', a group that engages with potential critics in the NGO sector, to defend its reputation (NBPOL 2004: 8, 11–12). Higaturu Oil Palm is similar.

Koczberski et al estimated that, at Hoskins in 2000, there were over 3,000 women on the Mama card scheme, earning an average of 1440 Kina per year, which represented 26% of total smallholder oil palm revenues in that area (Koczberski, Curry & Gibson 2001: 173–174). Yet from the NBPOL accounts the average director's fee was more than 160 times the average Mama payment, 40 senior employees earned 70 times the average Mama payment, and payments to the 14 most senior managers were more than 270 times the average Mama payment. On top of this, post tax profits for NBPOL exceeded 80 million Kina per year. It is useful to keep this perspective, when speaking of equity in the industry.

A few years later, in 2003, income from the Mama Lus Fruit scheme was noted as having risen to an average of 49 Kina per week (Koczberski 2007: 1178), still one of the lowest rural options (see Table 3.1). Warner and Bauer (2002: 5, 10, 14) had noted that the 'mama cheque' added only 'slightly' or 'marginally' to household income, an increase of between 8% (in multiple household blocks) and 18% (in a single household block). Yet the benefits were said to be in the way 'that households handle money': referring to the well known pattern of women using money more for family needs, and men wasting it more on 'discretionary spending' (Warner and Bauer 2002: 6). However no household study accompanied this assertion, nor was any evidence given of how households managed money before the mama card scheme. For example, the possibility that 'mama card' money (and any other money) might have been simply handed over the male head of the household for distribution was not considered. In a similar vein, the assertions about the scheme possibly reducing household conflict or slowing the spread of HIV infection (Koczberski 2007; Seeley and Butcher 2006) were not based on any particular evidence.

Of greater importance, these hopeful theories on the unintended gender consequences of the 'Mama Lus Frut' scheme did not explore the reasons behind women's stated preference for participation in local fresh produce markets, nor did they compare the relative incomes (and therefore the trade–offs) involved. Perhaps it was assumed that only formal sector schemes count? In any case, we now know (Tables 3.1 and 5.3) that the informal sector roadside markets produce women's incomes which are on average three to five times greater than the returns on the Mama Lus Frut scheme. Many women would be, to some extent, aware of this; on the other hand, the promises of the oil palm industry may have misled them. They may also have felt husband pressure to pick up the 'loose fruit' and use the 'mama card' to supplement the family income. The poor returns on the Mama Lus Frut scheme seem to compound the problems of monoculture and limited crop diversity for subsistence gardens and other cash crops in informal markets. On balance it does not appear to offer strong support for either women's or family livelihoods.

SMALL FARMERS' VOICES

What do small farmers themselves say about oil palm? Any serious analyst has to listen to the voices of those involved in the industry, and of those nearby. Previous studies have noted the concerns of 'small holders' in PNG's oil palm business as including worries about (i) poor prices, (ii) the maintenance of other produce as sources of market income, and (iii) the maintenance of garden food, and concerns over food security. They say 'Now the price of oil palm has dropped, we rely on the chicken business and local markets'; 'garden food is something that is very important'; 'if the [oil palm] price drops significantly, then where will we find food to eat?'; and 'I worry about my children. What will they eat if we don't have garden food?' (Koczberski, Curry and Gibson 2001: 66, 150). In another report, elder Hubert Seheute of Hohota village, who has spent twenty years working oil palm, explained:

> 'I thought I would be a rich man, but I am still looking for it. I
> have no money at this time. I don't have feeder road to my block.
> Hunting, gardening and other vacant land are now needed for
> oil palm. Fertile flat lands are most suitable for oil palm and it is
> now consuming what used to be our gardening land' (in Aurere
> 2003: 3).

These concerns underline the precarious existence, the low returns for small farmers and the pressure on land created by the oil palm business.

In my pilot survey of small farmers on the Popondetta plains, as well as collecting economic data, I concluded by asking small groups of farmers their opinion of oil palm and of any particular concerns that they might have. I spoke with 16 oil palm farmers and 5 non–oil palm farmers, across eleven clan areas. There was very little positive said about oil palm, even from those with higher than average returns. They repeated the concerns noted by Koczberski et al, and added concerns over:

- Chemical, soil and water pollution;
- The appropriation and loss of customary land;
- Poor returns for the effort involved in oil palm cultivation;
- The 'crowding out' impact of the oil palm plantations on other crops, including gardens;
- The lack of support services;
- Injustices of the industry, including broken promises about the benefits and services to flow from engagement in oil palm cultivation;
- The impact of oil palm on biodiversity and wildlife management areas (WMAs);
- Health problems, which were attributed to oil palm in their area, usually linked to chemical, soil and atmospheric pollution;
- Problems of access to and the cost of transport, and inadequate or poorly constructed roads.

The comments of these 21 farmers are set out in the following table. Their family annual income (averaged out for a typical family of seven) from oil palm as well as other cash crops is in brackets, after their comments. Note that some families with low cash crop incomes have outside employment, and that income is not included.

Table 6.7: Comments by small farmers in Oro on the oil palm business	
Clan area	Comments
1. Ahora	Non oil palm grower – the Wildlife Management Area (WMA) has been affected by oil palm – Higaturu spraying weed killer affects us – rat baits are also washed into our rivers – our water is polluted (156)
2. Sorovi	We struggle very hard to meet our families needs – all our needs are not being catered for – it is very hard to get cash – we get no help from OPIC (7,000)

3. Kakandetta	Land has been taken by the state – we have limited land – chemical pollution has an impact – our gardens are next to a plantation – there has been a change in the size and quality of vegetables – I have mixed feelings, oil palm has taken a lot of land/space and we have to buy chemicals (146)
4. Sorovi	Returns are not really what we are supposed to get – most costs are on the grower – chemicals, tax, shipments – the company gets most benefit – we have all the risks – the world price is 450 Kina per tonne and we get 121 Kina, and no money for the kernel – oil palm is not helping our people – there is no feedback from services (OPIC) – Higaturu doesn't do anything for us (6,000)
5. Kakandetta	Oil palm is not a good return for the work (3,937)
6. Kakandetta	We didn't know about the impact before growing oil palm – I am beginning to hate oil palm – the problems are transport, price and the single factory (7,420)
7. Gona	We knew it would change our lives, but I find it hard to believe we are going backwards – the effort we give, we are not getting what we expect – the problems? shortage of land and land disputes, the money is not sufficient, it goes quickly (this is where price comes in) and the health problems – babies and water – there is a lack of water and the water is not clean – it used to be clean (2,145)
8. Sosoba	Oil palm has brought injustice – the company didn't look at our needs – land was taken by the company (the Ambogo Estate) – they promised electricity, but didn't deliver – they destroyed our land with polluted water – there are now typhoid, diarrhoea, cysts, asthma – oil palm depletes the soil – I would like to get rid of oil palm, and move to other crops such as vanilla and cocoa (6,341)
9. Aeka	Local contractors pick it up (there is a bigger cost being further from the mill) – fruit is sometimes left to rot – it is grown as another option (it replaced cocoa, because of lack of support for cocoa) – there is much more effort in oil palm than buai and peanut – most time is spent on oil palm, more time than in the gardens – there is lots of abandoned oil palm lots in this area – it's just too hard – we are looking for an alternative, thinking to go back to cocoa, though there is no fermentary at the moment – oil palm has an impact on soil fertility, we tried to grow bush bananas with it, but they don't grow well together – gardens next to oil palm have problems (1,680)
10. Ahora	Oil palm was to have brought social development – but we have not got the maximum benefit – there is water pollution – people were encouraged to plant oil palm for 'better houses and services', but this has not happened – there are price problems and land degradation (372)
11. Ahora	Oil palm is labour intensive – not maximum benefits – there is water contamination – land degradation – palm seeds are getting into the native forests (796)
12. Gona	Oil palm is hard work for less money – the price varies – problems with pick ups – problems with water – not good drinking water and people are sick – an outbreak of TB (4,783)

13. Ahora	Labour is intense, less benefit – could be a good means of income but a hard task – not fit to work alone, need the whole family – more time is spent, little benefit – it cannot support the whole family – water is contaminated with chemicals – no buffer zones [next to rivers] – health problems – rotten fruit in the river too – air pollution, rain is acidic and attacks crops – pollution causes respiratory problems such as asthma, especially in babies – oil palm is a threat to native forest, it may take over rainforest and destroy it – no better drinking water, all water is contaminated (2,975)
14. Gona	Best cash crop but a very hard job – payment to growers is not adequate – families with many children have many problems [lack of income] – OK for families with two kids – oil palm gives us sickness (TB) and shortage of water – fish from river and sea are also damaged or sick – our environment and land has been damaged by oil palm (9,940)
15. Oro Bay	Non oil palm grower – no view on oil palm (n/a)
16. Ango	Non oil palm grower – will not have oil palm on my land – no extension services and no-one told me about the impact of oil palm – 'after 50 years all the land will be damaged' – that's why I don't plant oil palm – there has been chemical change from the estate and mini–estate – the river water was clear in the past and is now dirty – the culverts have been badly constructed, against my advice, causing erosion of my clan's land, the road will wash away in the next big rains – oil palm pollutes the river, I hate oil palm – there's not enough money in it and there have been empty promises of better housing, sanitation, etc – but from experience, the benefits have been less (602)
17. Ango	Just began growing oil palm – problems with payments and the environment – I was misled into planting oil palm and there will be no more, no expansion – now afraid of land being damaged and water polluted – protein in the rivers (fish and prawns) has been damaged – there might be a problem in the food chain (450)
18. Embogo	Non oil palm grower – no view on oil palm (1,225)
19. Dombada	Non oil palm grower – no view on oil palm (1,272)
20. Erora	Non oil palm grower – water has been affected here – algae growth in the rivers (Ambogo and Erora) – fish have been affected, they are unhealthy, small and have sores – a new type of snake has appeared (black with a white belly, poisonous) – in 2003–04 there was a big oil palm leak at Oro Bay when a ship was being filled – in the 1980s there was resistance and arrests when the Ambogo Estate was converted to oil palm from Cocoa (1,470)
21. Sorovi	I grow oil palm on an LSS block but am a firm opponent of oil palm – campaigning to draw attention to the damage caused by oil palm – 'I hate it' (2,184)

OIL PALM AND LIVELIHOODS

Despite it being a highly profitable industry for the few companies involved, oil palm is not a superior livelihood option for rural families in PNG. Average incomes are lower than many of the informal sector, the environmental costs are high and the inflexibility of the monoculture does not permit it to contribute effectively to the more valuable hybrid livelihoods.

The main problems facing small farmers in the oil palm industry are that they have poor information on the costs and benefits of oil palm cultivation, and the alternatives. The economic limits smallholders face are imposed by their weak market position in a long export industry value chain, and by their weak market relationship with a large price–fixing mill. The crop is also an inflexible form of land use, requiring land clearing and preventing companion planting. This contributes to pressure on gardens and lower cash crop diversity. The serious environmental impacts from soil erosion and chemical pollution is more pronounced in oil palm than with any other crop grown in PNG.

The main alternatives to small farmer engagement with the oil palm industry involve retaining control of customary land and using it for some more flexible combination of domestic and export crops, with some degree of specialisation and some degree of diversity. High value domestic crops include peanut, buai, various fruits, cucumber, taro, cooking banana, coconut and fish; while export crops which allow greater degrees of companion planting include copra, cocoa and vanilla. The hybrid livelihoods bringing highest returns to PNG's rural families seem to combine small businesses with well focussed domestic crops, some export options and some formal sector employment. Customary landowner-led collaborations in marketing – as well as in land care and environmental management – can also open better livelihood options.

The International Finance Institutions, in particular the World Bank, have driven and subsidised oil palm development (often with loans, that PNG must repay) because of their constitutional and ideological commitment to foreign investors. They do not have a livelihood focus, nor a focus on ecological sustainability. Small farmers in PNG now contribute a large share of oil palm fruit production, but they gain a very small share of the value from the industry. Successive reviews of the price-fixing/payout ratio have failed to significantly improve this.

These reviews have built in assumptions which favour the mills and undervalue the contributions of both customary land and the labour of the landowners.

Average family cash returns on VOP oil palm blocks remain half or less the average returns of roadside sellers, and others in the informal sector. For those on LSS blocks the returns are worse. Further, and due to the price–fixing power of the mill, a cash income 'ceiling' seems to apply to even the most hard working and productive of oil palm farmers. Even if they gain above average incomes, there is no evidence that they can reach incomes approaching those farmers engaged in very high income hybrid livelihoods, for example incorporating peanuts, buai, melon, cocoa, coconut and other more flexible crops.

The 'Mama Lus Frut' scheme, hailed as an important gender equity initiative, in fact provides one of the lowest income options in rural PNG, for some quite difficult work. Collecting spilt fruit is literally picking up the crumbs of a very lucrative industry. There is no real evidence to support the claims that the program has improved rural gender relations; and the advocates of this line have not seriously considered the informal sector alternatives for women.

Those families concerned about the problems they face with oil palm should seek out some independent advice on their alternatives, and ways they might phase out their commitment to this monoculture.

Village
cooperation

ও৩

The problems small farmers face in PNG's oil palm industry are not only to do with the monopoly power of the companies, nor the damaging character of that chemical-dependent monoculture; though these are serious enough. There is also the dilemma of how to productively engage or cooperate on wider basis, in a Papua New Guinean way in the post–colonial context, and beyond the traditional extended family. How can they build new options from a customary base? This is a question that has arisen in all the other plantation and agro-industries in rural PNG. Wider cooperation, of course, opens up new opportunities; yet the terms of engagement are critical.

Introduced and neo-colonial organisational models clash, not just with traditional values, but with the better traditional values. Yet is has proven difficult to disentangle the competing systems. Much of this is due to the incomplete decolonisation of agricultural relations. Land use systems from the colonial era persist. For example, through developments such as 'agro-nucleus' estates and semi-privatised plantations, agri-business in PNG has juxtaposed distinct conceptions of land (commodified, rather than inalienable), of management (hierarchical instead of collaborative), of production and benefit sharing (exclusionary and for private accumulation, rather than inclusionary for clan and family sharing). It is perhaps not surprising that such clashes of values have undermined many of PNG's larger agricultural ventures. There has been conflict and collapse in coffee and coconut plantations. Oil palm developments face resentment and resistance. So where then are the better future options for PNG's small farmers?

This chapter briefly considers the uneasy post-colonial legacy in PNG's plantations, along with some of the more promising village-level initiatives, before moving to a detailed case study of village cooperation. The Sausi community in Madang province, mostly without external support, has constructed wider forms of village cooperation which, it seems to me, deserve attention.

PNG AGRI-BUSINESS AND LOCAL INITIATIVES

Due to the character of PNG's independence process there was no sudden rupture with the colonial plantation systems, but rather a gradual attempt at 'nationalisation' and some redistribution of alienated lands. Historically, colonial PNG had been forced into commodity production through a process driven by Australian, British and German capital. This process included forced, semi-forced and often unpaid labour, and virtually no compensation for appropriated land (Gregory 1979). Yet, after independence, attempts to restore and extend PNG systems, or to effectively engage them with the plantation systems, have been slow and weak. Indeed, there has been a resurgence of similar systems through the neoliberal notion of 'agro-nucleus' estates for oil palm. Modernist ideas have assisted this neo-colonialism, by asserting an 'evolution' away from traditional systems and into an inevitable commercial and privatised logic.

This liberal modernism, which argued benefits for all, drew 'smallholder' families into the new schemes. Coffee, which spread through the Highlands and Morobe in the colonial 1950s and 1960s, was a crop that was easy to grow and transport, but subject to volatile prices. By the mid 1970s there were an estimated 50 million trees in PNG (Townsend 1977: 419). Copra and cocoa plantations drew in tenant farmers; and, after independence, oil palm estates took over alienated lands. Yet the semi-privatised experiments in highlands coffee plantations faced great internal problems, both in the boom times and in the late 1980s, when producer prices crashed (Connolly 2005: 19, 77). These problems had much to do with community rejection of private accumulation (whether by estate companies or by plantation 'big men') and its inability to contemplate wider benefit sharing. Profiting from community land, yet not sharing those profits with the community, is usually seen as an anti-social act, in PNG culture.

A few years after independence there were reviews of the attempts to return copra, coca and coffee plantation lands to nationals and to increase nationals as managers in plantations. This was a process at times called the 'decolonisation' of the plantations. Yet the deficiencies in including Melanesians as managers were fairly stark (Ndawala–Kajumba 1981; Mel 1981). The plantations generally did not present distinct PNG features. To the contrary, across the Melanesian countries, promises were being made to families about the great benefits of engaging with the entirely foreign structure of a giant oil palm company. Here the large company with a central plantation estate called on a periphery of small farmers to provide it with leased land and additional fruit, at prices fixed by the corporate estate. The contribution of PNG culture to this process was limited to cooperative production within families, on family land.

The opportunity costs of going down this road could be quite stark. In the Morovo Lagoon area of the Solomon Islands, Greenpeace demonstrated in the late 1990s that industrial logging and oil palm would displace more than three times its value in small scale productive activity such as fishing, local markets, eco-tourism, paper making, local crafts. Some of these activities included the adaptation of outside technologies (such as mobile saw mills for eco-forestry, and international eco–tourist marketing) into more traditional businesses (LaFranchi and Greenpeace 1999; Oliver and Greenpeace 2001). Nevertheless, the loggers descended and oil palm projects came in behind. Some years later, these same communities were complaining bitterly about environmental damage and broken promises over the supposed benefits of oil palm (Albert, Olivier and Fairley 2010).

This is a pattern from which it is difficult to break because, while new cooperative initiatives are popular and widespread, government policy has mostly followed the 'old economics' approach of pushing large formal sector projects and privileging 'export driven development'. This conditions the support given to such initiatives (Ingipa 2012). The result is that most smallholder credit and technical assistance goes into the export crops such as oil palm, coffee, cocoa and coconut.

Nevertheless, women's groups have gained some support for their cooperatives in vegetable marketing, taro markets, coconut oil processing, piggeries and poultry, crafts and floriculture (Malum Nalu 2010; Nari Nius 2011: 8). The latter, cultivation of flowers (orchids, potted plants and cut flowers) sells into local markets and tourist hotels as well as providing for export markets. And some government support for small fishing cooperatives has been an exception to the 'export driven' norm (NFA 2012). More recently the country's major agricultural support agencies (NARI, CCI, CIC, OPRA, OPIC and the FPDC) formed a new 'think tank' to develop new 'agriculture for development' ideas (Nari Nius 2011: 1–2). However five of those six agencies (i.e. all except the Fresh Produce Development Authority) are constituted to support export crops, so they will find a change in paradigm difficult.

Nevertheless, there are constant initiatives amongst farming families to build on their traditional base. A number of these were seen during the 2011 roadside seller surveys (see Chapter Five). Some were simple extensions of a family business, such as the man in Gabensis village (Morobe) whose family had two cocoa fermentaries, and bought additional cocoa bean from other small growers, then onsold it to a local company (Amos 2011).

It is perhaps not surprising that women have started many of the fresh produce cooperatives, because women already dominate vegetable growing and marketing. We heard of two such women's cooperatives in Morobe. They were looking for new markets for surplus production. These co-ops (Wansep and Omsis) have members which work together to ship their produce (fruit, coconut, vegetables and orchids) from

Lae through to the capital, Port Moresby. They coordinate and share in the hire of shipping containers. Some sales have been made to Fiji and Australia (Nawasio 2011). Further up the highway in the Eastern Highlands, a smaller group of women also jointly market vegetables to Port Moresby. They pay the costs of bus transport from Goroka to Lae, as well as container hire from Lae to the capital. At Port Moresby they pay porters and make use of relatives (aunties and cousins) to take their produce (carrots, cauliflower and sweet potatoes) to Gordon's market. There is risk and sometimes spoilage, but they factor this into the operation. They do not consider what they are doing a 'cooperative', but simply a form of working together (Atizo 2011). Probably the word 'co-operative' has some other meaning, as there has been government 'seed money' for such organisations; but typically that money just disappeared and the 'co-operative' never materialised (Aipapu 2009).

Another marketing initiative in Morobe, this time with NGO support, seems to have failed in its wider aims; but the technology was picked up and used by a number of families. A fish breeding project, backed by an aid agency (Bris Kanda) and drawing on some college training from Unitech, joined a number of Morobe families in fish breeding production and marketing. These are fresh water fish raised in ponds. The aim was to raise and sell 'fingerlings' (baby fish) to other communities across the province. However, due to management conflicts, the collaboration broke down and just one family proceeded with the sale of fingerlings. The other families maintain their fish farming for consumption and the retail market (Nawasio 2011). These fish farms are a relatively recent addition to small farming, and can be seen dotted across the highlands, Morobe and Madang.

Cross investment, in the various elements of hybrid livelihoods, can be seen amongst roadside sellers with local market sites. This included investment in small scale infrastructure. In Morobe's Goraku market, for example, the local sellers had constructed six pit toilets (four for women and two for men), for the customers and sellers, as well as shade for the stalls. At Yalu, revenue from the roadside sales (peanut, kulau and banana), combined with sales of chicken and cocoa, had been used to invest in forty (40) cocoa fermentaries. One family in this group was selling between 11 and 13 bags per month, at a current rate of K360 per bag (Sindana 2011). That amounts to more than 50,000 Kina per year, many times more than the highest oil palm farmer's family income. Notable here is that the start-up capital for cocoa processing was largely drawn from sales in local markets.

These same cocoa farming families also shared organic technologies on pest control and plant nutrition, to avoid costly and toxic chemicals. While the CCI (Cocoa Coconut Institute) had encouraged the use of weedicide and fertiliser in cocoa cultivation, and some had complied, others avoided it. Instead, they used some nitrogen fixing trees (*Gliricidia*), birds-eye chilli as insecticide, along with goat and fish waste as fertiliser. Chemicals were much more frequently used in oil palm, and sometimes in coffee (Sindana 2011).

Commerce in local markets across the provinces has been innovative. One particularly interesting collaborative development was in the lucrative buai (betel nut) trade, where typically highlanders buy buai and daka (mustard) wholesale from the coast, then ship it up to the highland provinces. The buai trader buses are a regular feature of highway life. Almost at the extreme ends of this trade, one clan in the East Sepik had been selling to Western Highlanders, by shipping buai (along with cocoa) by boat south to Bogia (in Madang province) and there by bus down to Madang and then up to the Highlands. What was distinct here was that the deals were done by mobile phone and the money wired, in advance, to the Sepik clan chief's bank account. A single transaction could be K30,000. The chief would then distribute the money amongst the clan including, at times, contributions to the local school and some community projects (Kayonga 2011).

Formal co-operatives are better entrenched in East New Britain (ENB), where they have grown from their export crop origins (in cocoa and coconut) into wider aims. The dozens of co–ops in ENB have extended into fresh food and finance. Many now have mixed social and commercial aims, apparently with some coordination by the churches. Cooperative and individual bank accounts have been used to finance school fees and church projects (Varagat 2011). The East New Britain Women and Youth in Agriculture Cooperative Association (ENBWYIACA) has attracted attention and some support, in recent years. In 2011 there were 25 registered cooperative societies in ENB, 13 of which were affiliated with the ENBWYIACA. They shared a focus on the range of local and export market produce, of importance to women

(NARI 2011: 8). Oil palm was not part of those activities, although that monoculture is more recently making some inroads into ENB.

Clan collaboration in commerce can be seen in ENB. The inland Baining people are now the dominant force in peanut wholesaling around Kokopo and Rabaul (Tongne 2011). They cultivate and sell on a substantial scale, but are rarely seen in retail markets. The retail business is carried out by women from the 'internal immigrant' families (from the Sepik or Bougainville, for example) who have less land and who originally came to ENB to work in the plantations. They buy large bunches and bags from the Bainings.

Many western writers share the modernist and 'evolutionary' assumption that small scale initiatives based on traditional systems cannot move much beyond that small scale, or cannot work in a wider context. For example, using 'game theory' and self-interest modelling Dwyer and Minnegal (1997) show that sharing by sago producers in Gwaimasi (in PNG's Western Province) has its limits. They demonstrate that clan sharing with others ('reciprocal altruism') may only persist if the eventual possibility of reciprocity (by the 'free riders') exists. I would have thought that this was fairly obvious, and that the more interesting element here is that this 'reciprocity' so easily breaks the temporal limits of conventional commerce.

We have seen a few examples of medium scale business developed through various forms of village cooperation. Let's now have a look at one community in Madang, which has developed its own forms of cooperation, including village co-finance.

SAUSI 'STARTS A FIRE'

The Sausi initiatives began as a reaction to planned expansion of oil palm onto their lands, but then turned into a creative phase. One of the participants said that Sausi had 'started a fire' (Letu 2009), with its firm resistance to oil palm and the decision to take another development path. This was a process referred to by another Madang man (paraphrasing an old expression) as 'building their own road by walking it' (Paol 2009). It is useful to look at this process in two parts: the initial campaign to block oil palm expanding onto their land, and the rise of their own development organisation: the Sausi Poverty Reduction and Alleviation Group (SPRAG). This account draws on my own interviews, between

2003 and 2009, and several reports prepared by Yat Paol, a member of the Madang–based Bismarck Ramu Group (BRG). Both Yat and the BRG have supported the Sausi community in their self-determination efforts since 1998.

Sausi is an area comprising Ward 11 of the Usino Local Level Government (LLG) area. It has organised itself into three zones, each of which has its own planning committee; yet the three zones come together into a combined committee for a number of key issues (Paol 2009). The whole Ward area has 14 or 15 clans (extended families), each clan has 10 to 20 families and total individuals in 2009 were about 1,200 (Marai 2009). The chief representative of Sausi has been Mr Aipapu Marai, who also became Chairman of the Ramu Valley Landowners Association (RVLOA), a group formed to defend customary land from a threatened corporate takeover. Aipapu also holds positions of responsibility in the Evangelical Brotherhood Church, the Sausi Primary School and has represented the Ward in local government since the mid 1990s. He and his wife Bima have five children.

The RVLOA represents the traditional landowners of a much wider area than Sausi, in fact several Ward areas about the size of Sausi, along the upper part of the Ramu River Valley (the 'Apa Ramu'). This takes in the areas of Sausi, Koropa, Yakumbu, Usiama, Boko, Urigina, Danaru, Usino, Sepu and Garaligut. So when talking about Apa Ramu resistance to oil palm, we are speaking of this larger group; when speaking of the Sausi initiatives, reference is to that smaller community of 14 or 15 clans.

In 1999 the Apa Ramu people were taken by surprise to discover that soil surveys and other assessments for oil palm development had been carried out on their land. Apparently this idea formed part of the Madang regional government's five year development plan. Along with a large nickel mine, tourist development in Madang town, upgrading of the wharf, roads and airport, and industrial development in Walium/Usino and Saidor, there were plans for a 35,000 hectare expansion of oil palm into the upper Ramu valley, just downstream from the large Ramu Sugar estate (alienated land which had been used as a sugar plantation). In June 2000 an agreement was signed, in Indonesia, between the PNG government and the Commonwealth Development Corporation (at that time the major shareholder in the Ramu Sugar estate) for this proposed oil palm project. Ramu Sugar Ltd was 'diversifying' into oil palm, and the Madang regional government had a 20% share in Ramu Sugar (Paol 2003; Paol 2004). The scale of this project (35,000 hectares plus the Ramu Sugar lands) could have created the largest oil palm area in PNG. Yet no–one had told the local landowners and, when they heard, they were both afraid and angry.

Aipapu explains the background:

> 'One white man from Australia [called John] who worked with the company ... saw one of [our] old men and told him 'Ramu Sugar will change into oil palm and they will get your land and plant oil palm from the edge of the hills through the whole of the Ramu valley. You will be pushed up the hills to live, you won't live on the valley anymore'.' (Marai 2009)

The old man didn't know whether to believe this, so he made some more enquiries. When the story seemed true, the old man sought out Aipapu and delegated him to lead on the oil palm issue. They organised a meeting at Kokopine village. 'How would we stop the oil palm? ... I got organized with the other nine ward councillors in Usino LLG and we formed an Association called the Ramu Valley Landowners Association (RVLOA).' After that the BRG got in touch with them and said they were a group who worked with landowners who opposed big corporate projects: 'So I was happy and got them to help us in our fight against the oil palm' (Marai 2009).

In August 2001 the RVLOA organised a meeting with the Madang provincial administration to discuss the oil palm plans. The meeting tuned 'sour'. Yet only one of the Upper Ramu landowners (FM, and a small group of his followers) was pro-oil palm (Paol 2004). In October the local media reported Minister Andrew Kumbakor saying that oil palm was 'the success story of PNG' (Paol 2004). Not only was there a difference between the government and the land owners, apparently the government felt it could ignore the clear wishes of the legally recognised customary owners of the land on which this development was planned.

This official arrogance towards the landowners, failing to even consult, hardened their position. First they would get rid of any dissent in their ranks, so they could present a united face. As in other areas, the oil palm companies would offer 'soft loans' of up to 10,000 Kina, to help the smallholder farmers get established, by purchasing seedlings and fertiliser. This money would be repaid to the company when the trees bore their first fruit and this was sold to the company. However there were rumours of other big money being thrown around, to divide them. On 9 January 2002 the RVLOA organised a big meeting in Sausi village. The aim was to develop strategies to protect their land. They built allies in the region and made sure their voice was heard by everyone.

When I first visited the Upper Ramu in February 2003 the anti-oil palm campaign was well underway. I met and then accompanied Aipapu on a visit to the district administrator, to present a letter on oil palm. I interviewed landowners outside Sausi, and they said the same: they were firmly against oil palm (Kapior 2003; Yambai 2003). The following month, the RVLOA took out full page advertisements in the Wantok and Post Courier newspapers. In no uncertain terms they declared:

'We the landowners ... wish to make it perfectly clear that
there will be NO OIL PALM project on OUR LAND!!! ...
The proposed oil palm project is an agreement by the National
Government, Provincial Government, Ramu Sugar Company
and overseas investors and DOES NOT INCLUDE THE
LANDOWNERS ... We, the landowners, are developing and will
continue to develop OUR LAND on our terms ... We therefore
sternly warn all those parties involved in wanting to use OUR
LAND for oil palm to STAY OUT! Any attempts to bring oil
palm on our land will be strongly resisted ... YOU HAVE BEEN
WARNED!!!' (Onot et al 2003)

A friend at the time reminded me that, under customary law, the theft of land was the most serious of crimes, attracting the most severe penalties. These warnings would have been taken seriously.

In June of that same year there was an oil palm conference in Kimbe, West New Britain (WNB). This was the site of the biggest oil palm development in PNG. The BRG suggested the RVLOA send some representatives to Kimbe, to see how other communities had been affected by the WNB oil palm industry. The Upper Ramu people were reluctant. They did not need any convincing that oil palm was a bad idea. They had lived down the road from the Ramu Sugar estate for many years, and saw few benefits and many problems from that. And many of their own people had travelled to work in the oil palm areas of West

New Britain and the Popondetta plains, and they had returned to say they did not want to see that on their land (Paol 2012). In the end, the RVLOA was encouraged to send two representatives (Beny Kapior and his sister Aikum Kapior) so that the other groups could see how the Upper Ramu resistance was being organised. Yat observed that these two, with limited education and limited English, came across as more confident and clear than many of the better educated landowners from other areas (Paol 2012).

With strong leadership and a united front, the RVLOA were staring down the government–corporate plans. In the next stage, they would announce their alternative 'model'. That is, they would not just oppose 'development' and do nothing; they would make it clear that they were 'developing' their land in a distinct way. This was best summed up in a Tok Pisin letter they set to government and then made available to the media. Headed 'Ol Papa Graun Bilong Upper Ramu (Koroba–Sepu) Ino Laikim Oil Palm Projek' [Upper Ramu landowners reject oil palm project]. The letter made some key points: (i) we are the landowners here, not you, the government (Mipela I papa bilong graun na ino yupela, gavman); (ii) this land, the bush, the water and everything in it is our life and that of our children; (iii) if this oil palm project came through, it would destroy life for us and our children, damaging the land, bringing in settlers and many social problems; (iv) we have our own development plan for our land. This plan involved the planting of cocoa trees, with help from some NGOs, and planting rice, vanilla, peanut, buai, daka, fruit and garden food (vegetables) for sale in the markets by the women (RVLOA 2004). The letter attracted wider attention, and Beny and others went on several radio stations (Radio Madang, Radio Australia, Yumi FM) to explain further (Paol 2004). The oil palm project for the Upper Ramu was halted. The re–badged Ramu Agri–Industries spread the crop on their on estate, and expanded slightly into customary land on the Morobe side, in the Markham valley.

What was different in the Upper Ramu was that the resistance was driven by landowners, with just some regional support. A government plan was forced to a halt by a strong public campaign, and the legitimacy of the landowners' position.

While the entire Upper Ramu area took up the 'alternative development plan' proposed by the RVLOA, pushing into cocoa and diverse crops for local markets, Sausi's plans were the most innovative, and built on a steady investment in cocoa and other crops. Not losing sight of the resistance to oil palm, Aipapu said:

'How are we going to stop Oil Palm? This land has to be planted with something else to show to the Government and the company that we have the plan for our land use ... so we formed a group to plant cocoa. The people agreed for each family to plant 1000–2000 cocoa trees. Now there are eight or nine cocoa driers in the community ... we plant rice, we have fish ponds ... eight fish ponds in the community ... 1000–2000 fish in each pond ready to be sold or for protein ... There are other things for cash income. We also have peanuts ... We plant water melon and betelnut to are sold ... we landowners sell cash crops and have control over our land.' (Marai 2009).

The cocoa trees were sources of cash income, but also 'signals' in the bush that the land was under landowner control. Sausi's fish ponds and rice fields were initially aimed at home consumption, but there were some commercial possibilities down the track. Maintaining control of clan land allows for this. The small farming projects intensified, and the revenue from peanut, melon and cocoa allowed Sausi leaders to contemplate wider investments, in their own community.

In 2008 the Sausi committee created a new group (effectively in place of a Ward Development Committee) which clearly borrowed some of the language of international finance agencies. The 'Sausi Poverty Reduction and Alleviation Group' (SPRAG) set up a series of programs which seem quite unique, and certainly 'home grown' (Letu 2009). While it handles large sums of money, the group is not incorporated, nor does it see any need to incorporate (Paol 2009). The group co–finances family and clan businesses, offers scholarships and supports community projects. In 2009 the Chairman was Charles Kupi and the Treasurer Nauns Letu, a pastor in the Kokopine Assembly of God Church. Nauns' family has three cocoa fermentaries and they have ambitious plans for up to 100 hectares of cocoa trees (Letu 2009). Aipapu said this of SPRAG:

'It all about people helping each other. We have organized for individuals in the community to contribute finance to projects in the community. We can give money to someone in the community to start a project in the community. This money belongs to him and he need not repay it to the group. He can look after his family and enjoy life ... [the group] will also minimize problems in the village. This money does not come from the member (local MPs) but from individuals in the community' (Marai 2009).

The initial projects funded were about consolidating the development strategy, such as community support for family cocoa fermentaries. The SPRAG put K2,000 Kina into the Tamamat clan fermentary, and K1,900 (of a total cost of 3,000) into the Wenex clan fermentary. The typical pattern is for the group to add to the clan investment. As Aipapu said, there are no loans, and no repayment demands. There are, however, expectations of reciprocity, either direct or indirect. For example, the SPRAG contributed K1,300 towards the Bomonot clan rice mill (a total cost of about 6,000), and contributing clans can expect to use the services of that mill for their rice, at a discount rate. The discount seems to be 2/3 the commercial price, or less (Sindana 2009). The SPRAG put in two amounts of K2,000 to the Masigrub clan, one for kaukau (sweet potato) seedlings, and the other for knapsacks and herbicide for their cocoa trees. In these cases there is no service that arises from their crops, but that clan is expected to contribute to the next round of funding (Letu 2009). The beneficiary clan has to provide a report, to show how well the money has been spent. However if they failed in this, the only sanction would be that a group might be excluded from future programs, and could be publicly criticised: 'you won't get our help again!' (Marai 2009).

The group has also put some money into its own functions (K1,900 to the Ward Development Committee) and was planning (in late 2009) to put K3,000 into the construction of two community water supplies (Letu 2009; Marai 2009). There is no SPRAG bank account, so far, and the money is generally contributed and then handed over, in cash, in open meetings. This re-investment in the community is in some respects a reaction to the idea they maintain of oil palm: that the benefits go to the company, and not to the local landowners (Letu 2009).

There is a bit more of a story behind transport, which is a big issue in rural PNG. Much of Sausi's money comes from markets, some in Sausi, but some also at the Ramu Sugar markets (half an hour up the road) and the Madang markets (three hours down the road), where the cocoa is also sold. There are regular buses (PMVs) along this main road (which runs from the Highlands to Madang) but, of course, they all charge money. Aipapu's wife, Bima Aipapu, explains that she and Aipapu had a succession of cars in the 1980s and 1990s, but then in 1997 the idea of a shared truck arose. One of the Sausi families bought the truck with finance from many (but not all) of the Sausi clans, two trucks were bought and sold until they purchased the current (as at 2009) truck in 1999. This is called 'Musurufana', which means 'Tuwat bilong meri' (in Tok Pisin), or 'women's sweat'. It is recognised that the money for the truck comes from women's work in the gardens and sales (especially peanuts and melons) at market. Bima explains:

> 'The mothers have worked so hard in the garden to produce enough to rush their food crops to the market. The Sausi mothers now spend most of their time to sell their garden produce at the market.

> This Musurufana, it helps us especially mothers and also the social activities too and helps transport the school materials and the building materials. Supports the Church groups as well. On the health aspects as well, when people are sick the truck provides the support by taking them to the Health Centre. When someone dies, the truck takes the body back home.' (Bima Aipapu 2009).

Apart from the social functions for which the truck has been used, there are reciprocal benefits for Sausi members. They seem to pay about 2/3 the fare of the local buses (Sindana 2009). At the time of these interviews the truck was eleven years old and had stopped making the longer trips to Madang. The family that owns and runs the Musurufana is saving for a new one, a six tonne in place of the three tonne truck, but the cost will be K120,000 (Sindana 2009). The Sausi group will make a contribution to this new vehicle, to continue this element of village cooperation.

There are some other SPRAG projects, including a guest house (making use of a ward level work group); but the most impressive is the tertiary scholarship program. Sausi families, like all families in PNG, face very high secondary school fees. As mentioned in Chapter Five, children's school fees are often cited as a principal reason for women going to sell produce at market. Primary school fees (at perhaps 250 Kina per year) are affordable, but secondary school fees start at 1,000 and can go up to several thousand Kina per child per year. The SPRAG has not tried to address this problem collectively, but has started scholarships for students who wish to go to Teachers College or University. This shows the commitment of the community to education for their children. At the time of my interviews there had been two graduations, and Aipapu's oldest son Jop was about to graduate from Madang Teachers College. That one scholarship cost K8,050, or K4,025 for each of his two years at college. The scholarships are rotated between each of the three zones of Sausi, one for each zone. However the supply has not yet met the demand.

The persistent failures of agri-business in PNG have been no accident. Neo-colonial plantation systems clash with traditional community values and are often seen as highly anti-social. Nor have outside models of cooperation fared that well. This begs the question: how can communities build on their existing strengths and develop new opportunities? PNG farmers are hardly standing still, there seems to be a range of initiatives, around the country, of cooperation, particularly in marketing. Yet with most government policy, extension services and finance going into export crops, much of that privileging corporate developments such as oil palm, there are few genuinely national models of how to build indigenous systems of cooperation. The Sausi community shows some important elements: keeping control of clans lands, developing diverse crops for home and local markets, supplementing these with more flexible export crops and then building systems of village co-finance. Encouraged by their successful resistance to oil palm expansion, Sausi has driven some surprising initiatives with very little outside support. What seems most important is that they are building a community focussed economy, with integrity, with their own resources and on their own cultural foundations. This may give their 'poverty reduction' approach firmer roots.

Customary Land:
reconciliation or resistance?

ℰℐ

As this book should have made clear by now, most of the better livelihood options for PNG's rural land owning families lie in maintaining control of their own land, developing 'hybrid livelihoods' which best suit their needs and looking for new possibilities in local level cooperation and marketing. None of the formal sector, corporate developments offer superior returns to landowner families. In the case of oil palm, families face much higher environmental costs for generally lower economic returns.

The rental of rural land seems the worst option of all. First, rural rents have no relation whatsoever to the productive value of land (see Table 8.1 below); second, there seems little prospect of this improving (see discussion below on the 'social relations of land'); and third, most leases in PNG mean dispossession, as compensation provisions for the 'improved value' of land make reclaiming leased ancestral lands all but impossible. In these circumstances, the question arises of 'reconciliation' with or 'resistance' to the constant demands for the dismantling of customary land systems.

'Reconciliation' in this sense means some level of acceptance of the assault on customary land relations, and some form of 'consent' to lease out clan and family land. We might call this the 'soft dispossession' of land. Such a dispossession, by pressured 'consent', could take place through land tenure conversion and sale, or through various types of leases in what has been called a 'middle way' (AusAID 2008: 15). Some of this is done under vague and mostly false promises; some of it is done under desperation, on the part of landowners, for access to cash.

First, some points need to be made about land valuation, in a country where rural land is hardly ever sold. 'Market values' are of no use in rural PNG, only providing a sorry indication of how cheaply some families' heritage has been given away. As Vanuatu Chief Selwyn Garu (2010) points out, it really makes no sense in a customary society to speak of the value of land, in the sense of sale or exchange, because the intergenerational value and ecological and cultural contributions of productive land make its contribution well beyond conventional calculation. However, for the purpose of demonstrating the serious undervaluation of land in the currently proposed schemes, it is worth referring to a short–term 'productive value of land'. This means: what value in basic products, such as food and cash income, can one unit of land (say one hectare) produce in a year? Through such calculations we can also gain some idea of an 'opportunity cost' valuation: that is, what would be lost, in a short–term economic sense, if that land were to be alienated (Anderson 2006 and 2006b)? Such calculations can give us an idea of the immediate costs of 'soft dispossession'.

Table 8.1 below shows rental returns on two lots of clan land that were fairly recently leased by incorporated land groups to Higaturu Oil Palm, in Oro Province (see further discussion on these leases in Section One below). Compare this rent to the other productive returns, per year, on the same one hectare of land.

Table 8.1 Returns on one hectare of rural land in PNG	
	Kina per year
Rental income (oil palm estate) with royalties (Oro) (i)	100
Subsistence production equivalent est. (2005) (i)	13,400
Subsistence production equivalent est. (2011) (ii)	10,700–18,900
+Lower local market income (2005) (iii)	1,000–3,000
+Higher local market incomes (2005–2011) (ii)	10,000–25,000
Oil palm company returns (net present value) (2009) (iv)	9,275
Small holder return on oil palm (VOP) (2010) (iv)	2,793
Sources: (i) Gou and Higaturu 1999, King 2001, Higaturu 2003; (ii) Anderson 2011; (iii) Anderson 2008; (iv) ITS Global 2011: 33–34	

If we add the subsistence value to the market income, it is plain that the rental returns in Oro are a very long way from compensating the land owners for foregoing other quite normal options. Through conventional activities, Table 8.1 shows that landowners could receive between 10 and 400 times more income and income equivalent from retaining and making use of their own land. Even through extremely limited activity, say by planting a few coconut trees, or a few betel nut plants, landowners would receive far more than 100 Kina per year.

These figures might help explain why most rural families resist land rental. However, to understand the pressures a little more, including why some families agree to such leases, we need to look a little deeper. This chapter begins by explaining the more recent ideas that suggest 'reconciliation' with pressures on customary land. Next, the obvious 'market failure' in rural land and the 'social relations of land' deserve attention. Finally, I discuss some different forms of 'resistance' (legal challenges, community organisation and farm management training) to the attempts to dismantle customary land tenure systems.

RECONCILIATION: 'SOFT DISPOSSESSION' AND LEASES

The leading exponent of neoliberal and neo-colonial ideas on land has been, perhaps unsurprisingly, the World Bank. As I explained in Chapter Six, the Bank is best understood as a lobby for private foreign investors. The basis for this is explained clearly in Article One of the Bank's constitution, maintained by the interests of its principal directors and sustained by its neoliberal ideology. Yet that ideology no longer presents a crude advocacy of land privatisation. Rather, some 'new economics' ideas (e.g. the rights of the poor and human development) are cleverly grafted onto the 'old economics' base, with a key reference point being national economic growth. The World Bank recognises that land regimes differ widely between countries, not least because of their different colonial histories. Nevertheless, in looking at these 'reconciliatory' views of customary land, we can identify the key modernist themes introduced back in Chapter Two. In both the World Bank literature and that of AusAID (the principal foreign aid agency on land in the Pacific) there has been relentless pressure to undermine customary land systems yet, in more recent times, a 'softer' language which claims to act in the interests of customary landowners. It makes sense to first look at the World Bank's global view of land, then at that of AusAID, in the regional context.

The principal theorist on land for the Bank in recent years has been Klaus Deininger. He prepared a major review of Bank policies in 2003, titled 'Land policies for growth and poverty reduction' (Deininger 2003). This report presented itself as the most substantial revision of land policy since the Bank's 'Land Reform Policy Paper' (World Bank 1975). The new emphasis was linking 'the empowerment of the poor' to new land administration regimes (Deininger 2003: 185). While it was recognised that land issues were 'highly country specific' (Deininger 2003: 189), and that some more flexibility in modernisation and formalisation was necessary, the report pressed standard modernist principles of registration and markets in land. Greater 'security of tenure' through formal systems and removing 'restrictions' on 'the functioning of markets' as well as 'transferability' were key themes (Deininger 2003: 76, 131). One revised theme was greater emphasis on rental markets. This has relevance to Melanesia, where pressure for 'tenure conversion' has shifted into 'opening up' new forms of leaseholdings. The report said that 'overemphasis on sales markets compared with rental markets is unwarranted' (Deininger 2003: 129, 187). Here we see a finessing of the distinction between ownership and control.

In a 2010 paper for the Bank, Deininger and surveyor Stig Enemark, further asserted the need for land modernisation and registration as an essential foundation for the Millennium Development Goals (MDGs). In a narrow reading of the MDGs, the eighth goal of 'global partnerships' (which includes the role of large corporations) is said to define 'the means' to achieve all the other goals (Deininger and Enemark 2010: xiii). From this, the role of land administrators is said to be 'central and vital', to the point that 'no development will happen without the footprint of the land professionals' (Deininger and Enemark 2010: xiii). While they concede, at times, that land systems vary, are specific to particular contexts and are 'basically political' (Deininger and Enemark 2010: xvii, xxvi); their approach remains modernist and hostile to traditional systems. Commercialising land to private or outside interests necessarily undermines a basic ethos of customary land systems, which is community sharing.

Indeed, in the course of re-stating some supposedly universal principles, Deininger and Enemark express a clear preference for the more highly commodified Australian (Torrens) and German land tenure systems, over the French and Latin European systems. The core assumptions are quite anti-pluralist:

> 'traditional cadastral systems cannot adequately provide security
> of tenure to the vast majority of the world's low income groups
> ... the land management paradigm makes a national cadastre [a
> centrally registered survey of lands] the engine of the entire land
> administration system, underpinning the country's capacity to deliver
> sustainable development' (Deininger and Enemark 2010: xvi–xx).

Notice that there is only one 'land management paradigm'. They rely on the modernist principles developed in colonial East Africa (see Chapter Two), but under the more contemporary heading of 'good land governance'. As in the 1950s, this means 'secure land tenure', combined with 'transfer of land at low cost through rentals and sales', use of land title as 'collateral' for bank loans, thus expanding credit (Deininger and Enemark 2010: xiv). Using this 'good land governance' to strengthen women's land rights' is thrown in at the end, for good measure, without any real explanation (Deininger and Enemark 2010: xiv). The weak basis for such assertions was discussed in Chapter Two.

In practice, the World Bank has moved rapidly into the worst 'land governance' of all: land grabbing, or the alienation of vast tracts of land to powerful interests. 'Land grabs' are an accelerated move by large corporations – particularly after the twin food and financial crises of 2008 – into land acquisitions in developing countries. The World Bank was at first slow to respond, then issued a report in 2010 which was described as 'both a disappointment and failure' (GRAIN 2010), as it downplayed the problem and said there was no cause for alarm. For all the 'risks' and 'dangers' there were said to be 'equally large opportunities'. The 'loss of livelihoods', 'displacement of local people from their land' and 'land being given away well below its potential value' were all recognised problems of the 'land grabs'; but they could be addressed through the Bank's previously stated principles of 'good governance' in land management (Deininger et al 2011: xlii).

The root of this apparent ambivalence lies in the tension between the World Bank's self–proclaimed role as advocate for the poor and broader development goals, and its clear constitutional role as a lobby for private foreign investors. It did not take long for analysts to discover that the World Bank was indeed supporting some of the 'land grab' investors. The International Finance Corporation (IFC), the Bank's private sector arm, had financed large acquisitions in several African and Latin American countries. One critical paper pointed out that the IFC, through its corporate subsidies, had put at risk the access to land and food security of many poor people in some of Africa's poorest countries: Liberia, Sierra Leone and Ethiopia (Daniel 2011: 1–19). Similarly, a ViaCampesina letter complained of a series of IFC interventions in South America. Large investor groups were backed by multi–million dollar loans to acquire vast tracts of land in Argentina and Paraguay (ViaCampesina 2011).

This 'land grabbing' spread to PNG, through the institution of Special Purpose Agricultural Business Leases (SPABLs). These make use of the 'lease-lease-back' mechanism under PNG law. One report calculated that 4.2 million hectares had been leased to private companies between 2003 and 2010 (Filer 2011: 2); another put the figure at 5.2 million hectares (Nalu 2011). In many cases the customary owners were not even aware that leases had been taken out on their land. An NRI report said the state had failed to administer these leases 'in a transparent and accountable manner' (Moore 2011: 10). At the time of writing in 2012, a new government led by Peter O'Neill claimed it had put a stop to these SPABLs.

As the principal foreign funder of land programs in Melanesia, AusAID has also had an important role in shaping what it likes to see as a 'consensus' on land reform, which includes central registration and commercialisation. The AusAID 'White Paper' of 2006, under a conservative government, showed a slight change in tone. Recall that land agendas driven by the World Bank in the late 1990s and early 2000s had met with fierce resistance; while Canberra's 2004 plans for land registration in The Solomon Islands was also resisted. In a tactical shift, AusAID's White Paper said:

> 'The issue of land tenure in the Pacific, although controversial, cannot be avoided if sustained growth is to be achieved. However, any changes will have to come from within the Pacific, and such changes will take considerable time' (AusAID 2006: 37).

This was a pre-cursor to the well-funded but modest-in-aims 'Pacific Land Program', implemented by the succeeding Labor government. The White Paper spoke of a 'Pacific Land Mobilisation Program' to explore ways to overcome 'the major tenure constraints to growth in the region'; of a 'Pacific Leadership Program' and of 'building demand for better governance', including of course governance in land administration (AusAID 2006: xii).

In early 2008, very soon after a Labor government assumed office in Canberra, AusAID released a document called 'Making Land Work' (AusAID 2008). Most likely prepared under the previous administration, this document was disavowed as a statement of government policy (it contained some AusAID chapters along with a number of 'case studies'), but was nevertheless referred to as presenting the broad ideas on which the $54 million 'Pacific Land Program' was based. The fund was to support AusAID designed land programs in Vanuatu, Papua New Guinea, the Solomon Islands and East Timor (McMullen 2008). The AusAID authored chapters of the volume spoke of a 'middle way' between the 'extremes' of 'maintaining existing [customary] institutions' and 'privatization: removing customary institutions'. Under this 'middle way', customary institutions would remain but would be 'linked' to formal economic and legal systems, 'allowing leases or other agreements for customary land to be used by individuals, organisations or corporations' (AusAID 2008: 15). This approach would 'protect customary rights, but also promote 'economic and social development' and help resolve disputes (McMullen 2008). All of this would be carried out by Pacific peoples themselves, it was claimed. AusAID seemed prepared for 'long timeframes' (AusAID 2008: 107). Nevertheless, this program was suspended in 2011, according to Foreign Minister Kevin Rudd because it 'didn't cut the mustard' (Rudd 2011); that is, it was not showing results. (Herein lies a dilemma for the AusAID administrators: having recognised the need for 'long time frames', they still face the dictates of all 'project' aid: short term results.)

This suggestion of a 'middle way' appears somewhat less than a frontal attack on customary systems, but is nevertheless an attempt to undermine those same systems. The new emphasis on leaseholds means that nominal customary title would be preserved, but its central ethos would be overthrown by the alienation of land through leases. The lessees would pay a small rent but would not substantially share with the clan, except by offering some low paid employment. Such leases are intended to allow a process of individual accumulation which excludes the community.

To see this 'reconciliatory' process in practice, let's look at both the old and the new leases in Oro Province. These are precisely the types of commercial processes in question; but they show pitiful outcomes for landowners.

In Oro the 'Sangara Crown lands', on which the Higaturu mill and estate and Popondetta township are built, have been under constant dispute since independence. An area of land amounting to more than 14,000 hectares was transferred from 'Natives to the Crown', beginning with deeds in 1910 and 1917 which purported to exchange a large amount of 'unoccupied … good agricultural land' for tobacco, axes, knives and matches (Papua 1917). After independence, and after numerous disputes, there was a 1979 National Lands Commission hearing into 14 different claims from the Sangara Pressure Group. At the final hearing in 1981 the landowners were awarded 200,000 Kina. This money was paid to Mr McKenzie Jovopa on behalf of the landowners on 26 January 1982. The settlement covered several villages (Hohorita, Kakandetta, Ahora, Soputa, Mangi, Waru, Iwore, Koipa, Hamburata, Kanari and Dobuduru villages). The state said it wanted to 'stop once and for all' any further claims (Secretary for Lands and Physical Planning 1995). But there are still land and environmental damage claims, for example from the Kakandetta and Ahora groups (K. Koja 2005).

In 1999, Higaturu acquired 20 year leases on some additional land for the development of mini-estate palm oil plantations. This was an extension of the estate on leased customary land under the lease-lease-back system. All such leases have to go through a formal process of the land being leased to the state for a peppercorn rent (say 10 Kina) then leased back to the company, with the state supposedly playing a protector's role. In practice, the 'terms and conditions' of the lease are a market relationship between a powerful company and a group of asset–rich but cash poor landowners, with no experience of modernist land transactions.

The Gou and Heropa leases show us the agreed and the actual returns to customary landowners. The 1999 Gou lease to Higaturu, for mini-estate oil palm land, involved a 20 year lease on 91 hectares of land, with a set rent of 20 Kina per hectare and royalties at 10% POPA (10% of the farmer gate price) per tonne FFB (subject to review) (Gou and Higaturu 1999). The agreement on 88 hectares of Heropa land went through some negotiations, beginning with a 20 Kina per hectare per year offer, then suggesting three options: either 50 or 100 or 150 Kina per hectare per year, and royalties ranging from 20% to 30% POPA per tonne (Heropa Enterprise 1999). Actual payments on the Heropa agreement up to 2001 suggest that rents were settled at 20 Kina per hectare per year. Higaturu paid the Heropa group 3,400 rent in 1999, 600 Kina in 2000 and 1,160 Kina in 2001 (based on 53 hectares of trees planted up to the end of 2000). An initial payment in 1999 seems to have been part of the agreement. In addition to these paid amounts, the Higaturu manager noted that 'outstanding rental of 120 Kina from 1999 and 2000 is to be paid on 23 March 2001' (King 2001). Documents on royalty payments to Heropa in 2003 show that the group was paid 277.76 Kina royalty on 15.99 tonnes of fruit in March 2003 (17.37 Kina per tonne), and 430.07 Kina on 29.56 tonnes of fruit in April 2003 (14.55 Kina per tonne) (Higaturu 2003). These figures look to be about 10% or 15% of the farm gate price for 2003. The landowners did not get their claimed higher rents and royalties. Summed for one year (at an average of 350 Kina) and divided by 53 planted hectares (the figure from 2000, there may have been more planted by 2003) we come up with an annual royalty estimate of about 80 Kina per hectare. Putting the rent and royalty figures together we come up with a combined land value payment of about 100 Kina. That is the figure used in Table 8.1 above, an amount which bears no relation whatsoever to the short–term value from other productive uses of land.

'MARKET FAILURE' AND THE SOCIAL RELATIONS OF LAND

A rental payment of 100 Kina per hectare per year might seem significant for 'unused' land held by cash poor families; however it is a very small fraction of the potential earning capacity of good agricultural land in PNG. Further, the alienation of this land limits the capacity of the clans to provide for growing populations. If they had held onto their land they could have, with little effort, earned more income in the meantime and would had retained access to the land for future needs. These leases are a great 'success' for the company but a devastating blow to the communities. We should recognise that this type of market has failed. The failure to produce lasting benefits for rural PNG communities has led to great dissatisfaction with existing leases and the various plantation schemes. As Chapter Six showed, this dissastisfaction emerges as complaints of environmental damage to land and surrounding areas (e.g. from logging and mining), complaints over the failure of promised benefits from land development (e.g. promised roads or health centres) and complaints over the unfair sharing of benefits of commercial development (e.g. from plantation cash crops).

In the economic liberal sense, market transactions should benefit all parties and, where this does not happen, 'market failure' is suggested. Without necessary adopting this paradigm, but for the purpose of a liberal explanation, we can consider 'market failure' in PNG's rural land. I suggest this is best understood through the social relations of land. A better appreciation of these relations can help explain why communities might be vulnerable to the poor logic of substituting viable, emerging hybrid livelihoods, based on customary land, for low paid formal sector options. In brief, rural land 'markets' in PNG are highly limited, the customary land owners are asset-rich, cash poor and have very little information on (and are often culturally disinclined to consider) the real opportunity cost value of their land and the range of cash economy options open to them.

Several elements are at work. First, landowners generally lease just some of their land, maintaining enough for houses and gardens. This is not necessarily 'surplus' land, as prime fertile agricultural or forest land is most often targeted by companies. However, at the same time, land that has not been developed for gardens is not necessarily given an exchange value, and the strong custom of sharing assets has generally not contemplated a 'market premium'. That is, a customary approach is probably incined to systematically 'undervalue' land, in the western commercial sense. Second, the lessees are most often a single large company, often backed by the regional and national government. There is no real competition, in the sense of another bidder for the lease, and there is very limited information on the terms of leases, or on alternative options. In addition, false promises over the likely benefits from 'development' are common. Logging and mining companies make promises which often do not materialise. They do not properly advise of environmental and social impacts. Oil palm companies promise inflated income opportunities. Rural families are vulnerable in the face of such misinformation. Thus competition and full information, key ingredients of the liberal theory of 'allocative efficiency' in markets, are missing.

Third, cash poor, asset rich families are vulnerable in exchange, as there are pressures to earn money to pay their children's school fees and health service fees. They are vulnerable to cash offers, and can easily undervalue their assets. In addition, cash crops are valued in exchange terms, but undeveloped or potential cash crops are often not factored into the calculations of customary land owners. Similarly, the subsistence value of land is usually regarded as a given (until it is taken away) rather than an equivalent exchange value, which might have to be compensated. This is particularly the case for customary land owners with little information and limited education. Not only are the customary landowners vulnerable to cash offers and not well educated in matters of exchange value, their own traditions often militate against such exchange calculations. They are inclined to freely share, even with outsiders; but they then expect reciprocal benefits. Such reciprocity is not reflected in the typical western lease.

Finally, there is fraud in the setting up of Incorporated Land Groups (ILGs) and the leasing of customary land. One such case at Collingwood Bay (Oro Province) was overturned by the courts, in 2002 (Tararia and

Ogle 2010). Combinations of these factors, I suggest, have led to a massive undervaluing of customary land in PNG, on the few occasions that there have been transactions. The track record is stark. From colonial times to recent years, there is no evidence that rural landowning families in PNG have ever gained any substantial benefit from leasing their lands.

RESISTANCE: MAINTAINING CONTROL OF CUSTOMARY LAND

Many families and communities have reached similar conclusions, as to the undesirability of leases, and have decided to defend and maintain control of their ancestral lands. However, as this involves opposing large and often unscrupulous corporations, often backed by governments, the methods of resistance require some skill and organisation. In Chapter Seven I described successful resistance by the Sausi community. In this section I want to indicate some themes of resistance: legal campaigns, community organisation and management training.

LEGAL CAMPAIGNS

In the late 1990s two Port Moresby based organisations were set up to assist landowners in their struggles with large companies. The Environmental Law Centre (ELC) has since taken action against logging companies in several provinces. The Centre for Environmental Law and Community Rights (CELCOR) has taken on some similar legal cases, as well as running education and advocacy campaigns. CELCOR has also made use of the internal review processes of the World Bank, in relation to oil palm developments. Court cases are usually long and expensive, but they also have some demonstrative and educative value as 'test cases'. Following are just two examples, court cases against logging companies in Collingwood Bay (Oro Province) and in the Middle Fly River area (Western Province).

The Collingwood Bay case was brought by Maisin landowners against a fake 'incorporated land group', the Keroro Development Corporation (Ltd) and the Malaysian logging company Deegold (PNG, Ltd). The fake ILG had organised a 'special agricultural business lease' for Deegold, under which logging and then oil palm development would be carried out. Most landowners first knew of the deal only when bulldozers and other logging machinery arrived on their beaches. The Environmental Law Centre represented 43 landowners in a case which stretched from 1999 to 2002. They at first secured an injunction to stop the logging and then demonstrated that the ILG did not actually represent the landowners of the area in question. After long hearings the National Court declared the lease void (Tararia and Ogle 2010: 24). The case demonstrated that lease law could be subverted by corrupt practice and – while PNG's courts demonstrated sufficient independence to find in favour of little people – vindication this way was a long and difficult path.

In another case CELCOR (assisted by the Environmental Defenders Office of NSW) represented landowners from the Middle Fly River area, over illegal logging on their land. There were two defendants: a landowner group, Paiso (Ltd), that had made out the lease and the logging company, Concord Pacific (Ltd). As in the Collingwood Bay case, the Incorporated Land Group wrongly presented itself as representing all affected landowners. 'Selective logging' had been authorised, under an environmental plan, alongside a road development proposed to connect the towns of Aiambak and Kiunga. This roadside logging was to offset the costs of building the road. However the logging was far more extensive than planned, the road was poor quality and never linked the towns. The 'corridor' for logging was supposed to be up to one kilometre on either side of the road for its full length of around 200 kilometres. In fact, as landowners claimed and satellite imagery confirmed, logging had gone as far as 20 kilometres from the road. The total area affected was closer to 200,000 hectares than the permitted 50,000 (Curtis 2011: 64–65).

Consultant Ian Curtis was engaged to estimate damages. Making use of an 'opportunity cost' valuation developed by this writer (Anderson 2006 and 2006a), he calculated damage to the excess 150,000 hectares of land, in terms of its fuller productive capacity. That is, he was not limited to the value of the timber extracted, which had been estimated at between K137 million and K157 million. His finding – based on the extent of damage, productive value per hectare and a discount rate – was over 500 million Kina (Curtis 2011: 66–73). The National Court, relying on this method of valuation, awarded 225.2 million Kina to the landowners (EDO 2011).

The Middle Fly case is significant, not just because it acted to discipline illegal loggers but because PNG's courts considered the wider productive value of customary land. Recall that the oil palm companies ignored the rental value of customary land in their pricing formula (Chapter Six, Section 3.2); and that 'old economics' in PNG borrowed a nominal rent from Fiji, when arguing the need for widespread land registration (Chapter Three, Section 2). PNG's customary land was valued more highly by the country's courts than by its economists.

COMMUNITY ORGANISING

Probably the most remarkable community group in PNG is the Madang–based Bismarck Ramu Group (BRG), which was created to help organise communities. These days the BRG calls its core work 'community facilitation', in recognition of the fact that the communities really organise themselves (Chitoa 2003; Paol 2003). Community organisation is central to successful 'resistance' of the pressures on customary land as large companies, hungry for access to land, can easily take advantage of divided communities. A little history is necessary to understand how the BRG and its forms of facilitated 'resistance' operate (for a fuller explanation see Anderson 2005).

The BRG grew out of, and in reaction to, two integrated conservation and development projects (ICADs) in PNG. These ICAD projects aimed 'at building linkages between the welfare objectives of local communities and biodiversity conservation goals by providing communities with development support' (McCallum and Sekhran 1997: 4). They generally involved some sort of material incentive for local communities to agree to protect natural areas; the incentive was seen as compensation for foregone exploitation of that part of the natural environment. However these projects had a sorry history around the world and the two from which the BRG emerged were no different.

The Lak ICAD Project in the early 1990s was backed by the PNG Department of Environment and Conservation and the UNDP (New Ireland Province); while the Bismarck–Ramu ICAD Project was backed by the PNG Department of Environment and Conservation, the Christensen Research Institute and the UNDP (Simbu and Madang Provinces) (McCallum and Sekhran 1997: 2). John Chitoa, a Bougainville man, worked in the Lak ICAD and became the coordinator of the BRG.

He says that the Lak project tried to compete with logging companies, offering an 'early reward scheme' to groups of people who were already receiving royalties from logging. The idea was to get villager–landowners to agree to leave certain forested areas still standing, and still have access to royalty equivalents.

> '[But the landowners] couldn't really understand what was the ICAD project ... basically people were confused, they thought that the integrated conservation and development idea was just like another developer' (Chitoa 2003)

Eventually the ICAD ran out of money, the logging company 'outbid' them and the people voted to go with the loggers.

The Bismarck-Ramu ICAD Project began in a similar way to the Lak Project but very quickly members of the group were dissatisfied with the design of the project, and indeed the whole ICAD approach. While they were committed to environmental protection, the majority of the group felt that projects planned by outsiders and based on science (focussing on biodiversity 'hotspots') and incentives to local villagers would not work. Any new developments would have to be 'driven' by the landowning communities themselves. Several of the project team left (or 'decolonised') the UNDP project and created the Bismarck Ramu Group.

The group retained support from some outside funders and began a new process. They planned the terms of their engagement ('community entry') with select groups of villagers in the region. Their 'entry' process involved listening to villagers' problems and concerns first, sharing PNG history and culture sessions and taking a great deal of time listening before suggesting their own ideas. They abandoned all material incentives. No money or 'cargo' (eg. motor vehicles) were to be associated with their entry into and engagement with a community (Van Helden 2001: 247). In addition, by 1999, almost all international workers left the project; it was to be run by Papua New Guineans. Finance Manager Tamana Tenehoe, a Bougainville woman, explained:

> 'If we have a foreigner in the team, the first picture that people in the village will get, they will expect something from outside ... whereas when we have our own local people going into the communities I don't think it raises their expectations.' (Tenehoe 2003)

The BRG thus began to stress the Melanesian nature of its approach, with an emphasis on customary relationships, building self–reliance and an environmental management based on traditional principles (Guman 2003a). However they retained some international influences, such as the writings on participatory democracy in development, by Ann Hope and Sally Timmel. These authors drew attention to broad community–level consultation, the 'weaving together of a social fabric' and the importance of women's roles in a process of meaningful development (Hope and Timmel 1984: 4–6).

The centrality of and respect for small landowners and their land–based relations became a clear and central feature of BRG indigenous practice. The group places land custodianship at the heart of a strategy of self reliance and ecological management. The focus on self reliance is also an indigenous feature, which builds on customary land management and maintenance of kinship systems (Paol 2003). The BRG is strongly against 'support' for communities that encourages dependence (Tenehoe 2003). However they recognise that communities often do need resources. John Chitoa says:

> 'Basically we are not against money ... but you do not start with
> money ... we know that times are different now, people are
> pressured to have money for school and health fees ... but we
> want to help them get up on their own two feet and use their own
> resources' (Chitoa 2003).

Communities are asked to identify their problems, rather than their needs; it was felt the latter would be 'feeding into the cargo/dependency mentality that we are trying to break' (BRG 1997: 22). The formation of committees was also avoided, as organising decisions could be made in different ways by different communities (BRG 1997: 22). The importance of time taken to build relationships was constantly stressed, a point repeated by BRG workers (Guman 2003b; Paol 2003; Tenehoe 2003). At the same time, the community organisers would make a point to leave so as to allow the community time to work independently and together. Importantly, conservation is not introduced by the community organisers as an initial or central theme, a clear break from the ICAD approach. The sole initial task is to help the community organise, and to empower itself, using its own resources (BRG 1997: 22–39).

The BRG, of course, is not a blank slate. They have their own 'agenda'. They make it clear that they seek to promote self–reliant strategies including communities holding and properly managing their own land, 'good' cultural values including 'recognising the strength and value of women', and explaining 'the negative impacts of large scale development and the tricks used by companies' (BRG 1997). They see few benefits from the corporate projects, but rather a hard reality of long term dispossession and environmental degradation. For this reason, they do not assist communities who wish to contract big corporate developments.

The BRG 'model' of community facilitation might be summed up as: firstly, developing indigenous partnerships with villager-landowners, through a well thought out process of 'community entry'; secondly, assisting villager-landowners to develop self–reliant strategies based on customary land tenure; and, finally, assisting villager-landowners in community planing, including resource management and conservation options. They have had some notable successes in helping some groups develop conservation areas, but are as proud of helping them develop schools, health centres and farm-based enterprises (see Anderson 2005).

The BRG has also played a lead role in organising other community groups to resist what are seen as inappropriate initiatives from NGOs, particularly some of the big international NGOs (BINGOs). For example, in 2003 five groups including the BRG wrote to the Worldwide Fund for Nature (WWF) to demand that that group withdraw its proposal for a 'forest summit', and that the group cease its association with mining companies and the World Bank (BRG et al 2003). The WWF in a 'concept note' had proposed a forest summit, to be privately backed by the World Bank (WWF 2002). The five groups argued that the World Bank had consistently attacked customary title, and for that reason had attracted widespread hostility in PNG. People had fought and won this battle with the World Bank; they had successfully defended customary title. Citing a range of examples, the groups said that, by collaborating with the World Bank, the WWF was 'undermining local organisations and disempowering local people' (BRG et al 2003). The WWF withdrew its proposal.

As it has become better known, the BRG has had to deal with increased requests from other PNG groups for training in community engagement and facilitation, and also in a range of practical skills related to community organisation and landowner support. The key themes developed by the BRG are community self–reliance (drawing on their resource base of customary land) and indigenous community empowerment. To this they have added a challenge to 'desocialised' methods of conservation and some new elements of group process (Anderson 2005). The group's contributions to community resistance have become legendary within PNG.

MANAGEMENT TRAINING

Finally, there is resistance involved in building the capacity of landowning families and clans to productively manage their own land. Most government agencies (such as 'extension services') offer technical support for some export crops; but farm management is a much wider matter. With little support from government or aid agencies for small farmers, families are mostly left to their own creative skills. There is only occasional outside help.

However Steve Rere, a former academic from the Eastern Highlands, has focussed on farm management training for a decade. Disillusioned with the way agriculture was being taught at university, thinking it had little to do with PNG's realities, he resigned and started a small college on the outskirts of Goroka. Here he teaches farm planning, production and financial management and a philosophy of self–reliance. I spoke with Steve at his college in late 2004, then again in 2011. His training has contributed to a string of livelihood breakthroughs for those prepared to make good use of their family land (Rere 2004).

In late 2004 Steve had 16 students at the 'Open Learning Institute', a 30 hectare, no-fee college. He began by recruiting street kids and those who had dropped out of school, including some who were involved with drugs. Somehow he got small groups sufficiently interested to enrol in a two year course and develop their skills between classes at the college and practice on their family land. To graduate they had to show accounts from successful farm projects. The eight graduates for 2004 had earned between K2,000 and K11,500 in their second year, from enterprises based on their family gardens. The young women with the highest income had earned it through a contact to sell carrots to a major supermarket in Lae (Rere 2004).

At our 2011 meeting Steve explained that he had moved away from training young people and preferred group training of more mature people. Groups have come from various parts of PNG and even Australia. His college has grown but the emphasis was the same. The first two days of a two week course were about the 'mindset' of self-reliance and empowerment. Financial independence, he says, is 'all within our means' and 'people can be who they want to be'. He does not teach farming, but rather farm management, steady production and marketing. His emphasis is also on wholesale production, not local or roadside markets. He sends out fieldwork supervisors to see the students working their family lands (Rere 2011).

Steve does not teach students how to grow things; he says they already know that. But while his students may seek training from agencies such as the Fresh Produce Development Corporation (the one government agency that provides support for local market produce), he makes them develop a farm plan, with constant production objectives, such as 20 bags of potatoes per week. Steve wants students to work in groups, to produce a steady stream of wholesale product for suppliers. He stresses budgeting and working with bank accounts, and less use of cash. This approach tries to link cultural realities to production plans. One particular scheme he supports is giving children coffee trees when they start school, By fourth grade the trees will be able to sustainably finance all their school fees. The college itself is something of a model, as all the buildings and vehicles have been financed by sale of crops from the college land, most visible the cassava crops, but also chicken, fish and some other produce. What happened to the young woman who earned K11,500 in 2004, I asked? She is now a millionaire with multiple businesses including restaurants, Steve replied; but she still sells wholesale vegetables (Rere 2011). This little college fills a gap in the PNG training landscape. It serves to direct attention away from outside projects and livelihoods back to the rich resources and great potential that PNG families already have.

The attempts to 'reconcile' PNG landowning families with the loss of their land seem unlikely to stop. Land is more valuable than ever in a world full of food, energy and financial crises. The ideological assault is clever and backed by powerful forces. A great challenge for PNG rural families is to better understand these pressures and consider which forms of resistance are best to help them to build strong and resilient hybrid livelihoods.

Food security:
a cautionary tale

❧

Papua New Guinea, and the Melanesian countries more generally, have a natural advantage in providing their citizens with sustainable access to good quality food. Production and distribution of staple and fresh foods is much better than income levels might suggest. While there are some particular problems of nutrition, unlike many dozens of other developing countries, the Melanesian countries were not devastated by the high prices of the 2008 global food crisis. The challenge must be to maintain and extend that natural strength.

Yet food security strategies in the Pacific are often confused, in part because debates often collapse the diverse character of the various island countries, in part because nutrition has a lot to do with education, but also importantly because there is a strong economic liberal influence on food and agriculture debates. Two wealthy, food exporting nations, Australia and New Zealand, have views on land and agriculture that are quite distinct to those of the smaller Pacific islands.

As discussed throughout this book, the 'modernist' view of land as just another economic commodity has never sat well with the Melanesian cultures. On top of this, the Australian and New Zealand approach to food security advocates corporate-driven agricultural liberalisation and trade; that is, income from exports as a means to purchase 'food security'. This is a view held by only a handful of countries. Most countries, wealthy and developing, ground their ideas of 'food security' in policies to consolidate local agricultural production, so as to feed their own populations. Here trade comes second. The views of Australia and New Zealand are distinct because of the influence of their agri-business companies and their status as major food exporters, Furthermore, these wealthy country views on agriculture and food have an impact on regional debates because of their role as the dominant aid providers and major investors.

This chapter tries to disentangle the distinct 'liberalisation' influences on Pacific food security debates. It then warns of the corrosive influence of agricultural liberalisation on global food security. This is not a current threat to Papua New Guinea but, if there were substantial growth in large-scale, export-oriented monocultures, it could be. There are countries such as Morocco and Haiti which, in the space of just one generation, have lost the capacity to feed themselves. They gave this up to focus on export crops. When those crops did not live up to expectations, they were left without both decent income and basic food. They were hit hard by both the volatility and the rising prices of traded food. In that sense, much of this chapter is a cautionary tale.

PACIFIC FOOD SECURITY DEBATES

It is a common feature of many societies that they look to what they do not have and perhaps take for granted or undervalue what they do have. In any case, in the Melanesian context, it would be a tragedy to ignore the great strength that the institution of customary land lends to national strategies for food security. Customary land is both a productive engine and (because land in PNG is generally well distributed) a powerful distribution mechanism. Few countries retain such a natural advantage.

Approaches to food security in independent Papua New Guinea took a rather natural course, looking first at the problem of a rising dependence on food imports, particularly in rice. At the time of the first Food and Nutrition Conference in 1983, national policy aimed to reduce dependence on imported food and improve the nutritional status of the people (Igua 2000: 71). The latter, also critical for health and especially child health, has as much to do with nutritional education as food supply. The increased food import dependence was mostly to do with the adoption of rice as a staple. Staple roots, vegetables, fruit and other foods were abundant within the country. One response to this problem, at a local level, was the rather spontaneous beginnings of small scale rice farming, especially in the highlands (Igua 2000: 72).

Australia was the main exporter of rice to PNG and, despite being the major aid donor, never expressed any real interest in programs to assist PNG's own rice production. Through its interest as a major grain exporter, and its ambitions to open greater 'market access' in global trade, Australia committed itself to agricultural liberalisation in the final 'Uruguay Round' of the GATT (1986–1994). This project influenced its approach to 'food security', which was mainly for other countries. With surplus production and a welfare system, Australia had no real food security problems of its own. For these reasons, and unusually, Australia's food security policy was expressed through its Department of Foreign Affairs and Trade (DFAT). This asserted, in 1996, 'the important role that trade liberalisation can play in reducing poverty and increasing food security' (DFAT 1996: vii). The Canberra department saw 'no indication of a looming crisis in world food security' and argued that there was 'ample evidence that broad-based trade liberalisation is an important vehicle for economic growth and the alleviation of poverty. It thus makes a major contribution to food security' (DFAT 1996: viii, x).

By the logic of this economic liberal view, it is income gained from trade that allows access to food. (Notice that this logic leaves to one side the additional problems of assuring a reliable food supply at stable prices, and of then distributing export income so that it can be used to purchase that food for the tables of hungry people.) The department argues against 'self-sufficiency' in food, suggesting instead a 'self-reliance' which the country could achieve from higher incomes 'in the long run' (DFAT 1996: x). Australia was both using economic liberal logic against the big powers and at the same time seeking common cause with developing countries at the newly formed WTO. It criticised the heavy subsidies on agriculture in Europe and the US, saying these were keeping food prices artificially low, thus hurting exporting farmers. 'Free trade [in agriculture] would increase world prices .. by 16 per cent for coarse grains, 10 per cent for wheat and 6 per cent for rice. Grain production ... would rise in developing countries. In general the self–reliance of developing countries would be enhanced.' (DFAT 1996: x). Contrary to the usual 'free trade' logic, which suggests lower prices for commodities, this agricultural free trade would mean (IF the big powers dropped their subsidies) higher prices. This was seen as an advantage to farming countries, or at least to the agricultural export sectors of those countries.

The same argument about 'self-reliance' and 'open market oriented' agricultural trade was made some years later in another Canberra document on food security, this time by AusAID. The language was finessed somewhat. AusAID said that 'some developing countries have improved their competitive position and exploited opportunities resulting from trade liberalisation. However some resource-poor countries have lacked the capacity to do so' (AusAID 2004: 5). Australia said it was committed to a 'multi-factored' idea of 'self-reliance' which included emergency assistance, government food programs but also 'open market oriented' agricultural trade. 'While trade liberalisation alone cannot solve food insecurity, the root cause of which is poverty, it offers the best opportunity to achieve long–term food security' (AusAID 2004: 9–10). To this end Australia was pushing for agricultural liberalisation at the WTO and elsewhere.

The 2008 global food crisis, brought on by sudden rises in prices, did not dampen Canberra's enthusiasm for a liberalisation which would raise food prices still further. The price rises of 2007–2008 had nothing to do with the EU and the US abandoning subsidies; indeed they had not. The rises were most strongly linked to oil prices, premiums on commodity trading and the rise of the biofuel industry. In face of the crisis of high food prices in dozens of countries, DFAT officials argued for greater liberalisation, knowing this would lead to yet higher prices. The crisis had roots, they said, in:

'the combination of huge production subsidies and high market barriers over several decades of a number of developed countries, especially the EU and the USA. These distortions kept prices low for a long period, and have discouraged investment and slowed productivity growth in agriculture for much of the developing world' (Brown, Laffan and Wight 2008: 13).

Although the WTO talks had collapsed two years earlier, with the overwhelming majority of developing countries taking specific objection to a renewed Agreement on Agriculture (see e.g. Castle and Landler 2008), DFAT was firmly committed, in the name of 'development', to this same process. Liberalisation was argued with the same logic as that of the 1990s: it would 'strengthen the incentives' for developing countries 'to increase their investment in their agriculture and food systems' and thereby increase both production and trade (Brown, Laffan and Wight 2008: 13). It was even asserted, two years after the collapse of the WTO's Doha Round, that there was 'an emerging global consensus' and that 'all the key players agree on the need to free up trade through early conclusion of the Doha Round' (Brown, Laffan and Wight 2008: 20). Well, we have to concede that these are loyal public servants, boldly and hopefully supporting the official line.

A little detail on the fanaticism in Canberra for agricultural liberalisation was needed to show why elements of this re-appear in regional declarations and reports to do with food security. However, given that this enthusiasm is only really shared by New Zealand, and not by any of the other island states, it often appears in muted form. Nevertheless, land registration and agricultural liberalisation appear, for instance in Pacific Community declarations. For example, in 'Towards a Food Secure Pacific', we see 'food security' become a platform for private sector partnerships (in Australian terms this means privileging agri–business corporations), 'enhanced land tenure' and export oriented agriculture. In the first and second of seven 'framework themes' the approach to food security is both regionalised and linked to large corporations: 'strong national and regional partnerships to face current and future challenges to our food system .. [and] partnerships and collaboration between the public and private sectors for the formulation, implementation and enforcement of food legislative frameworks' (Pacific Community 2010: 5). Theme Seven specifies 'access to and proper utilisation of land', as well as asserting that 'access to, management of and proper utilisation of land underpins food security'. The old modernist theme of 'security of land tenure' (in Australian terms this means central registration and commercialisation of land) is said to be required for 'unlocking the economic development potential of land for food security and other commercial exploitation' (Pacific Community 2010: 6, 11). Of course, agri–business companies and their demands for land have everything to do with export–oriented agriculture, not local food needs. The economic liberal approach to food security does not see this common sense point; it does not appear to them as a contradiction. The Pacific Community document mixes this logic ('country-led initiatives that enhance land tenure systems', etc) in with its other influences.

In this way, a rather incoherent mixture of ideas circulates Pacific debates on food security. We can see some of this reflected in a recent document, 'Food for Thought', by the Vanuatu–based Pacific Institute for Public Policy. Here the various problems of the islands are bundled together but not disentangled (e.g. Kiribati and Tuvalu have water problems, PNG does not); educational problems (junk food in the cities) are collapsed into agricultural problems; highly contentious histories (e.g. the 'green revolution', which the Pacific is said to have 'missed out on') are mentioned but not explained; and the demands of old economics ('growth' and trade–oriented 'comparative advantage') are poorly engaged with brief references to livelihoods (PIPP 2011: 1–4). Australian-dominated regionalism seems to confuse rather than assist in the building of effective national strategies. For this reason, a more detailed critique of agricultural liberalisation seems necessary.

THE DANGERS OF AGRICULTURAL LIBERALISATION

Agricultural liberalisation has played an important part in preparing the ground for the sustained food crisis we face. The WTO's Agreement on Agriculture helped increase food trade, but did not alleviate global hunger. Even by 2007, those suffering hunger in the world had risen from a 1990–92 base of about 820 million to 923 million, making the Millennium Development Goal target of 420 million near impossible (FAO 2008a). Then, with strong food price rises in 2007–08, the numbers of undernourished rose sharply to 963 million 'and the ongoing financial and economic crisis could tip even more people into hunger and poverty' (FAO 2008b). In late 2008 and 2009 food prices fell, but stabilised at higher levels than before the 2008 crisis. By April 2009 food emergencies remained in 32 countries (FAO 2009d).

The recent high food prices have been driven by high oil prices, inflated premiums in oil and food derivative markets, demand for richer diets and pressure on land, including from the biofuel industry. More than a decade ago Patnaik (1996) pointed out that economic liberalisation, including in agriculture, had come at the expense of food grain production and food security in developing countries. So what responsibility is there for a process which has argued a 'food security' which opposes local food production and privileges trade?

This section argues that there are three interlinked 'high risks' for food security embedded in agricultural liberalisation. These are the rationalisation of land, exposure to price volatility and the unaccounted costs of large monocultures, including biofuels. The promotion of export oriented monocultures has led to corporate capture of land and food production, while passing on to society massive ecological 'externalities' such as soil and water degradation. The conclusion will be that, for those countries which do not both generate a substantial staple food surplus and have a strong social security system, a prudent approach must involve strengthening domestic staple food production and building effective domestic distribution mechanisms.

AGRICULTURAL LIBERALISATION AND GLOBAL FOOD MARKETS

The economic liberal approach to food security – promoted by large staple grain exporting countries such as Australia, Canada and the USA – suggests 'the important role that trade liberalisation can play in reducing poverty and increasing food security' (DFAT 1996: vii). The logic of this is that expanded specialisation and trade will enhance incomes and these in turn will provide the purchasing power necessary to alleviate poverty and purchase food. Food insecurity is assumed to be largely a consequence of income poverty and 'open markets' are relied on to organise production and distribute income.

Such conclusions are backed by the modelling of research agencies which have been conscripted into the search for new agricultural export markets. So for example Australia's ABARE suggests that a fifty percent reduction in agricultural support levels would lead to a US$53 billion increase in global gross domestic product. While most of this would go to the wealthy countries, US$14 billion is suggested as the benefit for developing countries (Freeman et al 2000: 1–2).

Since the agricultural exporters became an important part of the GATT–WTO process in the 1980s and 1990s, and even after the food-price crisis of 2007–08, senior WTO officials have urged further agricultural liberalisation. In 2009 WTO Secretary General Pascal Lamy spoke against moves towards 'food self-sufficiency' and import substitution in food, claiming that 'stability' was to be found in further liberalisation:

> 'The Doha Round's agricultural package, which reduces tariffs,
> reduces harmful internal subsidies that prevent in particular the
> developing world from fairly competing, and which eliminates
> export subsidies altogether, is no doubt worth pursuing.' (Lamy
> 2008)

Implicit to this approach are the ideas that increased trade expands income, income is reasonably distributed and a reliable source of good quality food is always available. This theory might work in a poor country where land remained widely accessible, or in a rich country with a strong social security system or a relatively even distribution of income. Wealthy countries which do not have good quality land, such as Singapore and Japan, would seem to be prime candidates for an economic liberal approach to food security. However even here we see strong counter movements, such as in Singapore's rooftop gardens (Wilson 2005) and, more definitively in the case of Japan, strong, legislated support for domestic rice production.

Japan subsidises domestic rice production even though it is routinely criticised for this 'inefficiency'. The principle of domestic production remaining central to a stable food supply is spelt out clearly in Article 2 of the Japanese 'Basic Law on Food, Agriculture and Rural Areas':

> 'In consideration of the fact that food is indispensable in
> maintaining human life … a stable supply of good–quality food
> at reasonable prices shall be secured .. [due to] certain unstable
> factors in the world food trade and supply/demand, this stable food
> supply … shall be secured with increase of domestic agricultural

production as a basis, together with an appropriate combination with imports and stockpiles.' (MAFF 2009)

Due to this firm principle, and even though Japanese rice production in 2007 declined to 40% of consumption, cultivated land shrunk (Tokyo Foundation 2008), and the cost of Japanese rice rose strongly. Domestic rice production retains strong government support. As part of its food security policy, the Japanese Government also maintains rice stocks equivalent to 'as much as 2.5% of annual rice production' (Tokyo Foundation 2008). All this is anathema to the liberalisers.

While the Cairns Group of agricultural exporters put agricultural liberalisation on the agenda of the GATT/WTO, strong divisions emerged over food security. Several Cairns Group members (Argentina, Australia, Canada and Thailand) are big net grain exporters, but most are not. Most export non-staple foods such as fruits, seafood and coffee. While they have all backed the campaigns against agricultural protection in Europe and the USA, several substantial grain importers (e.g. Brazil, Indonesia) remain sensitive to demands for further tariff reductions (see Table 1). They cannot compete with the EU and US over WTO–allowed subsidies that require direct government payment for a list of 'non trade distorting' purposes.

Table 9.1: Food grain balance, select Cairns Group members			
CG Grain exporters	Exports: m. tonnes	CG grain importers	Imports: m. tonnes
Argentina	21.096	Brazil	9.292
Australia	17.651	Chile	1.739
Canada	18.542	Colombia	3.600
Thailand	8.435	Indonesia	6.637
		Malaysia	4.871
		The Philippines	4.435
Source: FAO 2007: Table D3; figures for 2001–2003; millions of tonnes			

In the Doha Round of the WTO this division led to many Cairns Group members joining a new developing country bloc (the G22: led by China, India and Latin America) which opposed the round. The Agreement on Agricultural (along with investment privileges and intellectual property rights) was one of the main sticking points. It is notable that this WTO 'development round' was opposed by virtually all major developing countries.

To understand global food markets and their risks, rather than refer to liberal models, we need to take a critical, institutional approach. Risk assessment calls for a comprehensive review of all these institutional elements. It is logical, but not essential, to organise these elements in terms of their supply and demand side nature. The supply side features (restricted or more expensive supply will drive prices up) acting on the food prices at the root of the 2008 food crisis were: the rise in oil prices (and therefore also fertiliser and transport), speculative premiums in the derivative markets for both fuel and food, ecological constraints on the exploitation of new arable lands and a substitution effect on land and crops from the rapidly rising biofuel industry. The demand side features (strong demand will also drive prices up) were: rising populations, increasingly wealthy populations (e.g. in east and south Asia) with a demand for richer diets (such as meats and oil seeds), and the new and strong demand for biofuel crops, as a result of the parallel energy crisis.

It would be wrong to single out any one factor, and ignore the others or indeed the inter-related nature of some of these factors. Estimates have been made of their relative weight. Joachim von Braun, head of the International Food Policy Research Institute (IFPRI) estimated that income growth and the demand for richer diets was the main part of the reason for the 2007–08 price rises, suggesting that biofuels added another 30% (Borger 2008). At least, these were important. However he has not taken into account oil prices and the premium added by speculative markets.

Three other matters should be noted here: the domination of world grain markets by giant corporations based in the wealthy countries (McMichael 2009), the relationship between food trade and food production, and the special case of China.

Liberalisation of food grain trade is mainly of interest to a small group of large corporations in the wealthy countries. McMichael (2009: 292) has called this 'food regime ... an institutionalized structure of agri-food relations that feeds the rich and not the world'. Small farmers have never been big grain exporters and, contrary to some misconceptions, it is the wealthy countries that are the big food grain exporters. The list of countries that produce many times more than their consumption of food grains contains very few developing countries (FAO 2007: Table D3). Thailand, the world's largest rice exporter, is an exception. The same countries that demand trade liberalisation have most often secured their own domestic food grain production, and a number of them are large exporters (see Table 2). On the other hand, most of the countries with serious food security problems are those which are now food-grain-import-dependent.

Table 9.2: Food grain production as percentage of consumption, select countries		
>8x consumption	<1.6 x consumption	Less than consumption
Australia 18.85 Canada 11.81 Denmark 12.66 USA 9.82 France 8.77	China 1.55 Philippines 1.18 Nigeria 1.16 India 1.14 Indonesia 1.04	Venezuela 0.95 Kenya 0.84 Sri Lanka 0.71 Colombia 0.71 Sierra Leone 0.41 Haiti 0.37
Source: FAO 2007: Table D3; data for 2001–2003		

Global food production is much more substantial than trade, but trade remains important. Even though total food grain trade is only 15% of world grain production (FAO 2007), and rice trade is less than 5% of global rice production (FAO 2009b), trade has a powerful impact on domestic prices. Of course, the price impact varies as amongst countries and social classes. Grain exporters welcome higher prices, poor consumers are devastated by them. There is no 'win win' here.

Rice markets show us some of the extremes of this relationship. Global production of rice is about 400 million tonnes; world trade in rice has been about 30 million tonnes or just 6% of production (FAO 2009b). The recent food crisis is shown in a magnified firm, in rice price rises. By 2007 export rice prices had gained 60% from 2002–04 levels, up to $335/tonne. They then shot up in 2008 to 3.7 times that base level. By early 2009 they had settled down somewhat, but at 2.6 times that base level, or around $600/tonne (see Table 3).

Table 9.3: Rice prices, 2004–2009		
	Thai export rice, US$/tonne [1]	Rice price index [2]
2004	244	118
2005	291	125

2006	311	137
2007	335	161
2008 April	853	321
2008 June	870	370
2008 Nov	591	269
2009 March	637	269

FAO (2009c) 'The FAO Rice Price Update – April 2009', Food and Agriculture Organization, www.fao.org/ES/ESC/en/15/70/highlight_533.html ; (1) Thai white rice 100% B second grade f.o.b. Bangkok; (2) FAO price indices for all rice types (2002–04 = 100)

Rice is a special case, which may well be designated a special or sensitive product and so gain some exemptions from WTO liberalisation rules. However other staple food grain prices had similar upward trends. Average wheat prices rose steadily from 2000, from $118 per tonne to $199 in 2006, $263 in 2007, then peaking at $344 in 2008 before subsiding to $246 in 2009 (FAO 2009c).

China also represents a special case, as the world's most populous nation. This Asian giant has harvested rice for thousands of years and remains the world's largest rice producer and consumer. The country produces about 30% of world rice, and used to export some of its surplus; however in recent years China has moved from surplus to deficit production. This deficit is largely a product of China's success in industrialisation and urbanisation. Rice production rose strongly from the 1960s to the 1980s, slowed in the 1990s and then began to fall in the 2000s (Table 4).

Table 9.4: China's Rice Production, 1956–2006	
	m. tonnes
1956	81.5
1966	95.4
1976	125.8
1986	172.2
1996	195.1
2006	182.5
IRRI 2006	

The big increases of the past half century are said to have been mainly from 'increased grain yield rather than increased planting area', while the decline has been attributed to limits of land and water, climate change and labour shortages (Peng, Tang and Zou 2009). More specifically, in recent years, agricultural livelihoods have not kept pace with economic opportunities in the cities. Chinese agriculture is said to employ 'roughly half the labour force' yet rural incomes are 'just 30 percent' the urban average. This has led to rural diversification into more high value agricultural products (such as fish), which in turn further undermines rice production (van den Berg et al 2005: 34). It is not hard to imagine, then, the powerful impact on world rice prices that would follow from China shifting just a few percent more into rice production deficit. China's demand for just one tenth of its rice in imports would account for more than half the global trade in rice. Prices would skyrocket. Rice exporters would be cheering but the shift would be devastating for small, import dependent countries. Fortunately, China has its own strategic reasons to embed 'self–sufficiency' in its policies. A policy statement issued in 2008 required overall food self-sufficiency to remain above 95% , with self-sufficiency in rice and wheat (Gao 2010: 43).

The reactions by some governments (e.g. Russia, Argentina and Vietnam) to limit exports (BBC 2008) were clearly defensive moves in response to the logic of global markets. The food crisis cannot be blamed on such reactive protectionism. Indeed as Polanyi (1944) argued many decades ago, societies will always seek to defend themselves from the corrosive impact of such 'self regulating markets'.

THE 'HIGH RISKS' OF AGRICULTURAL LIBERALISATION

In this increasingly volatile situation, food security approaches must be conservative. The likely risks of agricultural liberalisation must be recognised, in particular those from well known threats:

- Rationalisation of land, including displacement and dispossession of communities from their traditional lands,
- exposure to import price volatility, and
- inadequate accounting of the costs of large monocultures.

The 'high risks' from each of these threats deserve separate consideration.

Most developing countries share a history of indigenous people being displaced from their lands, initially by conquest but later by a range of devices. This displacement and dispossession was, in all cases, disastrous for the development and security of those communities, including their food security. Yet in relatively recent times, modernist arguments have suggested that all countries would be better off with greater land rationalisation, typically followed by the 'more highly productive' large scale monocultures.

Rationalisation and displacement of communities from land has often been linked to problems of food security. Maxwell and Wiebe (1999: 830) note the 'conventional links' of a 'linear framework', that suggest land must be mobilised for large scale production, to generate more income; this income, in turn, can be used to purchase more food. This is a pattern relied on by liberal modernist writers (e.g. De Soto 2001). However the commercialisation of customary lands can rapidly feed into 'forced asset sales', rationalisation and displacement of large populations. This is exactly what occurred under the 1990s structural adjustment programs of Fujimori in Peru and Salinas in Mexico, aggravating rural poverty (Plaza and Stromquist 2006; Veltmeyer and Petras 2008; Sheahan 1997). Yet the disruption of small, diverse farming patterns can destabilise regional food production and traditional distribution mechanisms. A push to commercialise small land holdings 'may fail to serve either growth or equity purposes [whereas] diversification, rather than specialisation, is an imperative for food security' (Maxwell and Wiebe 1999: 841).

In Melanesia, where a fairly even distribution of land remains, serving as a natural mechanism for the production and distribution of food, liberalisation pressures have sought to undermine 'weak' tenure through similar modernist arguments: for greater security of title, agricultural productivity and rural credit. The situation is rather different for those small countries whose histories have seen both a breakdown in widespread land tenure, and the collapse of domestic food grain production. Even assuming a rational distributive mechanism within the country, such countries are highly vulnerable to the volatility of international food grain prices. On the tenth anniversary of the WTO's Agreement on Agriculture, and noting the post–1994 rise in food imports, the UN's Food and Agriculture Organisation commented:

> 'Although lower basic food prices on international markets bring
> short–term benefits to net food–importing developing countries,

lower international prices can also have negative impacts on domestic production in developing countries that might have lingering effects on their food security' (FAO 2004).

The food crisis of 2008 was the culmination of a double movement in price volatility, which had been brewing for some years. In the first phase, cheap subsidised grain imports killed local developing country markets. In the second phase, expensive grain imports starved whole populations. Until the recent crisis, small farmers had been hurt by cheap imports. When imported staple food is cheap, farmers cannot justify planting next season's crop. The earlier low prices were a result of heavy domestic subsidies by the big grain exporters, such as the EU, the USA and Australia, and pressures for agricultural liberalisation. Through the WTO's Agreement on Agriculture, the rich countries' subsidies are 'green boxed' and allowed as being not directly 'trade related'.

A good example of this price volatility can be seen in Haiti, a country which was almost self sufficient in staple food production in the early 1980s, but by 2008 was food import dependent and starving. Like many countries, Haiti had moved from more diverse staple foods (rice, corn, cassava, millet) to greater dependence on rice. Yet the country had been nearly self-sufficient in rice, until the 1980s. Then, under financial pressure from the US and the World Bank it began to dismantle its tariffs and other forms of protection (Georges 2004). Increases in U.S. food aid drove down the prices of Haitian agricultural goods in local markets. Rice production fell sharply in the early 1990s and at the same time imports rose strongly (Toler 1996). By 2000, US rice imports into Haiti had risen to more than 200,000 tonnes. This drove many local farmers out of business and, when prices rose again, poor people could not afford to buy rice (Georges 2004). Haiti was in a serious food crisis in 2003, with damaged agriculture, food aid dependence and almost 4 million hungry (FAO 2003). By 2008 the situation had worsened (UN 2008).

Low food prices damage local production. High food prices hit poor people who have to buy their food. This is the unstable situation created by trade-dependent food patterns. The 2008 experience – driven by high oil prices, the biofuel industry and speculators – demonstrates that this volatility has worsened and the consequences are grave. Dozens of poor countries were affected. The UN's World Food Programme (WFP) admitted that, with the price rises, it did not have the money to maintain its existing feeding programmes in 78 countries, let alone start new ones (Borger 2008). This was a predictable consequence of agricultural liberalisation, indeed a consequence predicted and hoped for by the big food exporters.

Compounding the problems of land rationalisation and traded price volatility, the claimed benefits of large monocultures are typically over-stated. Corporate investors encourage this. Yet the extraction of profits from local resources and labour is the main reason large monocultures are created. So, in political debates, the income benefits to local communities are often exaggerated and the environmental costs are played down (e.g. SSCM 2008). With its narrow focus on export incomes and assumptions of unlimited growth, agricultural liberalisation promotes large chemical-intensive monocultures and ignores two substantial issues: the social value lost through displacement of small farming and the environmental damage of the monocultures. These massive 'negative externalities' (costs not incorporated into market prices) are passed across by large agricultural corporations to local communities and to the environment.

Small farms are typically undermined and displaced by the monocultures; yet there are a range of social benefits from small farming. While the domestic and export market contributions of small farmers may struggle to match those of the monocultures, they add value through substantial subsistence production, widespread employment and social security. When the formal economy fails in developing countries, widespread small farms provide a refuge for livelihoods. Small farms also stabilise ecologies, with greater crop diversity and less damage to soil and water systems. U.S. food security expert Peter Rosset says:

> 'Small farms are 'multifunctional': more productive, more efficient and contribute more to economic development than large farms. Small farmers can also make better stewards of natural resources, conserving biodiversity and safeguarding the future sustainability of agricultural production' (Rosset 1999).

The additional social value provided by small farming communities has been referred to as 'multifunctionality'. Yet these 'positive externalities' (benefits not incorporated into market prices) are not accounted for in the arguments for expansion of chemically-intensive monocultures. The effect is to undermine strategies of sustainable development, and that is why it has been said that:

'the multifunctional view of agriculture ... offers the possibility of going beyond the questions concerning productivity and market competitiveness towards establishing a debate in terms of strategies for sustainable development... [multifunctionality] does seem to present an opportunity for numerous countries of the South to pursue their public policies on a new basis' (Losch 2004).

Furthermore, as Mazoyer points out, small farmers are affected both as consumers and producers in food crises. Both low and high prices can hurt.

'The majority of those suffering under nutrition are not purchasers and consumers of food, but rather producers and sellers of agricultural goods who have been reduced to extreme poverty through falling agricultural prices; secondly, because the poverty and under nutrition of non–farmers are indirectly but largely due to the impoverishment of under–equipped small farming communities' (Mazoyer 2001).

Monocultures have an ugly ecological footprint. The 'green revolution' of the 1960s, which promoted new seed varieties, chemical additives and irrigation, was hardly 'scale neutral'. It generally worked in favour of large monocultures, and the benefits were seriously overstated. The 'green revolution' was not 'green' in the contemporary sense of being environmentally friendly, indeed it was chemically–driven and as much as anything a move to avert the 'red revolution' suggested by radical land redistribution. We know now that these technological shifts brought with them serious environmental and health costs – damage to river systems, soil erosion, salinisation and chemically induced cancers. These costs were passed on to the wider community and were not accounted for in the economic statements of industrial agriculture. Further, productivity gains were 'uneven across crops and regions' and 'farmers benefited only where cost reductions exceeded price reductions' (Evenson and Gollin 2003). Most small farmers could not afford the more expensive inputs and consumers and small farmers alike have discussed for many years the need to get off this 'pesticide treadmill' (e.g. Hansen 1986; Nicholls and Altieri 1997).

A 'second green revolution' has been spoken of for some years now (e.g. Eicher 1995) yet in recognition of the environmental damage caused by intense fertilisation, and the non-renewable nature of many fertilisers, a better focus has been on improved seeds that can do without such fertilisers (Lynch 2006). Yet hopes for a new 'technological fix' to deal with the ecological and economic problems are misguided. The inputs, many from fossil fuels, have become increasingly expensive, due to 'peak oil' the energy crisis. Aileen Kwa points out that, in industrial agriculture:

> 'Yield increases from high yielding Green Revolution technologies have been decelerating, and in some cases stagnating and even contracting ... Traditional rice farming in Asia produced 10 times more energy in food than was expended to grow it. Today's Green Revolution rice production cuts the net output in half. In the long run, [chemical intensive] methods encourage desertification, soil erosion, pesticide contamination and the depletion of groundwater. Yet these ecological problems are ignored because of the difficulty in quantifying and assigning monetary values to ecological degradation' (Kwa 2001).

Monocultures reduce the diversity of production in a region, and reduce the capacity of small farmers to companion plant and spread their crop options. Sugar cane, soy beans and oil palm are similar in this regard. Land clearing erodes and degrades the soil, silting up rivers and choking surrounding marine reef systems. Much of the fertiliser used runs into the water, causing algae blooms. These are the substantial costs of an unstable system.

Finally there is the contribution of biofuels, which have raised competition between food for people and food for cars. Biofuels have generated a substitution of food crops for fuel inputs in recent years. Before the 2008 food crisis an International Food Policy Research Institute (IFPRI) study predicted that, with strong growth in biofuels, maize and oilseed prices would rise between 18 and 72 percent over the next decade (Msangi 2009). As it happened, they rose into that range in less than one year. A UN Special Rapporteur on the Right to

Food, Jean Ziegler, strongly opposed the biofuel industry and pointed to a startling opportunity cost: '232kg of corn is needed to make 50 litres of bioethanol. A child could live on that amount of corn for a year' (Biofuels Digest 2007).

CONCLUSION

Pacific debates on food security have been distorted by the well articulated interests, dressed up as universal creed, of the major regional power and major aid agency. Australian promoted agricultural liberalisation thus pervades regional debates on food security, drawing in corrosive elements of agri-business interest, land registration and export orientation. This does not help Papua New Guinea build on its own strong foundation in food security: one of well-distributed customary land and highly productive small farming.

On the contrary, agricultural liberalisation carries several 'high risks' for food security, and these can been seen playing out with devastating consequence throughout the world. Firstly, risk is inherent in a rationalisation of land, which disconnects and dispossesses populations from their traditional and sustainable sources of food and social security. Promises of success in more formal cash economies have generally not substituted for land. Secondly, risk is embedded in the exposure of cash poor populations to the vagaries of international staple food prices, which have become more volatile in recent years, for a powerful combination of reasons. Thirdly, risks are obscured by the unaccounted costs of large monocultures. The loss of small farming and the damage to soil, water and biodiversity regimes is rarely incorporated in the calculations of large scale commercial agriculture.

The general lesson here might be that, unless a country can both generate a substantial staple food surplus and maintain a strong social security system, a prudent approach to food security must involve the strengthening of domestic staple food production, ensuring (or maintaining) widespread access to land and building other sustainable measures of domestic food distribution and nutritional education. For PNG, the central challenge seems to be to defend and extend the country's natural advantage of a wide and even distribution of customary land.

Conclusion:
Rethinking land and
livelihoods in
Papua New Guinea

❧

Papua New Guinea's customary land systems, almost unique in the world and resilient over many centuries, face new challenges. They have long supported ecologically sustainable livelihoods, social inclusion and community control in flexible ways. However, along with the strong financial demands from schools and limited health systems, they face pressures from investor groups to dismantle these community controls. Financial agencies persist in trying to insert principles of individual appropriation, centralised registration, exclusive boundaries and universal rules.

Such things have been tried before. There was an attempt to transmit the British colonial land registration system of Kenya to Melanesia. This faced nationalist resistance and failed. Subsequently, the Kenyan process was shown to have not delivered on its claimed benefits: security of tenure, agricultural productivity, rural credit and enhanced land rights for women. Nevertheless, a second 'liberal wave' pushed for land 'modernisation' in the 1980s and 1990s; this also faced resistance and failed. In response, financial agencies adjusted their arguments, linking their ideas of 'land reform' to 'poverty reduction' and support for customary land owners. But their model was much the same: registration, individual title and greater commerce in land. Like the British in colonial Kenya, they claimed this would lead to greater security of tenure, higher agricultural productivity, rural credit and enhanced land rights for women. The fact that this had not happened in Kenya did not seem to bother them. A Papua New Guinea government, with foreign financial backing, again picked up the land reform 'banner' in 2005. Some local advocates have replaced the international agencies on the 'front line' of the land debate, but the arguments remain much the same.

Attached to these 'liberal modernist' ideas of 'land reform' is the language of 'old school' economics, with its narrow focus on economic growth, formal economies and exports. By this logic, the 'national economy' would benefit from land registration, more logging, more monocultures and greater export orientation. Never mind that family livelihoods might go backwards and local ecologies would be devastated. This is an economics that carries many contradictions, particularly in a country like PNG, with large rural populations and large subsistence and informal sectors.

However this book has outlined a 'new school' economics, which focuses on family livelihoods, makes use of human development indicators and takes seriously the concept of 'ecologically sustainable development'. This might provide a framework for outsiders and nationals to better understand PNG's real economy, including the central role of small farming. Based on this approach, this book has focused on the economics of rural livelihoods, rather than on economic aggregates. The 'old school' ideas better suit powerful interests, as they are associated with expanding formal sectors; but this book has argued that no sensible economic logic can exclude a focus on PNG's rural families and their livelihoods.

Many of these families are building better futures for themselves, based on clan and family control of customary land. Indeed, if we look at evidence from the most successful rural livelihoods, we see they are not in the new formal sector industries (like industrial estates, factories or monocultures) but rather mixtures of traditional, informal and formal enterprise, what I have called diverse or 'hybrid' livelihoods.

Many analysts fail to see these hybrid livelihoods, because they ignore both the richness of PNG's subsistence sector and the cash flows from informal markets. Instead, they adopt misleading clichés such as the idea that all traditional societies are moving 'from subsistence to the cash economy'. How wrong this is. In fact, most PNG families remain engaged in both. They engage in subsistence production and get cash income from marketing a mixture of crops for both domestic and export markets. Many also engage in other small businesses such as stores and livestock business, and some family members take on outside employment. Many families are widely engaged. Yet the basis of these livelihoods remains control of customary land.

Hybrid livelihoods may be 'basic', supplementing subsistence production with the sale of surplus garden produce, and perhaps some additional employment. However there are also more 'focused' hybrids. These sell more market specific domestic and export crops, perhaps combined with family participation in other business or employment. Then there are the 'diverse and efficient' hybrids, probably enhanced in their strategies by an 'education effect' and sometimes an 'adaptive response' to threat. These supplement their base in subsistence production with better focused domestic and export crops, other employment or business and effective management of the 'hybrid'.

The roadside market surveys discussed in this book draw attention to a neglected sector which provides much more employment than all the monocultures and mining projects put together. Furthermore, the incomes to these women vendors are higher than those of the workers in the formal sector industries. These surveys demonstrate that PNG's rural domestic markets, and the women that dominate them, play a key role in Papua New Guinea's mainstream economy, and a key role in supporting some of the more promising hybrid livelihoods. These vendors show an average income one and a half to three times that of the national minimum wage, and much higher than most actual wages. This activity goes on without prejudice to traditional subsistence and social exchange production, nor does it exclude other livelihood activities such as small business, export cropping and family involvement in some formal sector employment. Families of the sellers surveyed were already engaged in many of those activities. Most said their income from domestic markets was higher than that from the other activities. While most also grew export crops, these were a supplement to their main income from cropping for domestic markets. The most successful fresh produce sellers combined diversification in products with specialisation in some high value foods (such as peanuts and melons), popular addictive crops (tobacco and betel nut) or prepared foods (scones and fried food).

The informal sector, more generally, often offers families better livelihood options that most of the rural formal sector industries, such as oil palm, factories, shop employment and mining. Other informal small business, including wholesale marketing and transport, offer similar opportunities. The economic success of the roadside markets has much to do with access to good quality customary land and proximity to the main roads. Yet continued access to good quality customary land could be threatened by land leases or diversion of land into oil palm operations. On the other hand, problems of remote location could be alleviated by government investment in better roads. It is significant that women identify closely with this market activity, both for its social environment and because they maintain control of their customary land related activities.

The major industrial monoculture in PNG, oil palm, has attracted much support from financial agencies, but is far less accepted by rural families. On this matter we have to recognise that the advice of the World Bank, constitutionally and effectively a lobby group for private investors, is partisan. Despite oil palm being a highly profitable industry for the few companies involved, the crop does not (contrary to World Bank claims) provide a superior livelihood option for rural families. Incomes for customary landowners engaged in oil palm cultivation do not compare well with many other options in the informal sector.

Average family cash returns on VOP oil palm blocks remain half or less the average returns of the roadside sellers, and of other averages in the informal sector. For those on leased blocks the returns are worse. Even the better-off oil palm growers do not approach the incomes of those in the superior hybrid livelihoods, for example those selling peanuts, buai, melon, cocoa, coconut and other more flexible crops. The

'Mama Lus Frut' scheme for women provides one of the lowest income options in rural PNG, for some quite difficult work.

That still leaves open the question of whether oil palm might form one element of a superior hybrid livelihood? This is certainly not the case through rural rents, which provide the worst of all economic options for landowners. And there are serious disadvantages to planting oil palm on customary land. Firstly, the corporate mills control and limit the prices to 'smallholders'; secondly, oil palm cannot be companion planted and is therefore a very inflexible option; and thirdly, the ecological costs, particularly through soil and water damage, are very high. Small farmers would be better off retaining control of their land and using it for some more flexible combination of domestic and export crops, with some specialized crops and some degree of diversity.

Where then are the better future options for rural landowner families? Plantation systems of coffee, coconut and oil palm were never really 'decolonised'. Few built on PNG social values, and this created a fair amount of conflict. Most government and aid agency support still goes to the export crops, which are often only secondary elements of family livelihoods. Nevertheless, there are constant initiatives in marketing and cooperation at a grass roots level, around the country. The Sausi community in Madang, for example, has demonstrated a successful approach: keeping control of clan lands, developing diverse crops for home and local markets, supplementing these with more flexible export crops (in this case cocoa) and then building systems of village co–finance for family business and college fees. Building on a community's own cultural foundations can provide a sound basis for a durable model.

The evidence of this book has established that the better livelihood options for PNG's rural land owning families lie in maintaining control of their own land. Yet there are those who persist in seeking to 'reconcile' landowning families with an eventual dismantling of their customary systems and leasing out their lands. This includes AusAID's 'middle way', which seeks to bridge what it says are two 'extremes': that of maintaining customary tenure and that of land privatisation. Yet the evidence is quite clear that families would gain little and lose much from engaging in rural leases. There has been organised resistance to these pressures: legal challenges, community organisation and farm management training. PNG's rural communities need to understand these new arguments, and prepare strategies which best to help them stay focused on their strong and resilient hybrid livelihoods.

At the policy level, Food security debates in the Pacific have been distorted by a 'big brother' which has some special ambitions in global food trade. Australian has pushed agricultural liberalisation in international fora, for its own reasons. This approach is closely linked to land rationalization and the expansion of large, export–oriented monocultures. Canberra's financial influence means that these ideas always creep into regional policy statements. However, policy makers in PNG and elsewhere in the Pacific should remain clear about their distinct circumstances, and their distinct needs.

Food security is not yet a major problem for rural communities in PNG, who were barely affected by the global food crisis of 2008. However there is a cautionary tale from that crisis. Developing countries like Morocco and Haiti, because of their movement down the export orientation track, have lost the capacity to feed themselves, in the space of just one generation. When income from their export crops fell, they were left without decent income and without basic food. That is a tragedy that PNG must avoid. Papua New Guinea should not be misled: the country has a chance to build on its already strong foundation in food security, through a natural advantage in well–distributed customary land and highly productive small farming.

I hope this book has managed to dispel a few myths. Rural families in PNG are NOT 'moving from the subsistence to the cash economy'. They are productively engaged in both. Customary land owners do NOT have to 'mobilise their land' to assist the 'development' of the country. They can best protect and build their own family and community livelihoods. The government has plenty of money from mining and gas to build roads and support schools and health centres. It is wrong to suggest that customary land 'must be registered' to provide 'greater security of tenure, and that these centralised titles will assist in agricultural productivity, rural credit and women's rights'. I have presented evidence to show that there is no basis for this in the experience of those countries which have tried it. Are 'economic options are better in the formal economy'. Well, only for a very few. In general, the informal sector outperforms the formal sector, in rural PNG. Similarly, it is wrong to suggest that 'large scale monocultures (like oil palm) are more productive than small farming'.

The great productivity of small farmers has simply not been measured properly. Perhaps their contribution will be better recognised, in future.

Appendices

Appendix Table 5.1: December 2004 pilot farmer survey, Madang

Region	Prov	Gardens				Kina pa	
		L/ha	HMW	HMF	%F	Buai	Cocoa
Raicoast	MAD	6	7	15+	75	1000	2000
Aiome	MAD	1000	20	20+	100	2000	500
aparamu	MOR	3	5	15+	85	2000	0
Amele	MAD	7	9	9+	75	5000	2000
Tokain	MAD	3	7	15	75	2000	1400
Bogia	MAD	2	8	8+	75+	100	100
Raikos	MAD	300	30	30	na	500	0
southkos	MAD	200	20	30	na	0	500
Baitabag	MAD	2	7	7	na	480	0
Baitabag	MAD	1	na	na	65	150	0
Gumine	SIM	3	2	5	60	0	0
aa	MAD	65	7	10	75	7300	0
Bogia	MAD	12	5	7	75	800	3000
aparamu	MAD	20	7	15	85	3000	7000
aparamu	MAD	80	20	30	80	500	3000
Saidor	MAD	1000	50	50+	90	3000	5000
Transgo.	MAD	10	20	20+	75	2000	0
E	SIM	2	5	50+	75	0	0
cc	EHP	20	5+	10+	75+	0	0
TOTALS						29,830	24,500
AVERAGE							

V– vegetables	L/ha = land in hectares
P=peanut	HMW= how many people work this farm?
G=greens	HMF= how many fed by this farm?
T= tree crops	%F= what proportion of their food from farm?
B=brus/tobacco	P7P= annual income per 7 people (weighted family)
M=mustard	Supp?= support services

Cocon.	Coffee	Vanilla	Other	Other*	Total	P7P	Supp?
500	0	1000	V,P,G,T	7000	11500	5360	nil
0	3000	not yet	M,V,P,B	500	6000	2100	DPI
1500	0	not yet	P,M,B	12,000	15500	7200	nil
300	0	5000		6000	18300	14200	WV
2400	0	0		1000	6800	3170	nil
0	0	450		0	650	570	nil
2000	0	0		0	2500	580	nil
500	0	0		0	1000	230	nil
0	0	150		100	730	730	nil
0	0	0		70	220	na	nil
0	90	0	Pineap	110	200	280	nil
0	0	2400		0	9700	6790	nil
0	0	0		0	3800	3800	nil
1000	0	5000	P,B	20,000	36,000	16800	WV, DPI
100	0	320	P	5,000	8920	2080	WV, DAO
4000	0	3,000	various	10,000	25,000	3,500	DPI, BRG
1000	0	not yet	P	20,000	23,000	8,050	Unitech st
0	500	0	V,P	300	800	112	nil
0	400	0		0	400	280	na
		17,320		**82,080**		**75,832**	
				Av of 18 —>		**4,213**	
						(av of 18)	

DPI=Dept Primary Industry
WV=World Vision
DAO=District Agric Officer   * peanuts were the biggest 'other' crop
BRG=Bismarck Ramu Group

interviews in Madang, Dec 2004 – assistance from Howard Sindana

Appendix Table 5.2: August–Sept 2005 pilot farmer survey, Popondetta Plains (ORO)

	Region	Gardens				Kina pa (farm income)		
		L/ha	HMW	HMF	%F	Buai	Cocoa	Cocon.
1	Ahora	130	3	45	90%	0	0	0
2	Sorovi	2	2	6	75%	0	0	0
3	Kakandetta	5		120	65%	0	B4	0
4	Sorovi	6	2	7	75%	0	0	0
5	Kakandetta	55	16	16	75%	new	0	new
6	Kakandetta	15	15	15	75%	0	0	0
7	Gona	18	8	23	90%	1000	0	0
8	Sosoba	4	7	17	50%	400	0	0
9	Aeka	15,000	10	50	90%	5,000	B4	B4
10	Ahora	210	172	172	10%	300	0	550
11	Ahora	130	45	45	50%	500	new	1000
12	Gona	6	2	6	80%	750	0	0
13	Ahora	90	8	16	10%	500	0	750
14	Gona	10	2	5+	80%	1000	0	2,500
15	Oro Bay	98	3?	14	80%	0	0	0
16	Ango	1000+	35	50+	90%	500	400	500
17	Ango	1000+	50+	50+	90%	130	300	130
18	Embogo	200	10	10	80%	new	new	0
19	Dombada	10	11	11	60%	200	0	600
20	Erora	1 or 2	2	5+	25%	350	0	250
21	Soravi	10+	20	30+	50%	0	0	0
	TOTALS							
	AVERAGE							

L/ha = land in hectares

HMW= how many people work this farm?

HMF= how many fed by this farm?

%F= what proportion of their food from farm?

Interviews in Oro August 2005

Coffee	Vanilla	P'nut	Oil Palm	Other	Other*	Emp	Total	P7P	OP?
0	0	0	0	F,V	1000	y	1,000	156	na
0	new	0	6,000		0	n	6,000	7,000	LSS
0	0	0	2,500		0	y	2,500	146	LSS
0	0	0	6,000		0	y	6,000	6,000	LSS
0	new	0	7,800	Chkn	1200	n	9000	3937	VOP
0	new	0	15,000*	Chkn	900	n	15900	7420	LSS
0	new	0	3,300	F,V	2,750	yy	7050	2145	VOP
0	new	0	15,000*		0	n	15400	6341	LSS
0	1,000	1,000	5,000		0	y	12000	1680	vop
0	0	0	7,800	F,V	500	n	9150	372	vop
0	0	0	3,380	F,V	240	n	5120	796	vop
0	new	0	2600	F,V	750	n	4100	4783	vop
0	new	0	4,550	F,V	1000	n	6800	2975	vop
0	new	0	2,600	F,V	1,000	n	7100	9940	vop
0	0	0	0	F,V,fsh	??	y	n/a	n/a	na
2400	new	0	0	F,V	500	y	4,300	602	na
2400	new	0	new	F,V	260	y	3,220	450	not yet
0	new	0	0	F,V	1,750	n	1750	1225	na
0	0	0	0	F,V	1,200	y	2000	1272	na
0	0	0	0	F,V	450	yy	1,050	1470	na
0	0	0	7800	F,V	1,560	n	9,360	2184	LSS
								60894	
						Av of 20 —>		3045	

P7P= annual income per 7 people (weighted family)

Supp?= support services

Other = other farm income? (fruit, vege, chicken, fish)

Other* = other non–farm income? (work, pension, business)

Emp = outside employment

Appendix Table 5.3: Questions asked of the roadside sellers (Madang, Morobe, EHP, ENB)

1   Which items do you sell?

2   How many hectares gardens does your family have?

3   How many days per week are you at market?

4   What is your average income per week OR per day from market sales?

5   Which item gives you the best income?

6   How many people in your family share this income?

7   Do you grow other crops that you do not sell at this market? (cocoa, vanilla, coconut, etc)

8   How does income from those crops differ from your income at this market?

9   Could you estimate annual income from those other crops?

10   Do you get any outside help for your farming? (extension services)

11   Does your family have another sources of income? (shop, employment, business)

12   What are your (i) main problems and your (ii) main expenses for market selling?

Appendix Table 5.4: Madang rural roadside market survey, 2007, AWE

Market (no. sellers)	actual AWE	Daily rate	H.M. days/ wk	Market weight	Weighted seller AWE	main items sold (AWE> K100)
Watta Rais (30)	300	100	3	0.26 *	78	P, B
WR	200	100	2	'	52	B, CO
WR	1975	282	7	'	514	P, B
WR	1250	500	2.5	'	325	P, M
WR	1125	225	5	'	293	P
WR	2250	321	7	'	Na *	P, B
Sausi (40)	60	30	2	0.43	26	P
SA	45	15	3	'	19	P
SA	70	23	3	'	30	P
SA	50	17	3	'	22	P
Yakumbu (20)	35	23	1.5	0.43	15	
YK	25	10	2.5	'	11	
Usino (50)	50	17	3	0.53	27	
US	150	75	2	'	80	P
US	450	150	3	'	239	M, P
US	60	20	3	'	32	
Mambu (70)	60	15	4	0.75	45	
MA	120	60	2	'	90	B
MA	450	180	2.5	'	338	B, DA
MA	210	84	2.5	'	158	B, DA
4 Mile (200)	210	70	3	1.08	227	B
4M	500	250	2	'	540	B
4M	150	30	5	'	162	B
4M	280	112	2.5	'	302	B, DA
4M	225	75	3	'	243	B, DA
4M	270	180	1.5	'	292	B, DA
4M	640	142	4.5	'	691	CI
4M	250	100	2.5	'	270	B, DA
Maiwara (13)	55	22	2.5	0.14	8	
MW	25	13	2	'	4	

Cont.

MW	60	15	4	'	8	
MW	50	20	2.5	'	7	
Pau (120)	35	35	1	1.03	36	
PA	300	75	4	'	309	M, MA
PA	60	30	2	'	62	
PA	45	15	3	'	46	
PA	70	18	4	'	72	
Selon (40)	125	50	2.5	0.57	71	B, BR
SE	180	60	3	'	103	B
SE	50	17	3	'	29	
Nagada (10)	50	25	2	0.21	11	
NG	60	20	3	'	13	
Baitabag (20)	40	27	1.5	0.43	17	
BB	40	27	1.5	'	17	
AVERAGE	289		2.93	1	138	

* Exceptional high income earner in Watta Rais removed in weighting process, reduces 6 to 5 interviews

Appendix Table 5.5: Madang survey 2007, AWE Distribution, per market and main item sold

Kina/wk	No. sellers	Main items	WR	4M	US	MA	PA	SE	SA	YA	MW	NA	BA
0–49	8						2		1	2	1		2
50–99	14				2	1	2	1	3		3	2	
100–199	5	P, B, BR		1	1	1		2					
200–299	7	B, CO	1	5		1							
300–399	2	P, B, M, MA	1				1						
400–499	2	P, M, B			1	1							
500–999	2	B, CI		2									
1000+	4	P, B, M	4										
TOTAL	44												

Abbreviations:
MARKETS: WR = Watta Rais; 4M = 4 Mile; US = Usino; MA = Mambu; PA = Pau; SE = Selon; SA = Sausi; YA = Yakumbu; MW = Maiwara; NA = Nagada; BA = Baitabag.
MAIN ITEMS: B = Buai (betel nut); P = peanut; M = melons; CI = cordial/iceblock; CO = coconut; MA = Mango; BR = Brus (tobacco); NB. National minimum wage (urban and rural) is K37.20 (BPNG 2006)

Appendix Table 5.6: (following pages) Roadside seller surveys in Morobe, Eastern Highlands and East New Britain, 2011

PNG roadside surveys 2011 — data and weighted data

Morobe, 11-12 June

#	market	g	days	K/day	K/week	wt/wk
1	Zenag	f	6	17	100	34
2	100	f	4	50	200	68
3	6.84	f	2	80	160	54.4
4	20	f	1	30	30	10.2
5	0.34	f	1	90	90	30.6
6		f	1	100	100	34
7		f	3	20	60	20.4
8		m	6	17	100	34
9		f	6	10	60	20.4
10		f	3	33	100	34
1	Gurako	f	6	60	360	122.4
2	60	f	6	120	720	244.8
3	4.1	f	6	60	360	122.4
4	12	m	6	75	450	153
5	0.34	f	2	50	100	34
6		f	6	75	450	153
1	Gabensis	f	3	90	270	62.1
2	40	f	3	20	60	13.8
3	2.7	f	7	30	210	48.3
4	12	f	7	36	250	57.5
5	0.23	f	3	33	100	23
6		f	3	17	50	11.5
1	Nine Mile	f	3	17	50	57
2	300	f	7	70	490	558.6
3	20.5	f	4	50	200	228
4	18	f	7	43	300	342
5	1.14	f	7	100	700	798
6		f	6	42	250	285
7		f	3	33	100	114
8		f	3	13	50	57
9		f	5	20	100	114

East New Britain, 20-22 June

#	market	g	days	K/day	K/week	wt/wk
1	Vunadidir	f	6	15	90	18
2	10	f	6	35	210	42
3		f	2	60	120	24
4	0.2	f	3	50	150	30
1	Ratavul	f	6	50	300	60
2	10	f	2	30	60	12
3		f	4	50	200	40
4	0.2	f	3	55	165	33
1	Napapar	f	3	30	90	24.3
2	20	f	5	100	500	135
3	2.9	f	3	40	120	32.4
4	10.7	f	2	30	60	16.2
5	0.27	f	3	50	150	40.5
6		f	3	70	210	56.7
1	Keravet	f	6	50	300	342
2	100	f	6	80	480	547.2
3	14.3	f	6	70	420	478.8
4	12.5	f	6	130	780	889.2
5	1.14	f	1	70	70	79.8
6		f	5	120	600	684
7		f	5	80	400	456
1	Warangoi sawmil	m	4	50	200	66
2	20	f	2	75	150	49.5
3	2.9	f	4	40	160	52.8
4	8.9	f	2	75	150	49.5
5	0.33	f	3	30	90	29.7
1	Warangoi	f	3	50	150	30
2	10	f	2	70	140	28
3		f	2	15	30	6
4	0.2	f	3	30	90	18

Eastern Highlands, 14-15 June

#	market	g	days	K/day	K/week	wt/wk
1	Daulo	f	7	50	350	308
2	& Stone	f	7	50	350	308
3	25	f	7	60	420	369.6
4	19.2	f	7	30	210	184.8
5	21.8	f	7	70	490	431.2
6	0.88	f	7	60	420	369.6
7		m	7	42	300	264
8		m	7	70	490	431.2
9		f	1	20	20	17.6
10		f	7	30	210	184.8
11		f	6	60	360	316.8
12		f	6	40	240	211.2
1	Kontena	f	4	50	200	182
2	15	f	6	30	180	163.8
3	11.5	f	3	50	150	136.5
4	12.7	f	3	10	30	27.3
5	0.91	f	3	50	150	136.5
6		f	2	40	80	72.8
7		f	3	40	120	109.2
1	Kohero	m	3	40	120	253.2
2	& Ifufa	f	7	60	420	886.2
3	20	f	6	40	240	506.4
4	2.11	f	6	60	360	759.6
1	Aine	f	6	115	690	690
2	25	f	5	70	350	350
3	19.2	f	5	60	300	300
4	16.4	f	5	50	250	250
5	1.17	f	6	30	180	180
6		f	3	50	150	150
7		f	3	100	300	300
8		f	4	50	200	200
9		f	5	40	200	200

PNG roadside surveys 2011 — data and weighted data — PAGE TWO

Morobe, 11-12 June

#	market	g	days	K/day	K/week	wt/wk
1	Yalu (Sund	f	4	90	360	176.4
2	200	f	2	150	300	147
3	13.7	f	2	30	60	29.4
4	28	f	2	100	200	98
5	0.49	f	3	190	570	279.3
6		f	7	200	1600	784
7		f	7	100	700	343
8		f	7	85	600	294
9		f	7	85	600	294
10		m	4	30	120	58.8
11		f	3	30	90	44.1
12		m	6	20	120	58.8
13		m	5	100	500	245
14		f	3	30	90	44.1
1	5 mile (Sun	f	5	50	250	52.5
2	30	f	3	30	90	18.9
3	2.1	f	3	250	750	157.5
4	10	f	7	70	500	105
5	0.21	f	7	20	140	29.4
	TOTALS		340	5304	23915	10965
	AVERAGES		4.5	63.2	285.2	144

SAMPLED: 50
est sellers in markets sampled: 730
markets sampled: 50% of total in area
total popn - 1460

Notes:
weight of market = %total popn / % total interview
market size
% total popn
% total interviews
market weighting

East New Britain, 20-22 June

#	market	g	days	K/day	K/week	wt/wk
1	Malakuna No 4	f	2	90	180	36
2	10	f	3	20	40	8
3		f	2	30	60	12
4	0.2	f	3	60	180	36
1	Ballora	f	2	40	80	31.2
2	10	f	3	50	150	58.5
	0.39					
1	Nonga	f	3	60	180	41.4
2	20	f	5	30	150	34.5
3	2.9	f	2	50	100	23
4	12.5	f	1	50	50	11.5
5	0.23	f	1	50	50	11.5
6		f	4	80	320	73.6
7		f	3	30	90	20.7
1	Navunaram	f	5	125	625	168.8
2	20	f	3	60	180	48.6
3	2.9	f	3	40	120	32.4
4	10.7	f	2	80	160	43.2
5	0.27	f	2.5	15	37	9.99
6		f	3	70	210	56.7
1	Tomaringa	f	2	40	80	43.2
2	20	f	2	20	40	21.6
3	0.54	f	3	50	150	81
1	Takubar (Papind	f	6	75	450	904.5
2	100	f	6	65	390	783.9
3		f	7	60	420	844.2
4	2.01	f	3	40	120	241.2
	TOTALS					
	AVERAGES		328	5284	19129	15169
	SAMPLED: 56		3.4	53.8	198.3	143.7

est sellers in markets sampled: 350
markets sampled: 50% of total in area
total popn- 700

Eastern Highlands, 14-15 June

#	market	g	days	K/day	K/week	wt/wk
1	5 Mile	f	3	10	30	28.2
2	20	f	5	50	250	235
3	15.4	m	5	60	300	282
4	16.4	f	5	50	250	235
5	0.94	f	2	10	20	18.8
6		f	6	20	120	112.8
7		m	6	26	156	146.6
8		f	5	40	200	188
9		f	2	50	100	94
1	Korofegu (Hag	f	6	70	420	331.8
2	20	f	5	30	150	118.5
3	15.4	f	5	50	250	197.5
4	19.6	f	3	30	90	71.1
5	0.79	f	4	50	200	158
6		f	6	60	360	284.4
7		f	5	30	150	118.5
8		f	3	31	93	73.47
9		f	4	70	280	221.2
10		f	3	40	120	94.8
11		f	3	40	120	94.8
1	Pitinamu(Bena	m	6	40	240	165.6
2	5	f	7	20	140	96.6
3	0.69	f	5	30	120	82.8
	TOTALS		423	3888	18902	17770
	AVERAGES		4.9	45.9	230.7	230.9

SAMPLED: 55
est sellers in markets sampled: 130
markets sampled: 50% of total in area
total popn - 260

PNG roadside surveys 2011

market	int	M/F	day	K/day	K/wee	Items sold	best items	Other income	Highes	Problems
Eastern Highlands, 14-15 June										
1 Daulo	l	f	7	50	350	veges,flowers	potatoe	emp(ramu sugar	LM	frost,fert.,se Daulo and Stone
2	h	f	7	50	350	veges, potat,flowe	potatoes	no	LM	theft,fert.,seeds
3 Stone	y	f	7	60	420	bv,fried food	fried food	building material:	na	no
4	y	f	7	30	210	fvg,fried food	fried food	building material:	LM	no
5	y	f	7	70	490	Bfdrvg,st	buai and cigs	coffee (little)	LM	no
6	y	f	7	60	420	Bdfgv	Buai	building material:	na	no
7	y	m	7	42	300	Bvg,store goods	Buai	building material:	na	no
8	y	m	7	70	490	Bvg,store goods	buai, carrots	building material:	na	no
9	l	f	1	20	20	artefacts, flowers,	artefacts	no	LM	theft, costs
10	l	f	7	30	210	v,cuc, bees	potato,cabbag	Coffee	LM	theft, costs
11	h	f	6	60	360	pbv	kaukau	piggery,Coffee (	LM	transport
12	h	f	6	40	240	Bv,cuc	carrot	Coffee(1K)	LM	no
1 Kontena	y	f	4	50	200	vg,kaukau	carrots	Coffee (1K),emp	Coffee¢	transport,pric Kontena market
2	y	f	6	30	180	vg	carrots	Coffee (5K)	Coffee¢	no
3	l	f	3	50	150	bvgp,bilums	peanut, carrot	no	LM	theft,pigs
4	l	f	3	10	30	vgbpf,cuc,taro,etc	carrot, cabba(	no	LM	theft, pigs
5	l	f	3	50	150	vgbp,ginger,etc	kaukau	Coffee	LM	theft, pigs, transport
6	l	f	2	40	80	vgb,ginger,etc	greens	emp(teacher)	na	theft,pigs
7	l	f	3	40	120	vgbp,ginger,bilums	greens	Coffee	LM	theft,pigs
1 Kohero	l	m	3	40	120	v,flour	potato,cabbag	Coffee	LM	no	Kohero and Ifiuf
2	h	f	7	60	420	pv	kaukau	Coffee(2K),emp	LM	theft,surplus
3 Ifiufa	h	f	6	40	240	vpB	kaukau	Coffee (1K)	LM	seeds,fert costs
4	h	f	6	60	360	vf,cuc	peanut,kauka	Coffee (K1.5),bi	LM	theft, seed/fert. costs
1 Aine	y	f	6	115	690	fbvg,sugarcane	gv	Coffee(7K)	na	no	Aine market: ab
2	y	f	5	70	350	vcpfg	gv	Coffee(up to 10	na	no
3	y	f	5	60	300	vgf,seeds	peanuts	Coffee(5K)	na	no
4	l	f	5	50	250	vgc,ginger,etc	kaukau	no	LM	theft,pigs,transport,seed costs,
5	l	f	6	30	180	pv, ginger	carrot	no	LM	seedling costs,transport
6	l	f	3	50	150	vpb	kaukau	Coffee	LM	seedlings,fert costs, transport
7	l	f	3	100	300	veges	carrot,cabbag	Coffee	LM	theft,transport,seed costs
8	l	f	4	50	200	p,veges	capsicum	Coffee	LM	theft,transport,pigs
9	h	f	5	40	200	veges,p,b	peanut	Coffee	Coffee¢	fert costs
1 5 Mile	y	f	3	10	30	avocados	avocados	children employ	na	no	5 Mile market: c
2	y	f	5	50	250	vg,store goods	carrots,green	Coffee	C?	no
3	y	m	5	60	300	scones,store gds,v	fried scones	no	LM	surplus goods
4	l	f	5	50	250	vg	chinese cabb	Coffee, emp(sor	LM	transport,seed/fert costs
5	l	f	2	10	20	gv,smokes	greens	Coffee	LM	theft,pigs
6	l	f	6	20	120	sausage	sausage	no	LM	transport
7	l	m	6	26	156	B,r,lollies,spear roll	spear roll	Coffee	LM	transport
8	h	f	5	40	200	pbv	kaukau	chickens	LM	fert,chemical cost
9	h	f	2	50	100	veges	cabbage	emp(husb),chick	chicken	no
1 Korofegu	h	f	6	70	420	Bpb,orange	peanut	Coffee(600)	LM	Coffee price, **Korofegu marke**
2	h	f	5	30	150	pb,orange	peanut	Coffee(600)	LM	fert cost, theft
3	h	f	5	50	250	Bpdbfv	banana	Coffee (1K),emp	LM	theft
4	h	f	3	30	90	pb,orange	orange	Coffee(650)	LM	coffee price, theft
5	y	f	4	50	200	fvgp	peanut,corn,p	Coffee (8K)	Coffee¢	theft
6	y	f	6	60	360	pf,avocado	peanuts	no	LM	theft, land shortage
7	l	f	5	30	150	pvfb	pineapple	Coffee	LM	pigs, theft
8	l	f	3	31	93	B, smokes,lollies	smokes	Coffee	LM	buai decay,transport
9	l	f	4	70	280	pfv,bilum	orange	Coffee	LM	pigs,theft
10	l	f	3	40	120	pgvf	peanut	Coffee	LM	pigs,theft
11	l	f	3	40	120	pgfv,bilum	orange	Coffee	LM	pigs, theft
1 Pitinamu	h	m	6	40	240	p,corn,orange	peanut	no	LM	surplus not s Pitinamu(Bena)
2	l	f	7	20	140	pbfv	peanut,corn,c	no	LM	pigs, theft
3	l	f	5	30	120	pbgv	peanut,corn,c	Coffee	LM	pigs, theft

Items: buai (B), banana (b), peanut (p), veges (v), greens (g), melons (m), daka (d), tapioka (t), flour (f), cooked food (c), brus (r
  coconut (co); COFFEE (C), POULTRY (P) STORE (S) VANILLA (V) store (st), ice=flavoured ice-blocks, egg, cuc=cucu

Notes: (i) #=likely mis-estimate; **(ii)** a number of people list 'natural disasters' and the weather as a problem of local markets, I ha

PNG roadside surveys 2011

	market	inte	M/F	days	K/day	K/we	Items sold	best items	Other income?	Highes	Problems
	East New Britain, 20-22 June										
1	Vunadidir	y	f	6	15	90	Bbd	Buai, daka	Copra,cocoa(7K)	Copra,c	no
2		y	f	6	35	210	Bd,co,cooked food	Cooked food	Cocoa,copra(3K)	Copra	no
3		e	f	2	60	120	cooked food	cooked food	Cocoa,coconut,e	LM	no
4		e	f	3	50	150	cooked food,flour,ri	cooked food	fishing,boat	LM	surplus food
1	Ratavul	y	f	6	50	300	Brfb,ice,store,fried f	Buai, daka	emp(father,husb	na	no
2		y	f	2	30	60	Bp,cooked food	cooked food	no	LM	no
3		e	f	4	50	200	ice, cooked food,bu	ice blocks	Cocoa, emp(2 ch	na	high prices
4		e	f	3	55	165	flour,mustard,b,coc	banana, coconu	Cocoa,coconut, e	co,coco	cocoa borer,
1	Napapar	y	f	3	30	90	pvg,store goods	peanuts	Coconuts,copra,e	LM	no
2		y	f	5	100	500	Bdprvg,bread,store	peanuts	Coconuts and co	LM	no
3		y	f	3	40	120	Bdvb,coc,fp,store g	peanuts	Coconut, Cocoa	LM	theft
4		y	f	2	30	60	Bdpbvg, fried flour,	peanuts	Cocoa, coconuts	cocoa,c	theft
5		e	f	3	50	150	Bdbv	kalava,kaukau,l	Cocoa(5.4K)	cocoa#	theft
6		e	f	3	70	210	Bd,coked food, ice l	cooked food	Cocoa, sawmill b	LM	transport
1	Keravet	y	f	6	50	300	fried flour:poris,scol	fried goods	emp(husband)	LM	no
2		y	f	6	80	480	vg,brus	brus(tobacco)	emp(husband, 2	na	no
3		y	f	6	70	420	Bd,brus	brus	emp(son)	LM	no
4		y	f	6	130	780	fv,brus	brus	emp(husband)	LM	no
5		e	f	1	70	70	pbv,rice,coc	peanut	Cocoa, rice, coffe	Copra	transport,milli
6		e	f	5	120	600	fish	fish	coconut	LM	high costs (7!
7		e	f	5	80	400	Bdp, coc,tapiok	peanut	Cocoa,copra	LM	prices
1	Warangoi sa	y	m	4	50	200	brus,veges	brus	emp(4 family mei	na	no
2		y	f	2	75	150	pfv	kaukau,peanuts	no	LM	crop pests
3		y	f	4	40	160	vgBd,kambang	kumul(greens)	coconut,cocoa	LM	crop pests
4		i	f	2	75	150	veges,peanut,corn	peanuts	no	LM	theft
5		i	f	3	30	90	Bpv	peanuts	Copra(K2,copra(	COC/C	no
1	Warangoi	y	f	3	50	150	Bdfvg	all same	Coffee(7.2K), co	Coffee#	no
2		y	f	2	15	30	Bv,tapiok, cooked f	veges, cooked f	Cocoa(500), cop	Cocoa,c	no
3		i	f	3	30	90	vb,rice	veges and rice	Cocoa(500),Cop	LM	mine pollutior
4		i	f								
1	Malakuna Nc	y	f	2	90	180	peanuts, corn	peanuts	coconut,cocoa(4l	Copra#	no
2		y	f	3	20	40	Bd,veges,coco,cool	Buai,daka	Coconut,Copra(6	Copra	no
3		i	f	2	30	60	Kulau,pawpaw,pear	Kulau	Coffee,emp(husk	Coffee	theft
4		i	f	3	60	180	Bp,veges,kaukau	peanut,coconut	Cocoa(1.5K),Cop	Cocoa/(	theft
1	Baliora	y	f	2	40	80	Bdp,veges, cooked	peanut	Copra(3.4K),Coc	Copra#	no
2		i	f	3	50	150	vpb,kaukau	peanuts,kaukau	Cocoa,Copra,trac	LM	theft
1	Nonga	i	f	3	60	180	Bp,kulau,kaukau,or	Buai,peanut	Copra (1.5K)	Copra#	theft
2		i	f	5	30	150	Buai, cooked food	Buai	Copra (500)	Copra#	theft
3		e	f	2	50	100	Bdgv	Buai, daka	Coffee,Cocoa,Cc	LM	cocoa borer,
4		e	f	1	50	50	cooked food	cooked food	emp(husband)	LM	LM depends
5		e	f	1	50	50	Bd,orange	na	Copra, Cocoa	na	theft
6		y	f	4	80	320	Bdvf,fish,orange	oranges	Cocoa,Copra (3.l	Coco/C	theft
7		y	f	3	30	90	Bdbv,cooked food	banana chips/cc	Cocoa,Coconuts	Copra#	theft
1	Navunaram	i	f	5	125	625	pb, veges	kaukau,peanut,	Cocoa(500),Cop	Cocoa/(	pests
2		i	f	3	60	180	pg,veges,kaukau	veges,peanut	Cocoa(1K),Copra	Cocoa/(	theft
3		e	f	3	40	120	Bdb,beans	Buai, daka	Copra (2K),emp(	Copra#	theft
4		e	f	2	80	160	pv, kaukau, beans	kaukau	Cocoa	LM	no
5		e	f	2.5	15	37	Bdrb,kaukau	kaukau,bean	emp(children)	LM	theft
6		y	f	3	70	210	Bdfgb,veges	banana	coconut, copra(4	copra#	theft
1	Tomaringa	i	f	2	40	80	beans,buai, muli	bean	cocoa(500),copra	cocoa/c	no
2		e	f	2	20	40	Bdg,kaukau	greens	cocoa	LM	theft
3		y	f	3	50	150	Bdpv, kaukau	cabbages	Coconut,Copra, e	LM	theft
1	Takubar (Pa|	i	f	6	75	450	pbv, kaukau, cocon	coconuts,peanu	Cocoa(1.5K),Cop	Copra/c	pests
2		i	f	6	65	390	vbp	veges,banana	Cocoa(1K),Copra	Cocoa/(	theft
3		y	f	7	60	420	Bdr,kambang,cigare	Buai, daka	emp(husband)	na	no
4		y	f	3	40	120	Bdpgv	veges,greens	poultry project	na	transport

Items: buai (B), banana (b), peanut (p), veges (v), greens (g), melons (m), daka (d), tapioka (t), flour (f), cooked food (c), coconut (co); COFFEE (C), POULTRY (P) STORE (S) VANILLA (V) store (st), ice=flavoured ice-blocks, egg, cuc=c

PNG roadside surveys 2011

	market	inte	M/	days	K/day	K/wee	Items sold	best items	Other income	High(	Problems	
Morobe, 11-12 June												
1	Zenag	h	f	6	17	100	bpd	Bp	CPS	LM	theft	Zenag market: u|
2		h	f	4	50	200	Bbpmbvf	Bbf	C (6K)	LM	no	
3		h	f	2	80	160	Bbdt	Bd	C (3.6K) V,P	C#	domestic	
4		y	f	1	30	30	Bvg	Bg	C(3K)V,Gold	C	transport	
5		y	f	1	90	90	Bgv	B	C, Gold	C	transport	
6		y	f	1	100	100	gv, st,ice	cuc.	C, Gold	LM	transport	
7		y	f	3	20	60	vgb	b	C(5K) Gold	na	transport	
8		n	m	6	17	100	vr, eg, st	st,egg	farm,emp(wife	na	no	
9		n	f	6	10	60	bg	bg	C(3-5K)V,P	C	no	
10		n	f	3	33	100	Bbv	B	no	LM	no	
1	Gurako	h	f	6	60	360	Bpmbv	Bp	no	LM	theft	Gurako market:
2		h	f	6	120	720	Bpmbd,pi	p	C (1.5K)	LM	child health	peanu
3		y	f	6	20-1(	120-6(	p,co,v	p	no	LM	walking	6 publ
4		n	m	6	75	450	cu,corn,v	v	V, Gold	na	no	
5		n	f	2	50	100	pbv	p	no	LM	no	
6		n	f	6	75	450	pbv	v	fish	LM	no	
1	Gabensis	h	f	3	90	270	pmbv, coc	dry coc	V, cocoa	LM	theft, chil(	Gabensis marke
2		h	f	3	20	60	v,cu,coc,pi	dry coc	cocoa	LM	competition	
3		y	f	7	30	210	v,cu	v,cu	coc, cocoa	LM	no	
4		y	f	7	36	250	vp	p	V,coc,cocoa	LM	transport,theft	
5		n	f	3	33	100	b,papaya,co	dry coc	Coc, cocoa	LM	no	
6		n	f	3	17	50	pb,v,fruit	p	coc, cocoa	LM	no	
1	Nine Mile	h	f	3	17	50	Bbpvd	Taro,d	poultry	LM	theft	Nine mile marke(
2		h	f	7	70	490	pbv,taro	taro,p	C	LM	theft	
3		h	f	4	50	200	pmbvd, taro	taro,v	C(1k),cocoa,s(	LM	theft	
4		y	f	7	43	300	v,corn,fungi	fungi(wild)	cocoa	LM	transport	
5		y	f	7	100	700	only taro	taro	no	LM	transport	
6		y	f	6	42	250	b,g	b,cuc	C(3K)	LM	no	
7		n	f	3	33	100	taro,g	taro	no	LM	no	
8		n	f	3	13	50	taro,g	taro,g	st,poultry(12K'	st,po(	no	
9		n	f	5	20	100	bv,taro	g	emp,poultry (6	emp,	no	
1	Yalu (Sunda	h	f	4	90	360	pbv,taro	pb	cocoa,poultry	LM	no	Yalu(Sunday) ma
2		h	f	2	150	300	Bbv,coc	b,coc	cocoa (3.5K),(	coco(	cocoa theft	
3		h	f	2	30	60	p,cuc,beans	beans	no	LM	no	
4		h	f	2	100	200	taro,v,coc,b	coc	cocoa	LM	domestic	
5		h	f	3	190	570	pbgv	banana	cocoa(3K)	LM	theft,transport	
6		y	f	7	200+	1500+	bfvg,coc	cook banan	empl(husban(	LM	transport	
7		y	f	7	100	700	fg,water,clot	oranges	no	LM	transport,water	
8		y	f	7	85	600	only brus	brus(tobac)	no	LM	transport	
9		y	f	7	85	600	only brus	brus(tobac)	no	LM	transport	
10		y	m	4	30	120	pgv	peanuts	no	LM	no	
11		n	f	3	30	90	bv	b&g	empl(school)	LM	no	
12		n	m	6	20	120	bv	banana	empl(labour p	LM	no	
13		n	m	5	100	500	bvg	banana	store	LM	no	
14		n	f	3	30	90	bg, kaukau	poultry(12K)er	na	no		
1	5 mile (Sun(	h	f	5	50	250	pbv,kaukau	pv	no	LM	transport	5 mile (Sunday) r
2		h	f	3	30	90	bgv	vg	empl(husban(	na	garden theft	
3		y	f	3	250	750	bfd	daka(musta	empl(father)	na	no	
4		y	f	7	70	500	bvg,coc	coconuts	no	LM	no	
5		n	f	7	20	140	b,kaukau	kaukau	empl(school)	na	no	

Items: buai (B), banana (b), peanut (p), veges (v), greens (g), melons (m), daka (d), tapioka (t), flour (f), cooked
coconut (co): COFFEE (C), POULTRY (P) STORE (S) VANILLA (V) store (st), ice=flavoured ice-block
Notes: #=mis-estimate; K=1,000 kina; poultry farm wage for labourers is 217K/wk. 1,000 for supervisors

Appendix Table 6.1: Chemical use by Higaturu in 2004

Product name	Product type	Amount used	Value US$
L1700 x 10	Surfactant	80 litres	447
24D	herbicide	4,406 litres	12,406
Activator 90	surfactant	1,980 litres	7,100
Trichlor tables x 10kg	chlorine	70 buckets	6,192
Glyphosphate 450	herbicide	17,022 litres	51,847
Gramoxone x 5 ltr	herbicide	3,685 litres	16,816
(Alloy) Metsulfuron x 500g	herbicide	169 per container	8,901
Icon 10WP x 50g	Malaria control insecticide	287 pkts	3,359
Diuron 500 FW	Herbicide	200 litres	1,005
Icon 2.5Cs x 500mls	Malaria control insecticide	18 per container	269

Source: HOP (2005a) 'Chemical use in HOP 2004, unpublished log

Appendix Table 6.2: Fertiliser use by Higaturu Oil Palms in 2004

	Total tonnes	Tonnes per ha
Organic fertiliser EFB:	45,027	17.59
Inorganic fertilisers:		
Am Chloride	1,757	1.6
Am Nitrate	96	0.49
Am sulphate	18	0.45
Calcium Borate	9	0.06
Potassium Chloride	1,376	1.72
Kieserite	56	0.97
Sodium Borate	39	0.04
Sulphur	6	0.19
TSP	10	0.15

Source: HOP (2005b) 'Estate report: fertiliser applied', 18 July, Pacrim Higaturu Oilpalms, Agrisoft systems printout, Popondetta

Appendix Table 6.3: Calculations used in the 2001 'oil palm fresh fruit bunch pricing formula'

Payout ratio elements:

1. CIF oil palm prices	Monthly average prices from 'Oil World', for month preceding FFB payment
2. Sales costs	A deduction before POR, for company sales costs, includes – freight, sales commissions, brokerage, insurance, overseas port charges
3. Extraction ratios	Converts FFB to oil palm products by ratios: CPO: 22.88; PK: 4.97
4. Exchange rates	Bank of PNG $US and $A rates, averaged
5. Transport costs	Deducted by company from millgate prices, eg HOP: 18K/Mt
6. VAT	Charged through a credit to farmers on the POR; reclaimable by the company
7. Levies	OPRA fees: 0.9K; OPIC fee: 3.5K (companies applying PPF pay a matching fee); and a fee of 1K for pest control is paid by farmers at Hoskins
8. POR	The post–1996 55% payout ratio is represented by this formula: [A x (CPO CIF–US$ Sales costs)] + B x (PKO CIF–US$ Sales costs)] + C x [(PKE CIF–US$ Sales costs] / US$/Kina = FOB Palm product value x POR = millgate price – FFB transport, VAT & levies = Farm–gate price // A, B & C = industry standard extraction rates for CPO, PKO and PKE

Cost assumptions:

1. Labour costs	= 5.50K per day (previously 3.85K – 70% min rural wage)
2. OPRA levy	= 0.90K per ton FFB (previously 0.56K)
3. OPIC levy	= 3.85K per ton FFB (previously 3.50K, now includes 10% VAT)
4. Land rent	= 80K per block per annum (LSS only – previously not applied)
5. House	= 1,000K (for VOP block, prev. 950K) = 3,500K (LSS block, prev. 2,500K)
6. Growers Assn fee	= 24K per block per year (previously 12K)

Example:

Higaturu (Oro) 2001	Kina palm product value of 1 mt FFB = 238.89K; farmers payout at 55% = 131.39K; add 1% VAT = 1.31K; less OPRA levy = 0.90K; less OPIC levey = 3.5K; less VAT at 10% on OPIC levy = 0.35K; Mill–gate price = 127.95K; less FFB transport costs = 18K; = Farm–gate price = 109.95K

Source: Burnett & Ellingsen 2001: 25–28, 31

Appendix Table 6.4: Higaturu Oil Palm Limited, harvest revenues and payments to small holders

	1984	1986	1988	1990
Average farmgate price to small holder FFB (K/tonne)	76.87	9.04	30.99	7.06
price in US$ (a)	86.53	9.39	35.77	7.49
Annual average price of palm oil in US$/tonne (b)	704.18	279.69	450.92	298.57
Proportion of FFB payments to CPO world price: (a) as % of (b)	12.29	3.37	7.95	2.51
Higaturu sales revenues (US$000)	31,613	12,448	19,581	15,540
the same in '000 Kina	28,084	11,985	16,965	14,664
of which: Palm Oil (000Kina)	25,888	11,438	15,431	12,888
: Palm Kernel (000Kina)	2,198	547	1,534	888
: Palm Kernel Oil (000Kina)				
Total Higaturu FFB harvested (tonnes)	108,668	117,683	106,574	135,784
Total Smallholder FFB harvested (tonnes)	68,288	83,693	73,082	70,177

Source: HOP (2004) *2004 Year Book*, Higaturu Oil Palms Limited, Popondetta (PNG)

Appendix Table 6.5: New Britain Palm Oil Limited, some indicators for 2000–04

	2000
Revenue (000 Kina)	229,030
Pre–tax profit (000 Kina)	63,495
Profit after tax (000 Kina)	47,464
Tax paid (000 Kina)	
Average price CPO (US$/tonne cif)	346
FFB from estate plantations (tonnes)	560,093
FFB from outgrowers (tonnes)	275,902
Foreign exchange gain (000 Kina)	
Director's fees (6 directors) (000 Kina)	
Numbers of employees (not directors) paid more than 100,000 Kina pa	
Numbers of employees (not directors) paid more than 200,000 Kina pa	
Numbers of employees (not directors) paid more than 400,000 Kina pa	
Numbers of employees (not directors) paid more than 800,000 Kina pa	

Source: NBPOL (2004) Report to Shareholders, Kimbe (PNG), pp.6, 13, 14 [2004 figures are projections]

1992	1994	1996	1998	2000	2002	2004
22.24	36.48	58.39	136.22	74.37	138.45	158.38
24.09	36.09	43.85	65.5	25.67	34.01	47.87
393.38	453.48	573.55	632.8	382.62	390.57	424.45
6.13	7.97	7.65	10.36	6.72	8.72	11.29
20,421	22,557	32,109	32,370	18,736	25,744	33,096
18,859	22,804	42,754	68,304	54,280	104,808	109,502
15,732	19,054	38,297	61,888	49,732	97,992	100,631
1,891	2,013	3,984	6,418	0	0	0
				4,548	6,816	8,871
134,531	138,435	155,306	142,352	146,586	143,098	149,731
60,190	57,519	71,726	94,279	113,109	140,034	146,291

2001	2002	2003	2004
206,676	319,111	340,099	392,176
37,289	101,709	109,223	126,317
6,844	68,001	76,654	88,355
		32,569	37,799
297	387	446	420
498,865	502,533	552,284	614,960
265,500	259,144	264,967	288,878
		12,228	5,170
		1,480	1,489
		40	41
		28	27
		17	14
		2	3

Bibliography

ల

CHAPTER TWO

ABC (2011) 'Budget boosts foreign aid', PM radio, May 11, online at: http://www.abc.net.au/pm/content/2011/s3214203.htm

Adedokun, Olaide, Oyetunji Akande, Adeola Karim and Nancy Nelson-Twakor (2000) 'Economic Liberalization and Women in the Informal Sector in Rural Nigeria', in Dzodzi Tsikata and Joanna Kerr (eds) (2000) *Demanding Dignity: Women Confronting Economic Reforms in Africa*, The North-South Institute and Third World Network-Africa

Ahmed, Abdel Ghaffar M. (2022) 'Survival under stress: the Rufa'a al-Hoi of the southern Funj in the Sudan', in Mustafa Babiker (ed.) (2002) *Resource Alienation, Militarisation and Development, Proceedings of the Regional Workshops on East African Drylands*, Organization for Social Science Research in Eastern and Southern Africa (OSSREA), 77–95, online at: http://www.ossrea.net/publications/images/stories/ossrea/dhp–resource–alienation.pdf

AusAID (2001) 'Undertaking Land Administration Projects: a sustainability, affordability, operational efficiency and good practice guidelines', *Quality Assurance Series*, No 26, July, Canberra, online at: http://www.ausaid.gov.au/publications/pdf/qas26.pdf

AusAID (2000) 'Improving Access to Land and Enhancing the Security of Land Rights: a review of land titling and land administration projects', *Quality Assurance Series*, No 20, September, Canberra, online at: http://www.ausaid.gov.au/publications/pdf/qas20.pdf

AusAID (2006) 'Australian Aid: Promoting Growth and Stability – White Paper', Australian Government, online at: http://www.ausaid.gov.au/publications/pubout.cfm? Id=6184_6346_7334_4045_8043

AusAID (2008) 'Making Land Work, Volume One – Reconciling Customary Land and Development in the Pacific, Canberra, online at: http://www.ausaid.gov.au/publications/pubout.cfm?ID=3363_9223_6836_1452_8140

AusAID (2009) 'Aid Activities: Pacific Land Program ($8 million 2009/10)', Australian Government, July, online at: http://www.ausaid.gov.au/country/pacific/land.cfm

Berman, Marshall (1983) *All that is solid melts into air: the experience of modernity*, Verso, London

Bourke, R. Michael (2005) 'Agricultural Production and Customary Land in Papua New Guinea', in Jim Fingleton (ed.) (2005) *Privatising Land in the Pacific*, Discussion Paper Number 80, The Australian Institute, Canberra, June

Bourke, R.M., C. Camarotto. E.J. DSouza, K, Nema, T.N. Tarepe & S. Woodhouse (2004) *Production Patterns of 180 Economic Crops in Papua New Guinea*, Coombs Academic Publishing, Australian National University, Canberra

Bredmeyer, T. (1975) 'The Registration of Customary Land in Papua New Guinea', *Melanesian Law Journal*, 3(2), 267–87

Brown, Paula, Harold Brookfield and Robin Grau (1990) 'Land Tenure and Transfer in Chimbu, Papua New Guinea: 1958–1984 – a study in continuity and change, accommodation and opportunism', *Human Ecology*, Vol 18, No 1, 21–49

Burns, Tony, Bob Eddington, Chris Grant and Ian Lloyd (1996) 'Land Titling Experience in Asia', BHP employees, online at: http://sfrc.ifas.ufl.edu/geomatics/publications/land_conf96/Burns.PDF

Burton, J. (1991) 'Social Mapping' in P. Larmour (ed.) (1991) *Customary Land Tenure: Registration and Decentralisation in Papua New Guinea*, Bulletin 40, Australian National University, New Guinea Research Unit, Port Moresby

Chimhowu, Admos and Phil Woodhouse (2006) 'Customary vs Private Property Rights? Dynamics and Trajectories of Vernacular Land Markets in Sub-Saharan Africa', *Journal of Agrarian Change*, Vol 6, No 3, July, 346–71

Curtin, Tim (2003) 'Scarcity Amidst Plenty: the economics of land tenure in Papua New Guinea' in Tim Curtin, Hartmut Holzknecht and Peter Larmour (2003) *Land Registration in Papua New Guinea: competing perspectives*, Discussion Paper 2003/1, State Society and Governance in Melanesia, Australian National University, Canberra

Dickerman, Carol; Grenville Barnes, John W. Bruce, Joy K. Green, Greg Myers, Richard Polishuk, Douglas Stienbarger, and Andrew Sund (1989) *Security of Tenure and Land Registration in Africa: Literature Review and Synthesis,* Land Tenure Centre, University of Wisconsin-Madison, Madison USA

Deininger, Klaus (2003) 'Land Policies for Growth and Policy Reduction', World Bank Policy Research Report, Oxford University Press and the World Bank, Washington

Downs I. (1980) *The Australian Trusteeship: Papua New Guinea 1945–1975*, Australian Government Publishing Service, Canberra

Elhadary, Yasin Abdalla Eltayeb (2010) 'Challenges facing land tenure system in relation to pastoral livelihood security in Gedarif State, Eastern Sudan', *Journal of Geography and Regional Planning*, Vol 3(9), September, 208–18

Fingelton, Jim (2004) 'Is Papua New Guinea viable without customary groups?' *Pacific Economic Bulletin*, Vol 19, No 2, 96–103

Fitzpatrick, Daniel (2005) 'Best Practice Options for the Legal Recognition of Customary Tenure', *Development and Change*, Vol 36, No 3, 449–75

Foley, Gary and Tim Anderson (2006) 'Land Rights and Aboriginal Voices', *Australian Journal of Human Rights*, Special Issue: Marginality and Exclusion, Vol 12, Issue 1, pp.83–108

Garu, Selwyn (2010) Interview with this writer, Mele Village, Efate Island, Vanuatu, 14 June [Chief Selwyn Garu was at that time head of Vanuatu's Council of Chiefs]

Gibson, John (2000) 'The Economic and Nutritional Importance of Household Food Production in PNG', in R.M. Bourke, M.G. Allen and J.G. Salisbury (2000) *Food*

Security for Papua New Guinea, Proceedings of the Papua New Guinea Food and Nutrition 2000 Conference, PNG University of Technology, Lae, 26–30 June

Gibson, John, Gaurav Dutt, Bryant Allen, Vicky Hwang, R. Michael Bourke and Dilip Parajuli (2005) 'Mapping Poverty in Rural Papua New Guinea', *Pacific Economic Bulletin*: 20, 1, 27–43

Giddens, Anthony (1998) *Conversations with Anthony Giddens: Making Sense of Modernity*, Stanford University Press, Palo Alto CA

Gosarevski, Steven; Helen Hughes and Susan Windybank (2004) 'Is Papua New Guinea Viable?', *Pacific Economic Bulletin*, 19 (1) 134–48

Grant, Chris (1999) 'Lessons from SE Asian Cadastral Reform, Land Titling and Land Administration Projects in Supporting Sustainable Development in the Next Millennium', BHP Engineering, Melbourne, online at: http://www.fig.net/figun/sessions/session8/grant.pdf

Gregory, C.A. (1982) Gifts and Commodities, London, Academic Press

Healy, Sean (2001) 'Papua New Guinea: People Rebel Against World Bank', Green Left Weekly, July 4, online at: http://www.greenleft.org.au/node/24766

Hyndman, David (2001) 'Academic Responsibilities and Representation of the Ok Tedi Crisis in Postcolonial Papua New Guinea', *The Contemporary Pacific*, Volume 13, Number 1, Spring 2001, pp. 33–54

Hughes, Helen (2004) 'The Pacific is Viable!', *Issue Analysis* No 53, Centre for Independent Studies, online at: http://www.vanuatu.usp.ac.fj/sol_adobe_documents/usp%20only/pacific%20general/hughes2.pdf

Ikdahl, Ingunn, Anne Helum, Randi Kaarhus, Tor A. Benjaminsen and Patricia Kameri-Mbote (2005) 'Human rights, formalisation and women's land rights in southern and eastern Africa', Noragric Report No 26, Norwegian University of Life Sciences, Oslo, online at: http://www.ielrc.org/content/w0507.pdf

Koczberski, G; G. Curry and K. Gibson (2001) 'Improving Productivity of the Smallholder Oil Palm Sector in Papua New Guinea: a socio-economic study of the Hoskins and Popondetta Schemes', Australian National University, Canberra, November

Lakau, Andrew (1991) *State acquisition of customary land for public purposes in Papua New Guinea, Department of Surveying and Land Studies*, Papua New Guinea University of Technology, Lae

Lakau, Andrew A.L. (1994) 'Customary land tenure and economic development in PNG' in Ron Crocombe and Malama Meleisea (Eds) (1994) *Land Issues in the Pacific, Institute of South Pacific Studies*, University of the South Pacific, Suva

Lamont, Michele and Marcel Fournier (1992) *Cultivating Differences: Symbolic Boundaries and the Making of Inequality*, University of Chicago Press, Chicago

Larmour, Peter (1991) *Customary Land Tenure: registration and decentralisation in Papua New Guinea*, Monograph 29, Institute of Applied Social and Economic Research / National Research Institute, Port Moresby

Larmour, Peter (2002) 'Policy Transfer and Reversal: customary land registration from Africa to Melanesia', *Public Administration and Development*, Vol 22, 151–61

Lawrence, J.C.D. (1970) 'The role of registration of title in the evolution of customary tenures and its effect on societies in Africa', paper at the Seminar on Cadastre, Addis Ababa, UN Economic Commission for Africa

MAAHWR (1956) *African Land Development in Kenya: 1946–55*, The Ministry of Agriculture, Animal Husbandry and Water Resources, Nairobi

Meinzen-Dick, Ruth (2009) 'Property Rights for Poverty Reduction?', DESA Working Paper No. 91, United Nations Department of Economic and Social Affairs, New York, ST/ESA/2009/DWP/91, December, online at: http://www.un.org/esa/desa/papers/2009/wp91_2009.pdf

Narokobi, Bernard (1988) 'Concept of Ownership in Melanesia', Occasional Paper No 6, The Melanesian Institute, Goroka, 2nd printing 1999

Naupa, Anna and Joel Simo (2008) 'Matrilineal Tenure in Vanuatu: 'Hu I kakae long basket?' case studies of Raga and Mele, in Elsie Huffer (ed.) (2008) *Land and Women: the Matrilineal Factor: The Case Studies of the Republic of the Marshall Islands*, Solomon

Islands and Vanuatu, Pacific Islands Forum Secretariat, 73–122, online at http://www.forumsec.org/resources/uploads/attachments/documents/Land%20and%20Women.pdf

NLDT-SCCLD (2006) 'Recommendations and Report to the National Land Development Task Force', SubCommittee on Customary Land Development, National Land Development Taskforce, University of Papua New Guinea, Port Moresby, 17 July

Okoth-Ogendo, Kenneth (1982) 'The perils of land tenure reform: the case of Kenya', in J.W. Arntzen, L.D. Ngcongco, and S.D. Turner (1986) *Land Policy and Agriculture in Eastern and Southern Africa*, Selected Papers Presented at a Workshop, Held in Gaborone, Botswana, 14–19 February, The United Nations University, online at: http://fimbo.org/attachments/059_The%20perils%20of%20land%20tenure%20reform-%20the%20case%20of%20Kenya.pdf

Ostrom, Elinor (2010) 'Robust Property Rights Institutions to Manage Local and Global Commons', Presentation to the World Bank, April 26, online at: http://siteresources.worldbank.org/EXTARD/Resources/336681-1236436879081/5893311-1271205116054/ostrom.pdf

Place, Frank and S.E. Migot–Adholla (1998) 'The Economic Effects of Land Registration on Smallholder Farms in Kenya: evidence from Nyeri and Kakamega Districts', Land Economics, Vol 74 No 3, 360–73

Platteau, Jean–Philippe (1996) 'The Evolutionary Theory of Land Rights as Applied to Sub–Saharan Africa: A Critical Assessment', Development and Change, Vol 27, 29–86

Shaw, Barry (1985) *Agriculture in the Papua New Guinea Economy*, Institute of National Affairs, Port Moresby, Discussion Paper No 20, June

Shiva, Vandana (1993) *Monocultures of the Mind: Perspectives on Biodiversity and Biotechnology*, Zed Books, London

Sillitoe, Paul (1999) 'Beating the Boundaries: Land Tenure and Identity in the Papua New Guinea Highlands', *Journal of Anthropological Research*, Vol 55, No 3, Fall, 331–57

Tiffany, Sharon W. (1983) 'Customary Land Disputes, Courts and African Models in the Solomon islands', *Oceania*, Vol 53, No 3, March, 277–90

Reynolds, Henry (1987) *The Law of the Land*, Penguin, Melbourne

Richardson, Colin (2006) 'Land Stewardship in Island Economies', *Dissent*, [Review of Fingleton et al 2005] Autumn/Winter

Rodman, Margaret (1984) 'Masters of Tradition: customary land tenure and new forms of social inequality in a Vanuatu peasantry', *American Ethnologist*, Vol 1 No 1, February, 61–80

Rusanen, Liisa (2005) 'Customary Landowners Rights Under Threat in Papua New Guinea: An update on the land debate and amendments to forestry and mining legislation', Aid/watch, Background Paper No 10, December 13, online at: http://www.aidwatch.org.au/sites/aidwatch.org.au/files/png+land+dec+05.pdf

Simpson, Rowton (1976) *Land Law and Registration*, Cambridge University Press, Cambridge

Swynnerton, R.J.M. (1955) *The Swynnerton Report: A plan to intensify the development of African agriculture in Kenya*, Government Printer, Nairobi

UNDP (1999) *Papua New Guinea Human Development Report 1998*, Office of National Planning and United Nations Development Programme, Port Moresby

Weiner, James F. and Katie Glaskin (2007) *Customary Land Tenure and Registration in Papua New Guinea: Anthropological Perspectives*, ANU E–Press, Australian National University, Canberra

World Bank (1975) 'Land Reform Policy Paper', Washington

World Bank (1989) 'Land Mobilization Program: Papua New Guinea', Projects and Operations, Project ID: P004386, 12 April, online at: http://web.worldbank.org/external/projects/main?Projectid=P004386

World Bank (1999) 'Papua New Guinea: improving governance and performance', Poverty Reduction and Economic Management Sector Unit, East Asia and Pacific Region, Washington, October 22

Yala, Charles (2005) 'The Genesis of the Papua New Guinea Land Reform Program: selected papers from the 2005 National Land Summit, National Research Institute, Monograph No 42, Port Moresby

Yala, Charles (2006) 'Rethinking customary land tenure issues in Papua New Guinea', *Pacific Economic Bulletin*, Vol 21, No 1, 129–37

Yala, Charles (2010) 'Overview' in Charles Yala (ed.) (2010) 'The Genesis of the Papua New Guinea Land Reform Program: selected papers from the 2005 National Land Summit, National Research Institute, Port Moresby

CHAPTER THREE

Altieri, Miguel A. (2004) 'Linking ecologists and traditional farmers in the search for sustainable agriculture', *Frontiers in Ecology and the Environment* 2: 35–42.

Anderson, Tim (2006) 'On the economic value of customary land in Papua New Guinea', *Pacific Economic Bulletin*, Volume 21 Number 1 (2006), pp. 138–52, online at: http://peb.anu.edu.au/pdf/PEB21–1Anderson–focus.pdf

Anderson, Tim (2008) 'Women roadside sellers in Madang', Pacific Economic Bulletin, Vol 23, No 1, online: http://peb.anu.edu.au/pdf/PEB23–1–Anderson.pdf

Anderson, Tim (2011) 'Melanesian Land: The Impact of Markets and Modernisation', *Journal of Australian Political Economy*, No 68, pp.86–107

AusAID (2000) *Improving Access to Land and Enhancing the Security of Land Rights: a review of land titling and land administration projects*, Quality Assurance Series No 20, September, AusAID, Canberra

AusAID (2006) 'Australian Aid: Promoting Growth and Stability: A White Paper on the Australian Government's Aid Program', AusAID, Canberra, online at: http://www.ausaid.gov.au/publications/pubout.cfm?Id=6184_6346_7334_4045_8043

AusAID (2008) 'Making Land Work', AusAID, Canberra, online at: http://www.ausaid.gov.au/publications/pubout.cfm?ID=3363_9223_6836_1452_8140

Boserup, Ester (1965) *The Conditions of Agricultural Growth: the economics of agrarian change under population pressure*, G. Allen, Chicago

Bourke, R. Michael and V. Vlassak (2004) *Estimates of Food Crop Production in Papua New Guinea*, Australian National University, Canberra

Bourke, RM; A. McGregor; MG Allen; BR Evans; BF Mullen; AA Pollard; M Wairu and S. Zotalis (2006) *Solomon Islands Smallholder Agriculture Study, Volume 1: Main Findings and Recommendations*, AusAID, Australian Government, Canberra, January

BSP (c.2010) Business: Welcome to Port Moresby, Bank of the South Pacific, Port Moresby

Bun, Y.; T. King and P.L. Sherman (2004) 'China's Impact on Papua New Guinea's Forest Industry', *Forest Trends*, online at: http://www.forest–trends.org/documents/files/doc_154.pdf

Burnett, Duncan & Dennis Ellingsen (2001) *Review of the Oil Palm Fresh Fruit Bunch Pricing Formula, Final Report prepared for the Commodities Working Group of the Government of PNG*, National Resources Institute and ADS (PNG), Port Moresby, November

CELCOR and ACF (2006) 'Bulldozing progress: Human rights abuses and corruption in PNG's large scale logging industry', Centre for Environmental Law & Community Rights (CELCOR) and Australian Conservation Foundation (ACF), Port Moresby

Cotula, Lorenzo, Camilla Toulmin & Ced Hesse (2004) *Land Tenure and Administration in Africa: lessons of experience and emerging issues, International Institute for Environment and Development*, London

Cousins, Ben; Tessa Cousins, Donna Hornby, Rosalie Kingwill, Lauren Royston and Warren Smit (2005) 'Will Formalising Property Rights Reduce Poverty in South Africa's 'Second Economy'?', Policy Brief No 18, Programme for Land and Agrarian Studies (PLAAS), Cape Town, October

Danielsen F, Beukema H, Burgess ND, Parish F, Bruhl CA, Donald PF, Murdiyarso D, Phalan B, Reijnders L, Struebig M, Fitzherbert EB (2009) 'Biofuel plantations on forested lands: double jeopardy for biodiversity and climate', *Conservation Biology*, 23, pp.348–58

Deininger, Klaus (2003) 'Land Policies for Growth and Policy Reduction', *World Bank Policy Research Report*, Oxford University Press and the World Bank, Washington

Deininger, Klaus and Gershon Feder (1998) 'Land Institutions and Land Markets', *Policy Research Working Paper*, Development Research Group: Rural Development, World Bank, November

De Soto, Hernando (2000) *The Mystery of Capital*, Bantam, New York

De Soto, Hernando (2002) 'Law and Property Outside the West: a few new ideas about fighting poverty', *Forum for Development Studies*, Number 2, 2002, Volume 29, Norwegian Institute for International Affairs, Oslo

Dickerman, Carol; Grenville Barnes, John W. Bruce, Joy K. Green, Greg Myers, Richard Polishuk, Douglas Stienbarger, and Andrew Sund (1989) *Security of Tenure and Land Registration in Africa: Literature Review and Synthesis*, Land Tenure Centre, University of Wisconsin–Madison, Madison USA

EIA–Telapak (2005) 'The Last Frontier: Illegal Logging in Papua New Guinea and China's Massive Timber Theft', *Environmental Investigation Agency*, online at: http://www.eia–international.org/files/reports93–1.pdf

Fairhead, Lindsay; Gae Kauzi and Charles Yala (2010) 'Land Reform in Papua New Guinea: quantifying the economic impacts', *National Research Institute*, Discussion Paper No 108, Port Moresby

Gou and Higaturu (1999) *Agricultural lease between Gou Development Corporation (Oro Province) and Higaturu Oil Palms*, September, Port Moresby

Hanson, L.W., B.J. Allen, R.M. Bourke and T.J. McCarthy (2001) *Papua New Guinea Rural Development Handbook*, Australian National University, Research School of Pacific and Asian Studies, Department of Human Geography, Canberra

Hughes, H. (2004) 'The Pacific is Viable!', *Issue Analysis* No 53, Centre for Independent Studies, Sydney

Hunt, Diana (2004) 'Unintended Consequences of Land Rights Reform: the case of the 1998 Uganda Land Act', *Development Policy Review*, 22 (2), 173–91

IFRT (2004) *Towards Sustainable Timber Production: A Review of Existing Logging Projects: Draft Observations and Recommendations Report*, Independent Forestry Review Team, Report to the Inter–Agency Forestry Review Committee, Port Moresby

ITS Global (2006) 'The Economic Importance of the Forestry Industry to Papua New Guinea', *International Trade Strategies Ltd*, Report for the Rimbunan Hijau (PNG) Group, July, Melbourne, online at: http://www.forestryanddevelopment.com/documents/pdf/fd–ITSGlobalEconomicreport.pdf

ITS Global (2009) 'The Economic Benefits of Land Use in Papua New Guinea', *International Trade Strategies Global*, Melbourne, November online at: http://www.fiapng.com/PDF_files/PNG%20Land%20Use%20Report%20Final4%20Nov%202009.pdf

ITS Global (2010) 'A 'REDD+iness' Program for Papua New Guinea: a strategy to promote sustainability and growth', *A Report for the PNG Forest Industries Association*, November, online at:http://www.itsglobal.net/sites/default/files/itsglobal/A%20REDDiness%20program%20for%20PNG%20%282010%29.pdf

ITS Global (2011) 'The Economic Benefits of Palm Oil in Papua New Guinea', *International Trade Strategies Ltd*, March, Melbourne, online at: http://www.itsglobal.net/sites/default/files/itsglobal/The%20Economic%20Benefits%20of%20Palm%20Oil%20in%20PNG%20%282011%29.pdf

Jevons, William Stanley (1871) *The theory of political economy*, MacMillan, London

Keynes, John Maynard (1936) *The General Theory Of Employment Interest And Money*, Palgrave Macmillan, Basingstoke

Kimbrell, Andrew (2002) *Fatal Harvest: The Tragedy of Industrial Agriculture, Foundation for Deep Ecology, Sausalito*

Koczberski, Gina (2007) 'Loose Fruit Mamas: creating incentives for smallholder women in oil palm production in Papua New Guinea', *World Development*, Vol 35 No 7, pp.1172–1185

Koja, Anderson (2003) Interview with this writer, Popondetta, 4 March [the late Anderson Koja was Chairman of the Popondetta Oil Palm Growers Association]

Laurance, William F.; Titus Kakul; Rodney J. Keenan; Jeffrey Sayer; Simon Passingan; Gopalasamy R. Clements, Felipe Villegas and Navjot S. Sodhi (2011) 'Predatory corporations, failing governance and the fate of forests in Papua New Guinea', *Conservation Letters*, Vol 4 Issue 2, April–May, pp.95–100

Lawrence, J.C.D. (1970) 'The role of registration of title in the evolution of customary tenures and its effect on societies in Africa', paper at the Seminar on Cadastre, Addis Ababa, UN Economic Commission for Africa

Lavigne Delville, Phillipe (2006) 'Registering and Administering Customary Land Rights: PFRs in West Africa', Communication to the World Bank Conference on 'Land Policies & Legal Empowerment of the Poor', Session 'Improving Tenure Security: Methods and Impact', Washington, November 2 – 3, online at: http://siteresources. worldbank.org/RPDLPROGRAM/Resources/459596–1161903702549/S4_Lavigne. pdf

Lee, Gary and Tim Anderson (eds) (2010) *In Defence of Customary Land*, Aidwatch, Sydney

Matbob, Patrick (2011) 'Relief to unskilled workers. But employers?', *Islands Business*, accessed 6 September, online at: http://www.islandsbusiness.com/islands_business/ index_dynamic/containerNameToReplace=MiddleMiddle/focusModuleID=18595/ overideSkinName=issueArticle–full.tpl

Meier, Gerald M. and Dudley Seers (eds) (1984) *Pioneers in Development*, World Bank, Washington

Meinzen-Dick, Ruth (2009) 'Property Rights for Poverty Reduction?', DESA Working Paper No 91, United Nations *Department of Economic and Social Affairs*, New York, December, online at: http://www.un.org/esa/desa/papers/2009/wp91_2009.pdf

Menger, Carl (1871) *Grundsätze der Volkswirtschaftslehre (Principles of Economics)*, Ludwig von Mises Institute, Auburn Alabama (2007 edition)

Moxnes Jervell, Anne and Desmond A. Jolley (2003) 'Beyond Food: towards a multifunctional agriculture', Working Paper 2003–19, *Norwegian Agricultural research Institute*, Oslo, online at: http://www.nilf.no/Publikasjoner/Notater/En/2003/ N200319Hele.pdf

Okoth-Ogendo, Kenneth (1982) 'The perils of land tenure reform: the case of Kenya', in J.W. Arntzen, L.D. Ngcongco, and S.D. Turner (1986) *Land Policy and Agriculture in Eastern and Southern Africa, Selected Papers Presented at a Workshop*, Held in Gaborone, Botswana, 14–19 February, The United Nations University, online at: http://fimbo. org/attachments/059_The%20perils%20of%20land%20tenure%20reform–%20the%20 case%20of%20Kenya.pdf

Rosset, Peter (2000) 'The Multiple Functions and Benefits of Small Farm Agriculture in the Context of Global Trade Negotiations', *Development*, Volume 43, Number 2, June 2000 , pp. 77–82

Samuelson, Paul (1947) *Foundations of Economic Analysis*, Harvard University Press, Cambridge, Massachusetts

Samuelson, Paul and William Nordhaus (1948–2009) Economics, McGraw–Hill/Irwin, New York (by 2009, this text was in its 19th edition)

Seneviratne, Kalinga (1995) 'IMF Plan Rejected by PNG People', Third World Network, 6 September, online at: www.hatford–hwp.com/archives/24/083.html

Sen, Amartya (1983) Development: Which Way Now?, *The Economic Journal*, Vol. 93, No. 372 (Dec., 1983), pp. 745–762

Sen, Amartya (1999) *Development as Freedom*, Oxford University Press, Oxford

Shiva, Vandana (1993) *Monocultures of the Mind: Perspectives on Biodiversity and Biotechnology*, Zed Books, London

Sodhi, Gaurav (2008) 'Five out of Ten', Island Sun, Honiara, Feb 4, p.4 and Feb 8, p.5

Sowei, J.W., Lahari, W. and Vatnabar, M. (2003) 'Rural Informal Sector Survey Report', January, National Research Institute (Social and Environmental Studies Division), Port Moresby

Stilwell, Frank (2006) *Political Economy: The Contest of Economics Ideas*, Oxford University Press, Oxford

Swynnerton, R.J.M. (1955) *The Swynnerton Report: A plan to intensify the development of African agriculture in Kenya*, Government Printer, Nairobi

Tararia, Almah (2003) Interview with this writer, Senior Lawyer, Environmental Law Centre, Port Moresby

UNDP (1990) Human Development Report 1990, United Nations Development Programme, New York

Uni Tavur (2001) The Uni Tavur testimony', *Pacific Journalism Review*, 7: 1 , pp.1–13, http://www.asiapac.org.fj/PJR/issues/next/2001unitavur.pdf

United Nations (2006) United Nations Millennium Project, online at: http://www.unmillenniumproject.org/goals/index.htm

Walras, Léon (1874/1877) Éléments d'économie politique pure, ou théorie de la richesse sociale *(Elements of Pure Economics, or the theory of social wealth)*, Librairie generale de droit et de jurisprudence, Paris (1952 edition)

Warner, R. and Bauer, M. (2002) 'Mama Lus Frut Scheme: an assessment of poverty reduction', *ACIAR Impact Assessment Series* No.20, Canberra, online at: http://aciar.gov.au/files/node/2236/ias20.pdf

Wilcove, David S.; and Lian Pin Koh (2010) 'Addressing the threats to biodiversity from oil-palm agriculture', Biodiversity and Conservation, Vol 19 No 4, pp.999–1007, online at: http://www.springerlink.com/content/x2ku107711p6u777/fulltext.pdf

World Bank (1989) 'Land Mobilization Program: Papua New Guinea', Projects and Operations, Project ID: P004386, 12 April, online at: http://web.worldbank.org/external/projects/main?Projectid=P004386

World Bank (2007) 'PNG Smallholder Agriculture Development', Project P079140, 30 November, online at: http://web.worldbank.org/external/projects/main?Projectid=P079140&theSitePK=40941&piPK=64290415&pagePK=64283627&menuPK=64282134&Type=Overview

World Bank (2010) 'Papua New Guinea Smallholder Agriculture Development Project', online at: http://web.worldbank.org/WBSITE/EXTERNAL/PROJECTS/0,,contentMDK:22608600~menuPK:64282138~pagePK:64614770~piPK:64614834~theSitePK:40941,00.html

World Bank (2011) 'Papua New Guinea: smallholder agriculture development project: frequently asked questions', online at: http://web.worldbank.org/WBSITE/EXTERNAL/COUNTRIES/EASTASIAPACIFICEXT/PAPUANEWGUINEAEXTN/0,,contentMDK:22140271~menuPK:333773~pagePK:1497618~piPK:217854~theSitePK:333767,00.html

Yala, Charles (2010) 'Overview' in Charles Yala (ed.) (2010) 'The Genesis of the Papua New Guinea Land Reform Program: selected papers from the 2005 *National Land Summit*, National Research Institute, Port Moresby

Yambai, Oiyoi (2003) Interview with this writer, Uriginia Village, Upper Ramu, March [Oiyoi is a member of the Ramu Valley Land Owners Association (RVLOA), and a traditional owner in LLG Ward 13]

CHAPTER FOUR

ADB (2004) *Swimming Against the Tide? As Assessment of the Private Sector in the Pacific Islands*, Asian Development Bank, Manila

Aipapu Marai (2009) Interview with this writer, Sausi, Madang Province, Papua New Guinea, 18 November

Alatas, Syed Hussein (1977) *The Myth of the Lazy Native: A study of the image of the Malays, Filipinos and Javanese from the 16th to the 20th century and its function in the ideology of colonial capitalism*, Frank Cass and Company, London; also available online at: http://www.bandung2.co.uk/books/Files/Economics/The_Myth_of_The_Lazy_Native.pdf

Allen, Matthew G. (2000) 'Subsistence or cash cropping? Food Security on Malo Island, Vanuatu' in R.M. Bourke, M.G. Allen and J.G. Salisbury (2000) *Food Security for Papua New Guinea, Proceedings of the Papua New Guinea Food and Nutrition 2000 Conference*, PNG University of Technology, Lae, 26–30 June

Altieri, Miguel A. (2004) 'Linking ecologists and traditional farmers in the search for sustainable agriculture', *Frontiers in Ecology and the Environment* 2: 35–42.

Anderson, Tim (2003) The World Bank's claims of 'good governance' in Papua New Guinea, report for the Australian Conservation Foundation (ACF) and the Centre for Environmental Law and Community Rights (CELCOR) – 60pp

Anderson, Tim (2006) 'On the economic value of customary land in Papua New Guinea', *Pacific Economic Bulletin*, Volume 21 Number 1 (2006), pp. 138–152, online at: http://peb.anu.edu.au/pdf/PEB21–1Anderson–focus.pdf

Anderson, Tim (2008) 'Women roadside sellers in Madang', *Pacific Economic Bulletin*, Vol 23, No 1, online: http://peb.anu.edu.au/pdf/PEB23–1–Anderson.pdf

Anderson, Tim (2011) 'Melanesian Land: The Impact of Markets and Modernisation', *Journal of Australian Political Economy*, No 68, pp.86–107

Anderson, Tim and Gary Lee (eds) (2010) *In Defence of Customary Land*, Aidwatch, Sydney

AusAID (2006) 'Australian Aid: Promoting Growth and Stability: A White Paper on the Australian Government's Aid Program', *AusAID*, Canberra, online at: http://www.ausaid.gov.au/publications/pubout.cfm?Id=6184_6346_7334_4045_8043

AusAID (2008) 'Making Land Work', *AusAID,* Canberra, online at: http://www.ausaid.gov.au/publications/pubout.cfm?ID=3363_9223_6836_1452_8140

Bebbington, Anthony (1999) 'Capitals and Capabilities: a framework for analysing peasant viability, rural livelihoods and poverty', *World Development*, Vol 27 No 12, pp.2021–2044

Bebbington, Anthony (2000) 'Re-encountering development: livelihood transitions and place transformations in the Andes', *Annals of the Association of American Geographers*, 90(3), 495–520

Benediktsson, Karl (1998) 'Food Markets in the Eastern Highlands, Papua New Guinea: actors, power and rural development geography', *Geografiska Annaler*, 80 B (3), 159–172

Boserup, Ester (1965) *The Conditions of Agricultural Growth: the economics of agrarian change under population pressure*, G. Allen, Chicago

Bourke, R. Michael and V. Vlassak (2004) *Estimates of Food Crop Production in Papua New Guinea*, Australian National University, Canberra

Bourke, R. Michael (2005) 'Agricultural Production and Customary Land in Papua New Guinea', in Jim Fingleton (ed.) (2005) *Privatising Land in the Pacific*, Discussion Paper Number 80, The Australian Institute, Canberra, June

Bourke, R.M.; C. Camarotto; E.J. D'Souza; K. Nema; T.N. Tarepe; and S. Woodhouse (2004) *Production Patterns of 180 Economic Crops in Papua New Guinea*, Coombs Academic Publishing, Australian National University, Canberra

Bourke, RM; A. McGregor; MG Allen; BR Evans; BF Mullen; AA Pollard; M Wairu and S. Zotalis (2006) *Solomon Islands Smallholder Agriculture Study*, Volume 1: Main Findings and Recommendations, AusAID, Australian Government, Canberra, January

Brennan, G. (1992) 'Mabo & Others v State of Queensland', High Court of Australia, Australian Law Reports, 107, 6 July

Buno (2004) interview with this writer, Pikosa Village, Eastern Highlands Province, 7 December

Callick, Rowan (2005) 'Resource Issues as a Source of Conflict', *Pacific Economic Bulletin*, Vol 20 No 1, May

CELCOR (2002) *Para–legal Training Manual, Centre for Environmental Law and Community Rights*, Port Moresby

Chitoa, John (2004) Interview with this writer, Madang, 14 December

Cleaver, Harry M. (1972) 'The Contradictions of the Green Revolution', *The American Economic Review*, Vol 62, No 1/2 March, 177–186

Cotula, Lorenzo, Camilla Toulmin & Ced Hesse (2004) *Land Tenure and Administration in Africa: lessons of experience and emerging issues*, International Institute for Environment and Development, London

Cousins, Ben; Tessa Cousins, Donna Hornby, Rosalie Kingwill, Lauren Royston and Warren Smit (2005) 'Will Formalising Property Rights Reduce Poverty in South Africa's 'Second Economy'?, *Policy Brief* No 18, Programme for Land and Agrarian Studies (PLAAS), Cape Town, October

Curtin, Tim and David Lea (2006) 'Land titling and socioeconomic development in the South Pacific, Pacific *Economic Bulletin*, Vol 21 No 1, 153–180

Deininger, Klaus (2003) 'Land Policies for Growth and Policy Reduction', *World Bank Policy Research Report*, Oxford University Press and the World Bank, Washington

Deininger, Klaus and Gershon Feder (1998) 'Land Institutions and Land Markets', *Policy Research Working Paper*, Development Research Group: Rural Development, World Bank, November

De Soto, Hernando (2000) *The Mystery of Capital*, Bantam, New York

De Soto, Hernando (2002) 'Law and Property Outside the West: a few new ideas about fighting poverty', *Forum for Development Studies*, Number 2, 2002, Volume 29, Norwegian Institute for International Affairs, Oslo

DFAT (2004) 'Solomon Islands: rebuilding an island economy', Department of Foreign Affairs and Trade', Economic Analytical Unit, 157pp., online at: www.dfat.gov.au/eau (GET REF)

Dickerman, Carol; Grenville Barnes, John W. Bruce, Joy K. Green, Greg Myers, Richard Polishuk, Douglas Stienbarger, and Andrew Sund (1989) *Security of Tenure and Land Registration in Africa: Literature Review and Synthesis*, Land Tenure Centre, University of Wisconsin–Madison, Madison USA

Downer, Alexander (2006) 'from the Minister', *Focus Magazine*, Sept–Nov, Vol 21, No 3, online at: www.ausaid.gov.au/publications/focus/sep06/focus_sep06.doc

DTI (2001) Statistical Digest 2000, Department of Trade and Industry, Papua New Guinea, July 2001, Port Moresby

FAO (2011) 'The State of Food Insecurity in the World', Food and Agriculture Organization of the United Nations, online at: http://www.fao.org/publications/sofi/en/

Fairhead, Lindsay; Gae Kauzi and Charles Yala (2010) 'Land Reform in Papua New Guinea: quantifying the economic impacts', National Research Institute, Discussion Paper No 108, Port Moresby

Falconer, Julia and J.E. Mike Arnold (1988) Social Forestry network' forests, trees and household food security', Network paper 7a, Winter, online at: http://www.odi.org.uk/resources/download/5001.pdf

Forum Secretariat (2000) Forum Regional Security Committee Outcomes, Apia, Samoa, 10–11 August

FPDC (2002) Fresh Produce News, Edition 162, September/October, 'Urban market prices', Fresh Produce Development Corporation, Goroka

FPDC (2004) 'Total marketed fruit and vegetable demand 1995', Demand calculation based on 1995 survey and population growth figures, Fresh Produce Development Corporation, Goroka, unpublished table, Table 1c

Gibson, John (2000) 'The Economic and Nutritional Importance of Household Food Production in PNG', in R.M. Bourke, M.G. Allen and J.G. Salisbury (2000) Food Security for Papua New Guinea, Proceedings of the Papua New Guinea Food and Nutrition 2000 Conference, PNG University of Technology, Lae, 26–30 June

Grossman, Larry (1981) 'The Cultural Ecology of Economic Development', *Annals of the Association of American Geographers*, Vol 71, No 2, June, 220–236

Gou and Higaturu (1999) *Agricultural lease between Gou Development Corporation (Oro Province) and Higaturu Oil Palms*, September, Port Moresby

Gunditjmara (2010) *The People of Budj Bim*, em PRESS, Heywood (Victoria)

Gunn, Bernard (2004) interview with this writer, Goroka, 9 December [Bernard is Director of the Community Based Health and Development Cooperative, at Kiam in the Western Highlands]

Hance, Jeremy (2011) '5 Million Hectares of Papua New Guinea forests handed to foreign corporations', *Mongabay*, March 23, online at: http://news.mongabay.com/2011/0323–hance_png_sabls.html

Hughes, Helen (2004) 'The Pacific is Viable!', *Issue Analysis* No 53, Centre for Independent Studies, Sydney www.cis.org.au

Hughes, Helen and J. Warin (2005) 'A New Deal for Aborigines and Torres Strait Islanders in Remote Communities', Issue Analysis No 54, Centre for Independent Studies, Sydney www.cis.org.au

Hunt, Diana (2004) 'Unintended Consequences of Land Rights Reform: the case of the 1998 Uganda Land Act', Development Policy Review, 22 (2), 173–191

ITS Global (2009) 'The Economic Benefits of Land Use in Papua New Guinea', International Trade Strategies Global, Melbourne, November online at: http://www.fiapng.com/PDF_files/PNG%20Land%20Use%20Report%20Final4%20Nov%20 2009.pdf

Kelsey, Jane (2004) 'A Peoples' Guide to PACER', *Pacific Network on Globalisation* (PANG), Suva

Kimbrell, Andrew (2002) *Fatal Harvest: The Tragedy of Industrial Agriculture*, Foundation for Deep Ecology, Sausalito

Koczberski, G; G. Curry and K. Gibson (2001) 'Improving Productivity of the Smallholder Oil Palm Sector in Papua New Guinea: a socio–economic study of the Hoskins and Popondetta Schemes', Australian National University, Canberra, November

Koja, Anderson (2003) Interview with this writer, Popondetta, 4 March [the late Anderson Koja was Chairman of the Popondetta Oil Palm Growers Association]

Lakau, Andrew A.L. (1994) 'Customary land tenure and economic development in PNG' in Ron Crocombe and Malama Meleisea (eds) (1994) *Land Issues in the Pacific, Institute of South Pacific Studies*, University of the South Pacific, Suva

Lavigne Delville, Phillippe (2006) 'Registering and Administering Customary Land Rights: PFRs in West Africa', Paper at World Bank conference on 'Land Policies and Legal Empowerment of the Poor', Washington, November 2–3, online at: **GET REF**

Lawrence, J.C.D. (1970) 'The role of registration of title in the evolution of customary tenures and its effect on societies in Africa', paper at the Seminar on Cadastre, Addis Ababa, UN Economic Commission for Africa

Lea, David (2004) *Customary Land Tenure in Papua New Guinea: what does it really mean?*, National Research Institute, NRI Special Publication Number 35, Port Moresby

Mara and others (1999) *Lease of Land, between Anton Mara, Leo Mautu Bakani, Lucas Becho, Paul Kaumu, Thomas Malala and John Nomu, and the Independent State of Papua New Guinea*, 23 November [concerning 777 hectares of land at Garu Village in West New Britain]

Mazoyer, Marcel (2001) *Protecting Small Farmers and the Rural Poor in the Context of Globalization*, Report for the United Nations Food and Agriculture Organisation, Rome

Meinzen-Dick, Ruth (2009) 'Property Rights for Poverty Reduction?', *DESA Working Paper* No 91, United Nations Department of Economic and Social Affairs, New York, December, online at: http://www.un.org/esa/desa/papers/2009/wp91_2009.pdf

Méndez, V. Ernesto; Christopher M. Bacon; Meryl Olsen; Katlyn S. Morris; and Annie Shattuck (2010) 'Agrobiodoversity and Shade Coffee Smallholder Livelihoods: a review and synthesis of ten years of research in Central America', *The Professional Geographer*, 62(3), 357–376

Mosco, Mark (2005) 'Customary Land Tenure and Agricultural Success: the Mekeo case', in Jim Fingeleton (ed.) (2005) 'Privatising Land in the Pacific', Discussion Paper Number 80, *The Australian Institute*, Canberra, June, online at: https://www.tai.org.au/file.php?file=discussion_papers/DP80.pdf

Moxnes Jervell, Anne and Desmond A. Jolley (2003) 'Beyond Food: towards a multifunctional agriculture', Working Paper 2003–19, Norwegian Agricultural research Institute, Oslo, online at: http://www.nilf.no/Publikasjoner/Notater/En/2003/N200319Hele.pdf

Naidu, Vijay (1980) The Violence of Indenture in Fiji, 2004 edition, Fiji Institute of Applied Studies, Nadi

Narokobi, Bernard (1988) *Concept of Ownership in Melanesia*, Occasional Paper No 6, The Melanesian Institute, Goroka, 2nd printing 1999

NRI (2007) 'The National Land Development Taskforce Report: Land Administration, Land Dispute Settlement, and Customary Land Development', Monograph 39, *National Research Institute*, Port Moresby

Oruga, Thomas (2004) interview with this writer, Pikosa Village, Eastern Highlands Province, 7 December

Paol, Yat (2004) Interview with this writer, Madang, 14 December [Yat was speaking as a community leader of Tokain village, and a community worker with the Madang based Bismarck Ramu Group]

PIFS (2001) Land Issues in the Pacific, Pacific Islands Forum Secretariat, Suva, Fiji, August

Powell J.M. (1976) 'Ethnobotany', in K. Paijmans (ed.) (1976) *New Guinea Vegetation, Elsevier Scientific Publishing Company*, Amsterdam & ANU Press, Canberra

Power, Anthony (2001) 'Land Mobilization Programme in Papua New Guinea', PNGBUAI, www.pngbuai.com/300 social sciences/management/

Rere, Steve (2004) interview with this writer, Goroka [Steve is an educator, author and former university lecturer in Agriculture]

Reynolds, Henry (1987) *The Law of the Land*, Penguin, Melbourne

Rigg, Jonathan and Sakunee Nattapoolwat (2001) 'Embracing the Global in Thailand: activism and pragmatism in an era of deagrarianization', *World Development*, Vol 29 No 6, 945–960

Rosset, Peter (2000) 'The Multiple Functions and Benefits of Small Farm Agriculture in the Context of Global Trade Negotiations', *Development*, Volume 43, Number 2, June 2000, pp. 77–82

Roughan, John (2008) Interviews with this writer, Honiara, 2–12 February [US born John Roughan has lived in the Solomon Islands for 50 years]

Rusanen, Liisa (2005) 'In Whose Interests? The politics of land titling', Background Paper, AID/Watch, Sydney, May

Rynkiewich, Michael (ed.) (2001) *Land and Churches in Melanesia: Issues and Contexts*, Melanesian Institute, Goroka (PNG), Point No 25

Rynkiewich, Michael (ed.) (2004) *Land and Churches in Melanesia: Cases and Procedures*, Melanesian Institute, Goroka (PNG), Point No 27

Saunders, Kay (1984) *Indentured labour in the British Empire, 1834–1920*, Taylor and Francis

Seneviratne, Kalinga (1995) 'IMF Plan Rejected by PNG People', Third World Network, 6 September, online at: www.hatford–hwp.com/archives/24/083.html

Shiva, Vandana (1992) *The Violence of Green Revolution: Third World Agriculture, Ecology and Politics*, Zed Books, London

Shiva, Vandana (1993) *Monocultures of the Mind: Perspectives on Biodiversity and Biotechnology*, Zed Books, London

Sindana, Howard (2004) interview with this writer, Madang

Sinemila, Grace (2004) Interview with this writer, Madang, 15 December [Grace was speaking as a member of Noromba village, WHP]

Smith, Bruce D. (1989) 'Origins of Agriculture in Eastern North America', Science, Vol 246, 22 December, pp.1566–1571

Sodhi, Gaurav (2008) 'Five out of Ten', Island Sun, Honiara, Feb 4, p.4 and Feb 8, p.5

Sowei, J.W.; W Lahari and M. Vatnabar (2003) *Rural Informal Sector Survey Report*, National Research Institute (Social and Environmental Studies Division), Port Moresby, January

Storey, Donovan and Warwick E. Murray (2001) 'Dilemmas of Development in Oceania: the political economy of the Tongan agro–export sector', *The Geographical Journal*, Vol 167, No 4, December, 291–304

Swynnerton, R.J.M. (1955) *The Swynnerton Report: A plan to intensify the development of African agriculture in Kenya*, Government Printer, Nairobi

Thomas (2004) interview with this writer, Gauhuku Zuha Village, Eastern Highlands Province, 8 December

UNDP (1999) Papua New Guinea: Human Development Report 1998, Office of National Planning, Government of Papua New Guinea and the United Nations Development Programme, Port Moresby

UNESCO (2011) 'Kuk Early Agricultural Site', UNESCO World Heritage Centre, online at: http://whc.unesco.org/en/list/887

Van Helden, Flip (1998) *Between Cash and Conviction: the social context of the Bismarck–Ramu Integrated Conservation and Conservation Project*, UNDP and National Research Institute, NRI Monograph 33, Port Moresby

Warren, Patrizio (2002) 'Livelihoods Diversification and Enterprise Diversification: an initial exploration of concepts and issues', LSP Working Paper 4, Livelihoods Diversification and Enterprise Development Sub–Programme, Food and Agriculture Organisation, December, online at: ftp://ftp.fao.org/docrep/fao/008/j2816e/j2816e00.pdf

World Bank (1962) 'Current Economic Position and Prospects of Swaziland', March 6, Report No. EA 132a, online at: http://www–wds.worldbank.org/external/default/WDSContentServer/WDSP/IB/2002/07/12/000178830_98101902071173/Rendered/PDF/multi0page.pdf

World Bank (1989) 'Land Mobilization Program: Papua New Guinea', Projects and Operations, Project ID: P004386, 12 April, online at: http://web.worldbank.org/external/projects/main?Projectid=P004386

World Bank (1999) Papua New Guinea: improving governance and performance, Poverty Reduction and Economic Management Sector Unit, East Asia and Pacific Region, October 22

Yala, Charles (2010) 'Overview' in Charles Yala (ed.) (2010) 'The Genesis of the Papua New Guinea Land Reform Program: selected papers from the 2005 National Land Summit, National Research Institute, Port Moresby

CHAPTER FIVE

ADB (2002) Papua New Guinea Country Strategy and Program Update, 2003–2005, (this replaces the CAP 2000), August, www.adb.org/Documents/CSPs/PNG/2002/

Adedokun, Olaide, Oyetunji Akande, Adeola Karim and Nancy Nelson–Twakor (2000) *Economic Liberalization and Women in the Informal Sector in Rural Nigeria*, in Dzodzi Tsikata and Joanna Kerr (eds), 2000. *Demanding Dignity: Women Confronting Economic Reforms in Africa*, The North-South Institute and Third World Network-Africa

Albaniel, Rosalyn (2007) Ramu workers stage protest, Post Courier, 9 January, p.9

Anderson, Tim (2006b) *On the economic value of customary land in Papua New Guinea*, Pacific Economic Bulletin, Volume 21 Number 1 (2006), online: http://peb.anu.edu.au/pdf/PEB21–1Anderson–focus.pdf

Anderson, Tim (2006c) *Oil palm and small farmers in Papua New Guinea*, Report for the Centre for Environmental Law and Community Rights, May

Anderson, Tim (2008) 'Women roadside sellers in Madang', *Pacific Economic Bulletin*, Vol 23, No 1, online: http://peb.anu.edu.au/pdf/PEB23–1–Anderson.pdf

Anderson, Tim (2011) 'Melanesian Land: The Impact of Markets and Modernisation', *Journal of Australian Political Economy*, No 68, pp.86–107

Bourke, R.M., C. Camarotto. E.J. DSouza, K, Nema, T.N. Tarepe & S. Woodhouse (2004) *Production Patterns of 180 Economic Crops in Papua New Guinea*, Coombs Academic Publishing, Australian National University, Canberra

Bourke, R. Michael (2005) *Agricultural Production and Customary Land in Papua New Guinea*, in Jim Fingleton (ed.), 2005. *Privatising Land in the Pacific*, Discussion Paper Number 80, The Australian Institute, Canberra, June

BPNG (2006) Quarterly Economic Bulletin, June 2006 Issue, Vol XXXIV, No 2, Bank of Papua New Guinea, Port Moresby

CELCOR (2005) Oil Palm and Poverty, Centre for Environmental Law and Community Rights, Port Moresby

Gibson, John (2000) *The Economic and Nutritional Importance of Household Food Production* in PNG, in R.M. Bourke, M.G. Allen and J.G. Salisbury (2000) *Food Security for Papua New Guinea, Proceedings of the Papua New Guinea Food and Nutrition 2000 Conference*, PNG University of Technology, Lae, 26–30 June

Gibson, John and Scott Rozelle (2002) 'Poverty and Access to Infrastructure in Papua New Guinea', ARE Working Paper, University of California, Davis, paper 02/008

Gibson, John, Gaurav Dutt, Bryant Allen, Vicky Hwang, R. Michael Bourke and Dilip Parajuli (2005) 'Mapping Poverty in Rural Papua New Guinea', *Pacific Economic Bulletin*: 20, 1, 27–43

Gregory, C.A. (1982) *Gifts and Commodities*, London, Academic Press

Hayami, Yujiro ; Kawagoe, Toshihiko ; Yokoyama, Shigeki ; Bagyo, Al Sri ; Zakaria, Amar Kadar (1991) *Marketing Innovation for Vegetables: conditions of diversification in upland farming*, United Nations Economic and Social Commission for Asia and the Pacific, Bogor (Indonesia), http://www.uncapsa.org/Monograph_Detail.asp?VListNo=24&VPage=2

ILO (2000) *The Informal Sector*, International Labour Organization, Regional Office for Asia and the Pacific, Bangkok

Jagannatha, N. Vijay (1987) *Informal Markets in Developing Countries*, Oxford University Press, New York

Jarrett, Frank G and Kym Anderson (1989) Growth, Structural Change and Economic Policy in Papua New Guinea, National Centre for Development Studies, Australian National University, Canberra

Jenkins, Carol (1996) *Poverty, Nutrition and Health Care in Papua New Guinea: a case study in four communities*, report for World Bank, Washington

Koczberski, G; G. Curry and K. Gibson (2001) *Improving Productivity of the Smallholder Oil Palm Sector in Papua New Guinea: a socio–economic study of the Hoskins and Popondetta Schemes*, Australian National University, Canberra, November

Koja, Kenneth (2005) interviews with this writer, Popondetta, August

Korugland, Peter and Maureen Santana (2007) Madang Oil Palm project set to go, *The National*, 9 January, p. 4

Lakau, Andrew (1991) *State acquisition of customary land for public purposes in Papua New Guinea*, Department of Surveying and Land Studies, Papua New Guinea University of Technology, Lae

NBPOL (2004) Report to Shareholders, New Britain Palm Oil Limited, Kimbe (PNG)

Nurul Amin, A.T.M. (2001) *The Informal Sector in Asia from the Decent Work Perspective*, International Labor Organization, Bangkok

Sachs, Carolyn (1997) *Gendered Fields: Rural Women, Agriculture, and Environment*, Westview Press, Boulder Colorado

Sandaratne, Nimal (2002) *The Informal Sector in Sri Lanka: Its nature and Extent and the Impact of Globalisation*, International Labor organization, http://www–ilo–mirror.cornell.edu/public/english/region/asro/colombo/download/nmlfml01.pdf.

Shand, R.T. and W. Straatmans (1974) *Transition from Subsistence: cash crop development in Papua New Guinea*, New Guinea Research Unit, Australian National University, Canberra

Shaw, Barry (1985) *Agriculture in the Papua New Guinea Economy*, Institute of National Affairs, Port Moresby, Discussion Paper No 20, June

Sindana, Howard (2007) pers comm, 20 March [based on Howard's interviews with workers at RD Tuna and Ramu Oil Palm]

Sowei, J.W., W. Lahari and M. Vatnabar (2003) *Rural Informal Sector Survey Report*, National Research Institute (Social and Environmental Studies Division), Port Moresby, January

UNDP (1999) *Papua New Guinea Human Development Report 1998*, Office of National Planning and United Nations Development Programme, Port Moresby

World Bank (2004) *The impact of international trade on gender equality*, Prem Notes No 86, May, http://www1.worldbank.org/prem/PREMNotes/premnote86.pdf

CHAPTER SIX

ADB (1998) *Project performance audit report on the Agricultural Research and Extension Project in Papua New Guinea*, Asian Development Bank, www.adb.org
ADB (2000) *Country Assistance Plan*, Papua New Guinea, www.adb.org/Documents/CAPs/PNG/
ADB (2001b) 'Studies to develop agro–industry in Papua New Guinea': News Release: Project Information, *Asian Development Bank*, 20 December
ADB (2002) 'Papua New Guinea: Country Strategy and Program Update (2003–2005)', *Asian Development Bank*, August, online at: http://beta.adb.org/documents/papua-new–guinea–country–strategy–and–program–update–2003–2005?ref=countries/papua–new–guinea/strategy
Anderson, Tim (2006) 'On the economic value of customary land in Papua New Guinea', *Pacific Economic Bulletin*, Volume 21 Number 1 (2006), online: http://peb.anu.edu.au/pdf/PEB21–1Anderson–focus.pdf
Anderson, Tim (2006a) 'Oil Palm and Small farmers in PNG', *a report to the Centre for Environmental Law and Community Rights* (CELCOR), Port Moresby, in 'Nature and Poverty', online at: http://www.natureandpoverty.net/find/?eID=dam_frontend_push&docID=228
Asian Food Worker (2010) 'Cargill exists palm oil in Papua New Guinea with US$175 million', 30 April, online at: http://asianfoodworker.net/?p=1014
Atwood, D.A. (1990) 'Land registration in Africa: the impact on agricultural production', *World Development* 18 (5), 659–671
Aurere, Harry (2003) 'Oil Palm in Papua New Guinea: the Oro case', *Centre for Environmental Law and Community Rights*, Port Moresby, February–March
Bretton Woods Project (2011) *Open for business: World Bank to reinvest in palm oil amid criticism*, 14 April, online at: http://www.brettonwoodsproject.org/art-568287
Burnett, Duncan & Dennis Ellingsen (2001) *Review of the Oil Palm Fresh Fruit Bunch Pricing Formula, Final Report prepared for the Commodities Working Group of the Government of PNG*, National Resources Institute and ADS (PNG), Port Moresby, November
Casson, Anne (2003) *Oil Palm, Soybeans and Critical Habitat Loss*, WWF Forest Conversion Initiative, Switzerland
CELCOR (2005) *Oil Palm and Poverty*, Centre for Environmental Law and Community Rights, Port Moresby
CSR (2005) *PNG Palm Oil Industry fights back*, Corporate Social Responsibility in Asia, Asia Weekly Vol.1 Week 18, 4 May, http://www.csr–asia.com/index.php?p=4095
De Soto, H (2000) *The Mystery of Capital: Why Capitalism Triumphs in the West and Fails Everywhere Else*, Basic Books, New York
Filer, Colin (2000) *The Thin Green Line: World Bank leverage and forest policy reform in Papua New Guinea*, National Research Institute, Monograph 37, Port Moresby
Fried, Stephanie Gorson; Shannon Lawrence and Regina Gregory (2003) 'The Asian Development Bank: in its own words: an analysis of project audit reports for Indonesia, Pakistan and Sri Lanka', *Environmental Defense*, Washington, July
Gou and Higaturu (1999) *Agricultural lease of Part of Portion 1961C*, Milinch of Sangara (NE) Fourmil of Buna, Oro Province, Vol 9 Folio 238, 6 September
Heaslip, J. and J. Maycock (1990) *Consultants report to the Working Group for the Review of the Oil Palm Fresh Fruit Bunch Pricing Formula*, Agricultural Development Services, Singapore, May
Heropa Enterprise (1999) 'Heropa Mini Oilpalm Estate: terms and conditions', negotiating document, Popondetta
Hevari, John (2005) *Letter to lawyers at CELCOR*, Centre for Environmental Law and Community Rights, 17 July

Higaturu (2003) *Payment printouts for Heropa Estate*, March & April

Holzknecht, H.A. (2002) 'Land, people and governance: conflicts and resolutions in the South Pacific', *Development Bulletin* 60, December, 8–12

HOP (2004) 2004 Year Book, Higaturu Oil Palms Limited, Popondetta (PNG)

HOP (2005a) 'Chemical use in HOP 2004, Higaturu Oil Palms, unpublished log

HOP (2005b) 'Estate report: fertiliser applied', 18 July, Pacrim Higaturu Oil Palms, Agrisoft systems printout, Popondetta

IFC (2010) 'The World Bank Group's Framework for Engagement in the Palm Oil Sector, DRAFT For Consultation', International Finance Corporation, World Bank Group, online at: http://www.ifc.org/ifcext/agriconsultation.nsf/AttachmentsByTitle/Draft+Framework+Paper+for+consultations/$FILE/WBG_Framework_for_Palm_Oil–DRAFT+FOR+CONSULTATION.pdf

ITS Global (2011) 'The Economic Benefits of Palm Oil in Papua New Guinea', International Trade Strategies Ltd, March, Melbourne, online at: http://www.itsglobal.net/sites/default/files/itsglobal/The%20Economic%20Benefits%20of%20Palm%20Oil%20in%20PNG%20%282011%29.pdf

JCU (2011) 'Improving palm oil production for PNG' James Cook University, online at: http://sustainability.jcu.edu.au/features/improving–palm–oil.html

King, Graham (2001) 'Letter to The Chairman, Heropa Land Group, Ango Village, Oro Bay, from Higaturu Oil Palms (Pacific Rim Plantations Ltd), 23 March [Graham King was Field manager, Expansion for HOP]

Koczberski, G;, G. Curry and K. Gibson (2001) *Improving Productivity of the Smallholder Oil Palm Sector in Papua New Guinea: a socio–economic study of the Hoskins and Popondetta Schemes*, Australian National University, Canberra, November

Keu, Stephen Talania (2001) 'Review of previous studies on the environmental impacts of oil palm plantation cultivation on people, soil, water and forest ecosystems', www.arst. uwaterloo.ca/ANTHRO/rwpark/WNB/SKeu%20R..

Knetsch, J. and M. Trebilcock (1981) 'Land policy and economic development in Papua New Guinea', *Discussion paper No 6*, Institute of National Affairs, Port Moresby

Koczberski, Gina (2007) 'Loose Fruit Mamas: Creating Incentives for Smallholder Women in Oil Palm Production in Papua New Guinea', *World Development*, Vol 35, No 7, pp.1172–1185

Koja, Anderson (2003) Interview with this writer, Popondetta, 4 March [the late Anderson Koja was Chairman of the Popondetta Oil Palm Growers Association]

Koja, Kenneth (2005) Interviews with this writer, Popondetta, August

Larmour, Peter (2002) 'Policy transfer and reversal: customary land registration from Africa to Melanesia', *Public Administration and Development 22*, 151–161 (2002), Wiley Interscience

Lea, David (2004) *Customary Land Tenure in Papua New Guinea: what does it really mean?*, National Research Institute, NRI Special Publication Number 35, Port Moresby

Mamoko, Andrew (2003) Interview with this writer, Port Moresby, 2 December [Andrew is Chairman of the Ahore/Kakandetta Pressure Group, from the Popondetta area in Oro Province]

Mazoyer, Marcel 2001. 'Protecting small farmers and the rural poor in the context of globalization', FAO, Rome, available at: http://www.fao.org/DOCREP/007/Y1743E/Y1743E00.htm

MPOB (2005) 'Average annual prices of oil palm products' and 'Monthly prices trend of crude palm oil', Malaysian Palm Oil Board, econ.mpob.gov.my

MPOC (2010) *Annual Report 2010: Leveraging on Sustainability, Malaysian Palm Oil Council*, online at: http://www.mpoc.org.my/pubs_view.aspx?id=3135953f-8771–436b–9dab–899773b2dc0b

MPOPC (2005) 'Data on palm oil production', Malaysian Palm Oil Promotion Council, www.mpopc.org.my

NBPOL (2004) *Report to Shareholders*, New Britain Palm Oil Limited, Kimbe (PNG)

Paol, Yat (2003) Interview with this writer about a proposed oil palm development in the Upper Ramu Valley, Madang, February

Papua (1917) 'Transfer of Land by Natives to the Crown' (Horata, Beliripa, Bengita, Tubatapa, Soi–iwa, Jove, Comberaba, Sagari, Ida, Sahuru, Zadocari, Zaurat Sogiri), 10 May, Port Moresby [colonial document setting out an exchange of an 'unoccupied' 8,280 acres of 'good agricultural land' along the Sambogo river for goods to the value of 'one hundred pounds, eighteen shillings and sixpence'; the goods were said to comprise tobacco, axes, knives and matches]

Philemon, Bart (2002) *Budget Speech 2003*, Minister for Finance and Treasury, 28 November 2002, http://www.treasury.gov.pg/budget2003/PM_Budget_Speech.2003.pdf

PNG Landowner Statement (2004) 'Papua New Guinea landowner statement on impacts and expansion of oil palm plantations and nucleus estates', press release signed by 31 landowners from Oro, East New Britain, West New Britain, Madang, New Ireland, East Sepik, West Sepik, Morobe, North Solomon, Milne Bay and Central Province, 6 August, Walindi, Kimbe, West New Britain

PNGSPS (2003) Anonymous senior PNG public servant, interview with this writer, Port Moresby, February

Ponzi, Daniele (2002a) Letter to Ms Lee Tan of the Australian Conservation Foundation, 5 August [Daniele is an Environmental Economist and a PNG Project Team Leader with the ADB – dponzi@adb.org]

Ponzi, Daniele (2002b) Letter to Ms Lee Tan of the Australian Conservation Foundation, 6 August

Prebisch, Raúl (1962) 'The Economic Development of Latin America and its Principal Problems', *Economic Bulletin for Latin America*, 7(1): 1–22

PTQ (2001) 'Oil Palm seen as Papua New Guinea Success, Pacific Tradewinds Quarterly, Vol 9 No 3 & 4, July–Dec

Radetzki, Marian (1990) *A Guide to Primary Commodities in the World Economy*, Basil Blackwell, Oxford

Rosset, Peter 1999. On the Benefits of Small Farms', *Institute for Food and Development Policy Backgrounder*, Winter 1999, Vol. 6, No. 4, available at: http://www.foodfirst.org/pubs/policybs/pb4.html

Ruki, Leo (2003) Interview with this writer, Popondetta, 3 March [Leo is Project Manager of the statutory authority, the Oil Palm Industry Corporation (OPIC), at Popondetta]

Secretary for Lands and Physical Planning (1995) 'Brief: Sangara Crown land – Oro Province', brief to Minister for Lands and Physical Planning, Department of Lands and Physical Planning: Northern Region, July 25

Seeley Janet and Kate Butcher (2006) 'Mainstreaming HIV in Papua New Guinea: putting gender first', *Gender and Development*, Vol 14, No 1, March, 105–114

Sinemila, Grace (2003) Interview with this writer, Madang, 9 December [Grace is a trainer with the Bismarck Ramu Group]

Singer, Hans Walter (1950) 'U.S. Foreign Investment in Underdeveloped Areas: The Distribution of Gains Between Investing and Borrowing Countries', *American Economic Review*, Papers and Proceedings 40: 473–85.

Snyder, Robert; Daniel Williams; and George Petersen (2003) 'Culture loss and sense of place in resource valuation: economics, anthropology and indigenous cultures', in Jentoff, Milne and Nilsen (eds) (2003) **GET REF**

Somare, Michael (2003) 'Appropriate investment incentives for agriculture, as a means to sustain rural livelihood', Address to the New Britain Palm Oil Limited and the business community in Kimbe, West New Britain, Web site of the Prime Minister of Papua New Guinea, www.pm.gov.pg/pmsoffice/, 5 June

Tan, Lee (2004) *Asian Development Bank Technical Assistance Loan to Papua New Guinea for Nucleus-Agro Enterprises*, ADB Environmental Monitoring Report prepared for the NGO Forum on the ADB, Australian Conservation Forum, Melbourne

Tararia, Almah (2003) Interview with this writer, Senior Lawyer, Environmental Law Centre, Port Moresby

Tararia, Almah and Lisa Ogle (2010) 'Incorporated land groups and the registration of customary land: recent developments in PNG', in Tim Anderson and Gary Lee (eds) (2010) *In Defence of Melanesian Customary Land*, Aid/Watch, Sydney, pp.21–26

Twite, Peter (2005) *Letter to Ed Matthew of Friends of the Earth (UK)*, [Peter Twite is Programme Manager and Departmental Financial Officer for Britain's Department For International Development (DFID). He also manages 'Capital for development', the British government's body for investing in developing economies]

Van der Tak, Steven (2002) *Letter to Ms Lee Tan of the Australian Conservation Foundation*, 24 July [Steven is Principal Programs Officer/Economist, Pacific Department for the ADB]

Van Gelder, Jan Willem (2004) *European Buyers of Oil Palm: A research paper prepared for Friends of the Earth England*, Wales and Northern Ireland, Castricum, The Netherlands, 10 February

Warner, Robert and Marcia Bauer (2002) 'Mama Lus Frut Scheme: an assessment of poverty reduction', ACIAR Impact Assessment Series No 20, Canberra

World Bank (1989) IBRD Articles of Agreement, established 1944, as amended 16 February 1989, online at: http://siteresources.worldbank.org/EXTABOUTUS/Resources/ibrd-articlesofagreement.pdf

World Bank (2003) 'Initial Project Information Document (PID): Papua New Guinea, Smallholder Agricultural Development', Report No AB161, World Bank, Washington, online at: http://www-wds.worldbank.org/servlet/WDSContentServer/WDSP/IB/2004/06/10/000104615_20040610164416/Rendered/PDF/PID0P079140.pdf

World Bank (2007) PNG–Smallholder Agriculture Development, November, online at: http://web.worldbank.org/external/projects/main?pagePK=64283627&piP-K=73230&theSitePK=333767&menuPK=333802&Projectid=P079140

World Bank (c.2007) 'Papua New Guinea Smallholder Agriculture Development Project', online at: http://siteresources.worldbank.org/INTPAPUANEWGUINEA/Resources/PNGSADPProjectBrief090610.pdf

World Bank (2010) 'PNG: improving community participation in local development while increasing revenue flow from the already established local oil palm production industry', online at: http://web.worldbank.org/WBSITE/EXTERNAL/COUNTRIES/EASTASIAPACIFICEXT/PAPUANEWGUINEAEX-TN/0,,contentMDK:22608600~menuPK:333773~pagePK:2865066~piP-K:2865079~theSitePK:333767,00.html

WRM (2001) 'The Bitter Fruit of Oil Palm', *World Rainforest Movement*, Montevideo (Uruguay), www.wrm.org.uy/plantations/material/oilpalm2.html

WRM (2004) 'Plantations Campaign', *World Rainforest Movement*, Montevideo (Uruguay), http://www.wrm.org.uy/plantations/palm.html

WWF (2002) *Oil Palm Plantations and Deforestation in Indonesia: what role do Europe and Germany play?, A report by WWF Germany in collaboration with WWF Indonesia and WWF Switzerland*, November

WWF (2003) *Responding to Global Demands for Sustainable Palm Oil: Industry–WWF Collaboration*, paper for the International Planters Conference, 16–17 June

Yambai, Oiyoi (2003) Interview with this writer, Uriginia Village, Upper Ramu, March [Oiyoi is a member of the Ramu Valley Land Owners Association (RVLOA), and a traditional owner in LLG Ward 13]

CHAPTER SEVEN

Albert, Simon, Fred Olivier and Wade Fairley (2010) 'Message from Marovo, Solomon Islands', http://vimeo.com/album/1806605

Amos (2011) Interview with this writer, Gabensis Village, Morobe, 11 June

Atizo, Louisa (2011) Interviews with his writer, Goroka, 15 June

Bima Aipapu (2009) Interview with this writer, Sausi (Madang), 22 November

Connolly, Bob (2005) Making Black Harvest, ABC Books, Sydney

Dwyer, Peter and Monica Minnegal (1997) 'Sago games: cooperation and change among sago producers of Papua New Guinea', *Evolution and Human Behaviour*, 18, 89–108

Gregory, Chris (1979) 'The Emergence of Commodity Production in Papua New Guinea',
    Journal of Contemporary Asia, Vol 9 Issue 4, pp.389–409
Ingipa, Joseph (2012) 'Message from the Registrar Co–operative Societies Unit', Co–opera-
    tive Societies of PNG, accessed 30 January, online at: http://www.csu.gov.pg/
Kapior, Beny (2003) Interview with this writer, Upper Ramu (Madang), 18 February
Kayonga, Wina (2011) Interview with this writer, Lae, 12 June
LaFranchi, Christopher and Greenpeace Pacific (1999) Islands Adrift?, Greenpeace Pacific,
    Suva
Letu, Nauns (2009) Interview with this writer, Sausi (Madang), 22 November
Malum Nalu (2010) 'Flower Power for East New Britain Women', July 25, online at: http://
    malumnalu.blogspot.com.au/2010/07/flower–power–for–east–new–britain–women.
    html
Marai, Aipapu (2009) Interview with this writer, Sausi (Madang), 22 November
Mel, Michael (1981) 'What Coffee Plantations in the Highlands Need' in Michael Walter
    (ed.) (1981) What Do We Do About Plantations? Monograph 15, *Institute of Applied
    Social and Economic Research*, Boroko PNG, pp.196–199
NARI Nius (2011) Newsletter of the PNG National Agricultural Research Institute, Vol 14
    Issue 3, Jul–Sept, online at: http://www.nari.org.pg/sites/default/files/narinius/2011/
    NN_vol14_No3_2011.pdf
Nawasio (2011) Interviews with his writer, Lae, 12 June
Ndawala–Kajumba, Sam (1981) 'Problems of Decolonization of Plantation Ownership
    in Papua New Guinea and Tanzania' in Michael Walter (ed.) (1981) *What Do We
    Do About Plantations?* Monograph 15, Institute of Applied Social and Economic
    Research, Boroko PNG, pp.151–168
NFA (2012) 'NFA Supports Fisheries Co–operatives', National Fisheries Authority of
    Papua New Guinea, January 30, online at: http://fisheries.gov.pg.dnnmax.com/
    FisheriesAuthority/NewsandMedia/NewsandEvents/CurrentNewsandEvents/
    NFArecognizesandSupportPNGFisheriesCooperati/tabid/267/Default.aspx
Oliver, Pam and Greenpeace Pacific (2001) Caught Between Two Worlds, June, Greenpeace
    Australia-Pacific, Suva
Paol, Yat (2003) 'A People's Fight to Protect Their Land', Report, Bismarck Ramu Group,
    unpublished
Paol, Yat (2004) 'Upper Ramu Anti–Oil Palm Campaign', Report, Bismarck Ramu Group,
    unpublished
Paol, Yat (2009) 'Building Their Own Road by Walking It', Report, Bismarck Ramu Group,
    unpublished
Paol, Yat (2012) personal communication with this writer, 31 January
Onot, Bom et al (2003) 'No Oil Palm', Post Courier advertisement, 27 March
RVLOA (2004) 'Ol Papa Graun Bilong Upper Ramu (Koroba–Sepu) Ino Laikim Oil Palm
    Projek', letter to Provincial and National Government of PNG, 15 March
Sindana, Howard (2009) Interviews with this writer, Madang, December
Sindana, Howard (2011) Interviews with this writer, Lae, 12 June
Tongne, Elizabeth (2011) Interview with this writer, Kokopo, 22 June
Townsend, D. (1977) 'The 1976 Coffee Boom in Papua New Guinea', Australian Geographer,
    Vol 13 Issue 6, pp.419–422
Varagat, Patrick (2011) Interview with this writer, Kokopo, 22 June
Yamboi, Oiyoi (2003) Interview with this writer, Upper Ramu (Madang), 18 February

CHAPTER EIGHT

Anderson, Tim (2005) 'Challenging 'Integrated Conservation and Development' in Papua
    New Guinea: the Bismarck Ramu Group', *Pacific Economic Bulletin*, 20 (1), pp.56–66
Anderson, Tim (2006) 'On the economic value of customary land in Papua New Guinea',
    Pacific Economic Bulletin, Volume 21 Number 1 (2006), online: http://peb.anu.edu.au/
    pdf/PEB21–1Anderson–focus.pdf

Anderson, Tim (2006a) 'Oil Palm and Small farmers in PNG', a report to the Centre for Environmental Law and Community Rights (CELCOR), Port Moresby, in 'Nature and Poverty', online at: http://www.natureandpoverty.net/find/?eID=dam_frontend_push&docID=228

Anderson, Tim (2006b) 'Valuation and Registration of Customary Land in Papua New Guinea', paper at IASCP Conference, Ubud Bali, 19–23 June, online at: http://dlc.dlib.indiana.edu/dlc/handle/10535/1180

AusAID (2006) 'Australian Aid: Promoting Growth and Stability – White Paper on the Australian Government's overseas aid program', Australian Agency for International Development, Canberra, online at: http://www.ausaid.gov.au/publications/pubout.cfm?Id=6184_6346_7334_4045_8043

AusAID (2008) 'Making Land Work, Volume One: Reconciling Customary Land and Development in the Pacific', Public Affairs Group, Australian Agency for International Development (AusAID), Canberra, http://www.ausaid.gov.au/publications/pdf/MLW_VolumeOne_Bookmarked.pdf

BRG (1997) Bismarck Ramu Group (BRG), Guide for Community Development Team Members, Madang (50pp + app) [the 1997 edition has been updated, to c.2000]

BRG et al (2003) Letter to WWF Pacific, [from the Bismarck Ramu Group, the Centre for Environmental Law (CELCOR), the Environmental Law Centre, Alotau Environment, and Christians for Environmental Stewardship], 20 February

Burnett, Duncan & Dennis Ellingsen (2001) *Review of the Oil Palm Fresh Fruit Bunch Pricing Formula, Final Report prepared for the Commodities Working Group of the Government of PNG*, National Resources Institute and ADS (PNG), Port Moresby, November

Chitoa, John (2003) interview with this writer, Madang PNG, 8 December

Curtis, Ian (2011) 'Valuing the economic loss of or modification of the ecosystem services provided by the forest', *Australia and New Zealand Property Journal*, Vol 3, No 2, June

Deininger, Klaus (2003) 'Land policies for growth and poverty reduction', Report Number 26384, *World Bank, Washington*, Online at: http://www-wds.worldbank.org/external/default/WDSContentServer/WDSP/IB/2003/08/08/000094946_0307250400474/Rendered/PDF/multi0page.pdf

Deininger, Klaus and Stig Enemark (2010) 'Land Governance and the Millennium Development Goals', in Klaus Deininger, Clarissa Augustinus, Stig Enemark and Paul Munro–Faure (eds) (2010) *Innovations in Land Rights Recognition, Administration and Governance*, The World Bank, Washington, Introduction: pp.xiii–xxvii

Deininger, Klaus, Derek Byerlee, Jonathan Lindsay, Andrew Norton, Harris Selod and Mercedes Stickler (2011) 'Rising Global Interest in Farmland', *The World Bank*, Washington, online at: http://siteresources.worldbank.org/INTARD/Resources/ESW_Sept7_final_final.pdf

EDO (2011) '3. Historic decision in the Kiunga-Aiambak road case in Papua New Guinea: Logging company ordered to pay a record K225.2 million', Environmental Defenders' Office, Weekly Bulletin, 1 July, online at: http://www.edo.org.au/edonsw/site/bulletin/bulletin716.php

Filer, Colin (2011) 'The new land grab in Papua New Guinea: a case study from New Ireland Province', Discussion Paper 2011/12, State Society and Governance in Melanesia, Australian National University, online at: http://ips.cap.anu.edu.au/ssgm/papers/discussion_papers/2011_02_filer.pdf

Garu, Selwyn (2010) Interview with this writer, Mele Village, Efate Island, Vanuatu, 17 June

GRAIN (2010) 'World Bank report on land grabbing: beyond the smoke and mirrors', *Against the Grain*, September, pp.1–6, online at: http://www.grain.org/article/entries/4021–world–bank–report–on–land–grabbing–beyond–the–smoke–and–mirrors

Gou and Higaturu (1999) Agricultural lease of Part of Portion 1961C, Milinch of Sangara (NE) Fourmil of Buna, Oro Province, Vol 9 Folio 238, 6 September

Guman, Yanny (2003a) interview with this writer, Madang PNG, 26 February

Guman, Yanny (2003b) interview with this writer, Madang PNG, 7 December

Heropa Enterprise (1999) 'Heropa Mini Oil palm Estate: terms and conditions', negotiating document, Popondetta

Higaturu (2003) Payment printouts for Heropa Estate, March & April

Hope, Anne and Sally Timmel (1984) *Training for Transformation 1*, Mambo Press, Gweru Zimbabwe, 1996 edition

King, Graham (2001) 'Letter to The Chairman, Heropa Land Group, Ango Village, Oro Bay, from Higaturu Oil Palms (Pacific Rim Plantations Ltd), 23 March [Graham King was Field manager, Expansion for HOP]

Koja, Anderson (2003) Interview with this writer, Popondetta, 4 March [the late Anderson Koja was Chairman of the Popondetta Oil Palm Growers Association]

Koja, Kenneth (2005) Interviews with this writer, Popondetta, August

Lawrence, J.C.D. (1970) 'The role of registration of title in the evolution of customary tenures and its effect on societies in Africa', paper at the Seminar on Cadastre, Addis Ababa, UN Economic Commission for Africa

McCallum, Rob and Nikhil Sekhran (1997) *Race for the Rainforest*, PNG Biodiversity Conservation and Resource Management Programme and UNDP, Waigani (PNG)

McMullen, Bob (2008) 'Launch of Making Land Work – Pacific Land Conference', Speech by Parliamentary Secretary for International Development Assistance, 12 June, Vanuatu, online at: http://www.ausaid.gov.au/media/release. cfm?BC=Speech&ID=2528_8235_2115_7707_4349

Moore, Elizabeth (2011) 'The Administration of Special Purpose Agricultural Business Leases: customary land tenure and the lease–lease–back system', *Discussion Paper No. 118*, The National Research Institute, Port Moresby, June, online at: http://www. nri.org.pg/publications/Recent%20Publications/2011%20Publications/SPABL%20 Paper_JR_cleancopy_200511_Final.pdf

Nalu, Malum (2011) 'Gazettals reveal truths', *The National*, 6 April, online at: http://www. thenational.com.pg/?q=node/18224

Paol, Yat (2003) interview with this writer, Madang, 7 December

Papua (1917) 'Transfer of Land by Natives to the Crown' (Horata, Beliripa, Bengita, Tubatapa, Soi–iwa, Jove, Comberaba, Sagari, Ida, Sahuru, Zadocari, Zaurat Sogiri), 10 May, Port Moresby [colonial document setting out an exchange of an 'unoccupied' 8,280 acres of 'good agricultural land' along the Sambogo river for goods to the value of 'one hundred pounds, eighteen shillings and sixpence'; the goods were said to comprise tobacco, axes, knives and matches]

Rere, Steve (2004) Interview with this writer, Goroka (PNG), 11 December

Rere, Steve (2011) Interview with this writer, Goroka (PNG), 16 June

Rudd, Kevin (2011) 'Australia rejects re–engaging directly with Fiji military regime', ABC Radio, 11 may, online at: http://www.radioaustralia.net.au/pacbeat/stories/201105/ s3214157.htm

Secretary for Lands and Physical Planning (1995) 'Brief: Sangara Crown land – Oro Province', brief to Minister for Lands and Physical Planning, Department of Lands and Physical Planning: Northern Region, July 25

Tararia, Almah (2003) Interview with this writer, Senior Lawyer, Environmental Law Centre, Port Moresby

Tararia and Ogle (2010) 'Incorporated land groups and the registration of customary lands: Recent developments in PNG' in Anderson, Tim and Gary Lee (eds) (2010) *In Defence of Melanesian Customary Land*, Aidwatch, Sydney, available online at: http://www.aidwatch.org.au/publications/publication–in–defence–of–melanesian– customary–land

Tenehoe, Tamana (2003) interview with this writer, Madang PNG, 6 December

Uni Tavur (2001) The Uni Tavur testimony', Pacific Journalism Review, 7: 1 , pp.1–13, http:// www.asiapac.org.fj/PJR/issues/next/2001unitavur.pdf

Van Helden, Flip (2001) *Through the Thicket: disentangling the social dynamics of an integrated conservation and development project on mainland Papua New Guinea*, Wageningen University, Netherlands

ViaCampesina (2011) 'The World Bank funding land grabbing in South America, open letter to the IFC, 7 July, online at: http://viacampesina.org/en/index.php?option=com_content&view=article&id=1097:open–letter–to–ifc–pending–approval–of–the–project–calyxagro–proj–ref–29137

World Bank (1975) 'Land Reform Policy Paper', Washington

World Bank (2010) 'Rising global interest in farmland: can it yield sustainable and equitable benefits?', Washington, September, online at: http://siteresources.worldbank.org/INTARD/Resources/ESW_Sept7_final_final.pdf

WWF (2002) 'Concept Note: New Guinea Forest Summit', September, WWF South Pacific Programme

Yambai, Oiyoi (2003) Interview with this writer, Uriginia Village, Upper Ramu, March [Oiyoi is a member of the Ramu Valley Land Owners Association and a traditional owner in LLG Ward 13]

CHAPTER NINE

Anderson, Tim (2006) 'On the economic value of customary land in Papua New Guinea', *Pacific Economic Bulletin*, Volume 21 Number 1, pp. 138–152.

AusAID (2004) 'Food Security Strategy', Commonwealth of Australia, Canberra, May, online at: http://www.ausaid.gov.au/publications/pdf/food_security_strategy04.pdf

BBC (2008) 'Vietnam next to cut exports', BBC World News, 28 March, available at: http://news.bbc.co.uk/2/hi/business/7317989.stm.

Bello, Walden (1999) 'Asia, Asian Farmers and the WTO', Focus on Trade, No. 36, July.

Biofuels Digest (2007) 'UN Special Rapporteur on the Right to Food calls conversion of food stocks to fuel a 'crime against humanity'', October 29, available at: http://biofuelsdigest.com/blog2/2007/10/29/un–special–rapporteur–on–the–right–to–food–calls–conversion–of–foodstocks–to–fuel–a–crime–against–humanity/.

Borger, Julian (2008) 'Feed the world? We are fighting a losing battle, UN admits', *The Guardian UK*, 26 February, available at: http://www.guardian.co.uk/environment/2008/feb/26/food.unitednations.

Brown, Nicolas, Judith Laffan and Mike Wight (2008) 'High food prices, food security and the international trading system', paper for Informa national Food pricing Summit, Sydney, 29–30 September, Trade and Economic Analysis Branch, Department of Foreign Affairs and Trade, Canberra, online at: http://www.dfat.gov.au/trade/focus/081017_food_security.html

Castle, Stephen and Mark Landler (2008) 'WTO talks collapse over farm trade', New York Times, July 29, online at: http://www.nytimes.com/2008/07/29/business/worldbusiness/29iht-wto.4.14867782.html?pagewanted=all

Chao Xiao (2009) 'China Hopes early rice futures contract means bigger global price role', *China View*, 20 April, available at: http://english.people.com.cn/90001/90778/90857/90861/6640954.html.

Del Castillo, Laureano (2006) 'Property rights in peasant communities in Peru', Colloque International 'Les frontières de la question foncière – At the frontier of land issues', Montpellier, available at: http://www.mpl.ird.fr/colloque_foncier/Communications/PDF/Del%20Castillo.pdf.

De Soto, Hernando (2001) *The Mystery of Capital*, Bantam Press, London.

DFAT (1996) Food Security and Trade: a future perspective, Department of Foreign Affairs and Trade, Canberra.

Eicher, Carl K. (1995) 'Zimbabwe's maize–based Green Revolution: Preconditions for replication', *World Development*, Volume 23, Issue 5, May 1995, Pages 805–818.

Evenson, R. E. and D. Gollin (2003) 'Assessing the Impact of the Green Revolution, 1960 to 2000', *Science*, 2 May 2003: Vol. 300. no. 5620, pp. 758 – 762.

FAO (2003) Food crisis worsening in Haiti – more than 3.8 million hungry people, 31 July, available at: http://www.fao.org/english/newsroom/news/2003/21165–en.html.

FAO (2004) 'The implications of the Uruguay Round Agreement on Agriculture for developing countries', Food and Agriculture Organization of the United Nations, available at: http://www.fao.org/docrep/004/w7814e/W7814E08.htm.

FAO (2007) 'Food Balance – Cereals Excluding Beer (2001–2003)', Food and Agriculture Organization of the United Nations, Statistical Yearbook 2005–2006, Volume Two, available at: http://www.fao.org/statistics/yearbook/vol_1_1/site_en.asp?page=consumption.

FAO (2008a) The State of Food Insecurity in the World 2008, Food and Agriculture Organization of the United Nations, available at: ftp://ftp.fao.org/docrep/fao/011/i0291e/i0291e02.pdf.

FAO (2008b) 'Number of hungry people rises to 963 million', Food and Agriculture Organization of the United Nations, 9 December, available at: http://www.fao.org/news/story/en/item/8836/.

FAO (2009a) Rice Market Monitor, Food and Agriculture Organization of the United Nations, February 2009, Volume XII – Issue No. 1, available at: http://www.fao.org/es/ESC/en/15/70/highlight_71.html.

FAO (2009b) 'Countries by commodity: Rice, Paddy', Major Food and Agricultural Commodities and Producers, Statistics Division, Food and Agriculture Organization of the United Nations, available at: http://www.fao.org/es//ess/top/commodity.html?land=en&item=27&year=2005.

FAO (2009c) 'Annual Averages: Wheat (US No. 2, Hard Red Winter ord. Prot, US f.o.b. (Tuesday) Gulf)', from International Grain Council, Food and Agriculture Organization of the United Nations, available at: www.fao.org/es/esc/prices.

FAO (2009d) 'Food prices remain high in developing countries: Despite improved global cereal supplies food emergencies continue in 32 countries', 23 April, available at: http://www.fao.org/news/story/en/item/12660/icode/.

Freeman, Fran; Jane Melanie, Ivan Roberts, David Vanzetti, Apelu Tielu and Benjamin Beutre (2000) *The Impact of Agricultural Trade Liberalisation on Developing Countries*, ABARE Research Report 2000: 6, Australian Bureau of Agricultural and Resource Economics, Canberra.

Gao, Shutao (2010) 'Discuission on Issues of Food Security Based on Basic Domestic Self–Sufficiency', Asian Social Science, Vol 6 No 11, November, pp.42–48

Georges, Josiane (2004) 'Trade and the Disappearance of Haitian Rice', TED case studies No 725, available at: http://www1.american.edu/TED/haitirice.htm.

Gorham, Michael (1979) 'Japan's Policy of Food Security: an Alternative Strategy', Economic Review, Federal Reserve Bank of San Francisco, Summer, 30–45.

Hansen, Michael (1986) *Escape from the pesticide treadmill: alternatives to pesticides in developing countries*, Institute for Consumer Policy Research, New York.

Igua, Passinghan B.K. (2000) 'Food Security Strategies for Papua New Guinea', in Pantjar Simatupang and Euan Fleming (2000) 'Integrated Report: Food Security Strategies for Selected South Pacific Island Countries', Regional Co–ordination Centre for Research and Development of Coarse Grains, Working Paper 40, online at: http://www.uncapsa.org/Publication/cg40.pdf

IRRI (2006) 'Rough rice production' (000 t), Peoples Republic of China, by Province, 1950–2006, International Rice Research Institute, available at: http://beta.irri.org/solutions/index.php?option=com_content&task=view&id=250.

Jawara, Fatoumata and Aileen Kwa (2003) *Behind the Scenes at the WTO: the Real World of International Trade Negotiations*, Zed Books/Focus on the Global South, London and New York.

Kwa, Aileen (2001) 'Agriculture in Developing Countries: Which Way Forward?', Focus on the Global South, Trade–Related Agenda, Development and Equity (T.R.A.D.E.) Occasional Papers 4, June, available at: http://focusweb.org/publications/2001/agriculture_which_way_forward.html.

Lamy, Pascal (2009) 'Actions that result in stability must be pursued, Lamy tells agriculture conference', WTO News: Speeches – DG Pascal Lamy, World Trade Organization, available at: http://www.wto.org/english/news_e/sppl_e/sppl118_e.htm.

Losch, Bruno (2004) 'Debating the Multifunctionality of Agriculture: From Trade Negotiations to Development Policies by the South', *Journal of Agrarian Change*, Vol 4 issue 3, June, 336–360.

Lynch, Jonathan P. (2006) 'Roots of the Second Green Revolution', Paper at 18th World Congress of Soil Science, July 9–15, available at: http://acs.confex.com/crops/wc2006/techprogram/P14956.HTM.

MAFF (2009) 'The Basic Law on Food, Agriculture and Rural Areas (Provisional Translation)', Ministry of Agriculture, Forestry and Fisheries, Government of Japan, available at: http://www.maff.go.jp/soshiki/kambou/kikaku/NewBLaw/BasicLaw.html.

Maxwell, Daniel and Keith Wiebe (2002) 'Land Tenure and Food Security: Exploring Dynamic Linkages', *Development and Change*, Volume 30 Issue 4, Pages 825–849.

Mazoyer, Marcel (2001) 'Protecting small farmers and the rural poor in the context of globalization', FAO, Rome, available at: http://www.fao.org/DOCREP/007/Y1743E/Y1743E00.htm.

McMichael, Phillip (2009) 'A Food Regime Analysis of the 'World Food Crisis", *Agric Hum Values*, 26:281–295

Msangi, Siwa (2007) 'Biofuel revolution threatens food security for the poor', Science and Development Network, 6 December, available at: http://www.scidev.net/en/middle-east–and–north–africa/opinions/biofuel–revolution–threatens–food–security–for–the.html.

Nicholls, C.I., and M.A. Altieri (1997) 'Conventional agricultural development models and the persistence of the pesticide treadmill in Latin America', *International Journal of Sustainable Development and World Ecology* (United Kingdom), Vol 4(2), pp.93–111.

Pacific Community (2010) 'Towards a Food Secure Pacific: framework for action on food security in the Pacific', online at: http://www.foodsecurepacific.org/documents/FINAL%20TOWARDS%20A%20FOOD%20SECURE%20PACIFIC_June1.pdf

Patnaik, Utsa (1996) 'Export oriented agriculture and food security in developing countries and India', Economic and Political Weekly, Vol 31 No 35/37, September.

Peng, Shaobing; Qiyuan Tang and Yingbin Zou (2009) 'Current Status and Challenges of Rice Production in China', Plant Production Science (Tokyo), Vol 12, No 1, pp.3–8.

PIPP (2011) 'Food for Thought: exploring food security in the Pacific', Discussion Paper 19, *Pacific Institute of Public Policy*, Port Vila, Vanuatu, December, online at: http://www.oxfam.org.nz/imgs/whatwedo/grow/food%20for%20thought.pdf

Plaza, Orlando and Nelly P. Stromquist (2006) 'Consequences of Structural Adjustment on Economic and Social Domains: Two Decades in the Life of Peru', *The ANNALS of the American Academy of Political and Social Science* 2006; 606; 95.

Polanyi, Karl (1944) *The Great Transformation*, Beacon Press, London (2002 edition).

Rosset, Peter (1999) On the Benefits of Small Farms', *Institute for Food and Development Policy Backgrounder*, Winter 1999, Vol. 6, No. 4, available at: http://www.foodfirst.org/pubs/policybs/pb4.html.

Sachs, I. (1987) The Green Revolution Revisited, Allen and Unwin, London.

SSCM (2008) 'AMP Government invests on the production of alternative energy and generates 40,000 jobs in the districts', Secretariat of State for the Council of Ministers, RDTL, press release, 8 July, Dili, available at: http://www.laohamutuk.org/Agri/agrofuel/SSCM8Jul08En.pdf.

Tokyo Foundation (2008) 'The Perilous Decline of Japanese Agriculture', September 9, available at: http://testglobal.tokyofoundation.org/articles/2008/the–perilous–decline–of–japanese–agriculture–1

Toler, Deborah (1996) 'Harvest of Hunger: The United States in Haiti', *Institute for Food and Development Policy Backgrounder*, Fall 1996, Vol.3, No. 3, available at: http://www.foodfirst.org/en/node/240.

UN (2008) 'Haiti facing 'explosive situation' because of food crisis, UN official warns', United Nations News Centre, 18 April, available at: http://www.un.org/apps/news/story.asp?NewsID=26391&Cr=haiti&Cr1.

UNDP (2007) Human Development Report: Fighting Climate Change: Human Solidarity in a Divided World, United Nations Development Programme, New York.

Van den Berg, Marritt, Huib Hengsdijk, Wang Guanghuo, Joost Wolf, Martin van Ittersum and Reimund Roetter (2005) 'The future of rural income and rice production in China', *IIASS Newsletter*, No 38, September, p.34.

Veltmeyer, Henry and James Petras (2008) 'Peasants in an Era of Neoliberal Globalization: Latin America on the move', Theomai, No. 18, available at: http://revista–theomai. unq.edu.ar/NUMERO18/Veltmeyer.pdf.

Wilson, Geoff (2005) *Singapore's New Business Opportunity: Food from the Roof, City Farmer*, available at: http://www.cityfarmer.org/singaporeroof.html.

Wilson, Geoff A. (2007) *Multifunctional Agriculture: a transition theory perspective*, CAB International, Oxfordshire (UK) and Cambridge (USA).

Index

❧

217

Printed in Australia
AUHW010519100919
317094AU00002B/4

9 781925 333008